HRM AND PERFORMANCE

HRM and Performance

Achieving Long-Term Viability

Jaap Paauwe

OXFORD
UNIVERSITY PRESS

OXFORD
UNIVERSITY PRESS

Great Clarendon Street, Oxford OX2 6DP

Oxford University Press is a department of the University of Oxford.
It furthers the University's objective of excellence in research, scholarship,
and education by publishing worldwide in

Oxford New York

Auckland Bangkok Buenos Aires Cape Town Chennai
Dar es Salaam Delhi Hong Kong Istanbul Karachi Kolkata
Kuala Lumpur Madrid Melbourne Mexico City Mumbai Nairobi
São Paulo Shanghai Taipei Tokyo Toronto

Oxford is a registered trade mark of Oxford University Press
in the UK and in certain other countries

Published in the United States
by Oxford University Press Inc., New York

British Library Cataloguing in Publication Data
Data available

Library of Congress Cataloging in Publication Data
Data available

ISBN 0–19–927390–1
ISBN 0–19–927391–X (pbk.)

1 3 5 7 9 10 8 6 4 2

Typeset by Kolam Information Services Pvt. Ltd, Pondicherry, India
Printed in Great Britain on acid-free paper by
Biddles Ltd., King's Lynn Norfolk

To Roger Williams

Acknowledgements

I have happily collaborated for a number of years with a wide range of colleagues in the writing of papers and books. But a few years ago I got the urge to write a book just by myself, which would reflect my own personal ideas about HRM and performance and the factors that, to me, are decisive in shaping HRM policies and practices.

I was lucky to find that a number of others supported this idea. Roger Williams, my colleague and friend for many years, strengthened my conviction that I owed it to myself to write this kind of mid-career book. Our Research School at the Erasmus University (ERIM) agreed that there is some benefit from 'older' colleagues writing books, despite the fact that a single paper in an international refereed journal generates the same amount of credit.

Yet, reflecting on these past two years of writing, I realize that it is impossible to write a book on one's own without major support. First of all, I would like to thank Netherlands Institute for Advanced study in the Humanities and Social Sciences. (NIAS) for granting me a fellowship enabling me to study and write for almost an entire academic year. I would also like to thank the Dean of our School of Economics and the Board of the Erasmus University Rotterdam, which granted me a sabbatical. Ben Bakker and Frits Gosselink took over the management of our department so that I could concentrate on writing, and my teaching was left in the able hands of Marielle Sonnenberg and Wim Blauw. I am very much obliged to all four of them.

The staff at NIAS is perfect in 'pampering' academics who want to concentrate on a certain area. They are highly service-oriented, yet in a self-conscious way, which prevents them from becoming subservient, a very pleasant attitude. Many thanks to all of you, and my special thanks for Petry Kievit-Tyson, Anne Simpson and Saskia Lepelaar, who corrected my English and compiled the list of references. Although at first I had trouble getting used to the atmosphere of silence and devotion at NIAS, I soon settled in, and by the time it came to leave I felt I could have happily continued for years more. Part of the delight in working at NIAS is derived from the opportunity given during lunch breaks, etc., to converse and discuss with the others. The inspirational ideas from a variety of academic disciplines and topics that this gives rise to is amazing. My thanks again to all involved.

Acknowledgements

A second group of people I would like to thank are my former Ph.D. students, Ferrie Pot, Keimpe Schilstra and Paul Boselie, who all willingly agreed to collaborate with me on the empirical chapters. Their work is in line with my own thinking on HRM/industrial relations, and the thoroughness of their Ph.D. work underpins the more theoretical modelling that I undertook in this book. Thanks also to my fellow staff members Graham Dietz and Bas Koene for their important contributions.

Apart from the people who are directly involved in the writing of this book, a number have played a major role in the development of my thinking over the years: Karen Legge, with her distinction of the conformist and deviant innovator, and her stress on the necessity to distinguish rhetorics from reality; Lee Dyer, the first to make a plea for studying the process of how HRM policies and practices come about; and Shaun Tyson, who, apart from his own inspiration, introduced me to a whole range of inspiring academics in the UK during my stay at the London School of Economics and later at Templeton College Oxford. More recently I learned much from specialized small-scale conferences and meetings organized by David Guest (King's College, London), Ray Richardson (London School of Economics), John Purcell (University of Bath), and my US colleagues at Cornell University, Patrick Wright and Scott Snell. In the Netherlands I found support and inspiration from my colleagues of the Dutch HRM Network.

At Erasmus University Rotterdam we have the luxury of so-called student assistants, who help in every way one can imagine. In relation to this book, I owe a lot to Michelle Richelle, who (apart from the happy rhythm in her name) helped considerably in the finishing and final editing stages of the book. Thanks also to the editing staff at OUP, among whom I am grateful to David Musson and Matthew Derbyshire for their patience and support. Finally, I owe special thanks to my almost lifelong tutor, mentor, and good friend Roger Williams, to whom I dedicate this book.

J.P.

Rotterdam/Woerden
May 2004

Contents

Contents

Appendices

Figures

Figures

Tables

Tables

About the authors

Jaap Paauwe

Jaap Paauwe (PhD, Erasmus University Rotterdam) is Professor of Business and Organization at the Rotterdam School of Economics, Erasmus University Rotterdam. He has written and co-authored eleven books on human resource management and published numerous papers on HRM, industrial relations, and organizational change. Together with academics at other Dutch universities, he initiated the Dutch HRM Network. He was twice (1997 and 2001) in charge of editing a special issue on 'HRM and Performance' for the *International Journal of Human Resource Management* (UK). In 2004 a special issue on 'HRM and Performance' was published in the *Human Resource Management Journal* (UK), for which he also acts as a reviewer and guest editor. He is a research fellow and co-ordinator for the research programme on 'Managing Relationships for Performance' at the Erasmus Research Institute for Management (ERIM).

Before joining the university in 1988, Paauwe worked for both the Dutch trade union movement and a major employer. He was for some years head of the research department at the CNV group of trade unions, and before this he worked as staff member in the personnel department of the Dutch-based engineering company SHV/GTI. During that period he was involved in coaching works councils, training and development, and research into the measurement of HRM progress.

Having experienced both the employers' and unions' side, he decided to return to university in order to deepen his insights from a more academic and theoretical perspective. In 1991 he was an academic visitor at the London School of Economics (Department of Industrial Relations) and in 1996 he was a visiting professor at Templeton College at Oxford University. In 2001/2 he was a fellow in residence at the Netherlands Institute for Advance Studies in the Social Sciences and Humanities (NIAS), where he wrote the larger part of this book. His fields of interest are institutional theory, human resource management, organizational change, new organizational forms and corporate strategy. Contact details are *paauwe@few.eur.nl* or Erasmus University Rotterdam, P.O. Box 1738, 3000 DR, Rotterdam, the Netherlands.

About the authors

Paul Boselie (vignette Chapter 6)

Dr Paul Boselie is a post-doctoral researcher at the Rotterdam School of Economics, Erasmus University Rotterdam. He received a MSc. as well as a Ph.D. in economics from the Erasmus University Rotterdam. He is actively involved in executive education (the HR Leadership Programme at RSM and the Management Consultancy Programme) and undergraduate courses (Introduction to Organization Theory). His research interest is focused on issues related to human resource management, strategic management, and new institutionalism. His research has been published in journals including the *Human Resource Management Journal*, the *International Journal of Human Resource Management* and *Managing Service Quality*.

Graham Dietz (Chapter 7)

Dr Graham Dietz is a Research Fellow within the Erasmus Research Institute of Management (ERIM). He completed his Ph.D. on 'Partnership in British Workplaces: Four Case Studies in the Development of Trust' at the London School of Economics (LSE) in April 2002. His main research interests focus on how trust is developed, sustained, and enhanced (as well as what damages trust), and the impact of trust on organizational performance and employee well-being. His research has been published in the *Human Resource Management Journal*.

Bas Koene (vignette Chapter 6)

Dr Bas A. S. Koene holds a Ph.D. from Maastricht University in the Netherlands. Currently he is assistant professor in the area of human resource management and organizational behaviour in the Faculty of Economics and Business Administration of the Erasmus University Rotterdam. His research interests include the institutional development of the labour intermediation market and the control and co-ordination aspects associated with flexible work relationship for both user organizations and employment intermediaries.

Ferrie Pot (Chapter 8)

Dr Ferrie Pot received his Ph.D. in 1998 at the Erasmus University Rotterdam. His Ph.D. research entailed a comparative study of the organization–employment relationship in Dutch and American society. The study combined various of his areas of interest, including institutional economics, organization studies, and industrial organization/HRM. Since 2002 he has been engaged in performance auditing of government policies as senior auditor at the Netherlands Court of Audit.

Keimpe Schilstra (Chapter 7)

Dr Keimpe Schilstra holds a Masters' degree in sociologically oriented economics from the Erasmus University Rotterdam. His Ph.D. thesis (1998) was entitled 'Industrial Relations and Human Resource Management: A Network Approach'. He has for several years worked in an advisory capacity for the FNV federation of trade unions, focusing on collective bargaining agreements and negotiations within works councils.

Copyright Acknowledgements

We are grateful to the following for permission to reproduce copyright material: Figure 2.1 from R. Whittington (1993), 'What is strategy, and does it matter'. Reprinted with permission of Thomson Publishing Services. Table 2.3 and table 2.4 from B. de Wit and R. Meyer (1998) 'Strategy: Process, content and context'. Reprinted with permission of Thomson Publishing. Figure 2.2. from L. Dyer (1983) 'Bringing human resources into strategic formulation process', Human Resource Management, 22/3: 257–71. Copyright © 1983 John Wiley & Sons, Inc. Reprinted by permission of John Wiley & Sons, Inc. Table 2.5 from R. Schuler and S. Jackson (1987) 'Linking competitive strategies with human resource practices', Academy of Management Executive, 1/3: 209–13. Reprinted with permission of the Academy of Management. Figure 2.4 from C. Hendry and A. Pettigrew (1990) 'Human resource management: an agenda for the 1990s', International Journal of Human Resource Management, 1/1: 17–43. Reprinted with permission of Taylor and Francis Ltd. http://www.tandf.co.uk/journals/routledge/09585192.html. Figure 2.5 from M. Beer, B. Spector, P. Lawrence, D. Quinn Mills and R. Walton (1984) 'Human resource management: a general manager's perspective'. Reprinted with permission of B. Spector. Figure 2.6 from C. J. Fombrun, N. Tichy, M. A. Devanna (1984) 'Strategic human resource management'. Copyright © 1984 John Wiley & Sons, Inc. Reprinted with permission of John Wiley & Sons, Inc. Figure 2.7 from D. Guest (1997) 'Human resource management and performance: a review and research agenda', International Journal of Human Resource Management, 8/3: 263–76. Reprinted with permission of Taylor and Francis Ltd. http://www.tandf.co.uk/journals/routledge/09585192.html. Figure 3.1 from T. A. Kochan, H. C. Katz and R. B. McKersie (1986) 'The transformation of American industrial relations'. Reprinted with permission of T. A. Kochan. Table 3.1 from C. Oliver (1991) 'Strategic Responses to institutional processes', Academy of Management Review, 16/1: 145–79. Reprinted with permission of the academy of Management. Table 4.1 from D. Guest (1997) 'Human resource management and industrial relations', Journal of Management Studies, 24/5: 503–21. Reprinted with permission of Blackwell Publishing. Figure 4.2 from B. E. Becker, M. A. Huselid, P. S. Pickus and M. F. Spratt (1997) 'HR as a resource of shareholder value: research and recommendations', Human Resource Management,

36/7: 49–47. Copyright © 1997 John Wiley & Sons, Inc. Reprinted with permission of John Wiley & Sons, Inc. Figure 4.3 from D. Guest (1997) 'Human resource management and performance: a review and research agenda', International Journal of Human Resource Management, 8/3: 263–76. Reprinted with permission of Taylor and Francis Ltd. http://www.tandf.co.uk/journals/routledge/routledge/09585192.html. Figure 5.3 from J. B. Barney (1997) 'Gaining and sustaining competitive advantage'. Copyright 1997. Reprinted with permission of Pearson Education, Inc., Upper Saddle River, NJ. Figure 9.1 from J. Storey (1992) 'Developments in the management of human resources'. Reprinted with permission of Blackwell Publishing. Figure 9.2 from K. Kamoche (1994) 'A critique and a proposed reformulation of strategic human resource management', Human Resource Management Journal, 4/4: 29–43. Reprinted with kind permission from Human Resource Management Journal. Figure 9.4 from J. J. Phillips, R. D. Stone and P. P. Phillips (2001: 3) 'The human resource scorecard: measuring the return of investment'. Copyright © 2001 Elsevier Science Ltd. Reprinted with permission from Elsevier Science Ltd. Figure 9.5 from J. Peppard and A. Rylander (2001: 515) 'Using an intellectual capital perspective to design and implement a growth strategy: the case of ApiON', European Management Journal, 19/5: 510–25. Copyright © 2001 Elsevier Science Ltd. Reprinted with permission from Elsevier Science Ltd. Figure 9.6 from J. J. Phillips, R. D. Stone and P. P. Phillips (2001: 3) 'The human resource scorecard: measuring the return of investment'. Copyright © 2001 Elsevier Science Ltd. Reprinted with permission from Elsevier Science Ltd.

1   Introduction

The last decade of the twentieth century witnessed a phenomenal increase in the numbers of academics interested in human resource management and its relationship with performance. Earlier decades had seen bestsellers that focused on areas like marketing, strategy, and business process re-engineering. But the 1990s saw a wave of popular books embracing 'people management'. Catchy titles like *Competitive Advantage through People* (Pfeffer, 1994), *Living Strategy* (Gratton, 2000), and *HR Champions* (Ulrich, 1997) have sold in their thousands if not tens of thousands. Even more intriguing are the subtitles, for example *'Building Profits by Putting People First'* (Pfeffer, 1998), *'Linking People, Strategy and Performance'* (Becker *et al.*, 2001), and *'Putting People at the Heart of Corporate Purpose'* (Gratton, 2000). In every executive development programme, the topic of human resource management (HRM) is compulsory. The importance of managing people to achieve competitive advantage has by now become a generally accepted 'mantra' for corporate executives.

The interest in HRM and performance can be traced to the seminal work by Huselid (1995), which claimed that more advanced high performance work practices implied a substantial increase in sales and market value per employee. Add to this the global popularity of Pfeffer's (1994) book on 'competitive advantage through people', and the scene was set for an explosion in interest. Pfeffer (1994) emphasized the importance of what he described as sixteen best (human resource) practices. These practices, later to be reclassified by Pfeffer (1998) and reduced to seven, would, if implemented, contribute to sustained competitive advantage.

So by the mid-1990s the topic of HRM and performance was popular not only among managers, but also among academics on both sides of the Atlantic. By now numerous papers were being presented at a wide range of conferences, and many of these were to find their way into special issues of respected academic journals. There began to emerge a number of papers attempting to contemplate structures, set boundaries, and establish a landscape for other researchers to follow. Delery and Doty (1996), for example, developed the distinction between universalistic, contingency, and configurational approaches to understanding HRM practices. Guest (1997) discussed the idea of distinguishing between strategic, descriptive, and normative theories. Legge (1995) warned of the need to distinguish the rhetoric from reality and made a plea for a more critical approach. She was not alone: Paauwe and Richardson (1997), and later Boselie *et al.* (2001), following their reviews of work in this area, also emphasized the need for a more critical approach.

The search for links between HRM and performance was however to continue unabated, culminating in a search for metrics. Can we, writers were to question, prove—in relation to daily business life—that human resources do indeed matter, and that this proof can be expressed in terms of the hard currency of business? Once again, a number of best-selling books were to set the scene. This time, however, the emphasis was not just on understanding the relationship between HRM and performance, but on how we could measure progress and how we could measure the strategic contribution of HRM practices to performance. Books like *The HR Scorecard* (Becker *et al.*, 2001), *The Human Value of the Enterprise* (Mayo, 2001), and *The Human Resources Scorecard: Measuring the Return on Investment* (Phillips *et al.*, 2001) are just a few of the titles that were to become popular.

With regard to all this activity, a number of points need to be made. First, it is the US-based academics and consultants who dominate the field. Of course some UK academics also play a role, but in a more modest way; with a few notable exceptions, other geographical areas such as mainland Europe and Australasia are barely represented. Second, little attention is given to the way in which HRM practices and policies are *shaped*, and to the factors affecting that process. The focus to a large degree is simply on the kinds of practices that are related to achieving improved performance. Third, the concept of performance is defined mainly from a financial–economic perspective—as, for example, productivity, return on investment, and shareholders' value. Of course, such definitions are important, but they constitute a rather narrow approach to what the concept of performance should imply.

So it is little wonder that, despite the number of books, articles, recommendations, and insights into the area of HRM and performance that have appeared in recent years, there is much still to be done and considerable doubt about whether the real picture is being adequately captured. There are, it seems, important elements absent when HRM and its contribution to performance are discussed—for example, what sort of performance, and for whose sake? Similarly, if performance is defined only in financial–economic terms, what is this saying about how we view those who work in organizations? Is the only goal of HRM to increase shareholders' value? This book puts forward a different approach based on the following precepts.

Human resources are something more than just 'resources'.

They are active individuals with past experiences, internalized values, and norms that are not necessarily those of the employing organization. They belong to a range of different communities, both inside and outside the organization, and their behaviour is only partially governed by the institutions they work for.

Human resource management is not concerned solely with financial performance.

The HRM function, as one of the major organizational functions, also has a professional responsibility. It should ensure that the organization abides by all relevant trade unions agreements and national and international legislation. It must also play a role in developing a sense of corporate citizenship among all who work within the organization.

Human resource management focuses on the exchange relationship between employee and organization.

This exchange relationship involves not only labour, money, and time, but also (for example) competences, knowledge, information, learning, voice/participation, and well-being. People frequently spend more than eight or ten hours a day being involved in an organization, so they are heavily influenced by this exchange relationship. This number of hours is often more than the number of hours they can consciously spend with their spouses, children, relatives, and friends. So being involved in shaping that kind of exchange relationship is a very crucial and important task, which encompasses more and other criteria than just those dominated by economic rationality.

The shaping of the employment relationship takes place in an area of continuous tension between added value and moral values.

Added value represents the harsh world of economic rationality, but HRM is also about moral values. It is about achieving fairness and legitimacy. *Fairness*

3

relates to the exchange relationship at an individual level. People want to have a fair (equitable) balance between what they contribute to an organization and what they get back from it in return. Once again, this involves more than just the exchange of money for time and labour. *Legitimacy* refers to the exchange relationship at a more collective level and relates to the relationship between the organization and society at large. It is about the organization's attaining legitimacy in the eyes of relevant stakeholders—for example the government, shareholders, works councils, and trade unions.

These two sides of the same coin can be distilled from the very concept of 'strategic human resource management' itself. Concepts such as 'strategic' and 'resources' refer to the necessity of generating added value and contributing to productivity, and profitability, increasing shareholders' value and in this way safeguarding the continuity of the firm. However, in the very wording of 'strategic human resource management' we also encounter the concept of 'human', which refers to human beings, who want to be treated in a humane way. This is where we enter the domain of moral values, which are ingrained by institutions such as family, church, school, education, culture, trade unions, and legislation. Given that our focus is on the employment relationship, we limit ourselves here to moral values such as fairness and legitimacy, but these can easily be extended to include values such as sustainability, participation, solidarity, and trust. Figure 1.1 schematically depicts this tension between added value and moral values.

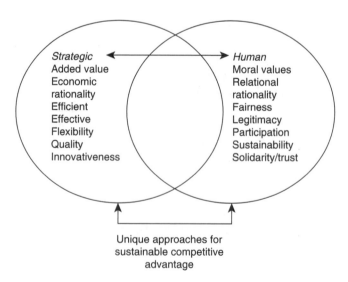

Fig 1.1. Added value versus moral values

At first sight the fields of added value and moral values might appear to be contradictory. However, the argument developed in this book is that these two can be aligned in such a way that the unique blending (*unique* because it will be custom made for every firm, company, and organization) results in a sustainable competitive advantage. So I do not consider these moral values as an impediment or hindrance. On the contrary, the creative and unique blending of the two can contribute to a sustained competitive advantage and viability of the organization in the long run. That is the thesis of this book. I am not alone in making this plea. For example, Paine (2003: xi) argues in *Value Shift* that the superior performers of the future will be those who can satisfy both the social and financial expectations of their constituencies.

Based on the above vision of human resources and HRM, the central theme of this book is the development of *a contextually based human resource theory*. At the theoretical level, this approach implies that we will make use of both *the resource-based view of the firm* (being the dominant research paradigm in the area of HRM and performance) and *institutional theory* (Paauwe and Boselie, 2003). Since I shall opt for a more pluralistic perspective on the concept of performance, I distinguish more goals than just those related to productivity, profitability, and shareholders' value; I also include goals like agility (see Dyer and Shafer, 1999), social legitimacy (see Boxall and Purcell, 2003), and individual and societal well-being (Beer *et al.*, 1984). This implies that my theoretical endeavour is not limited to just the level of the individual organization: it will also include, as will be seen in the more empirically oriented chapters, discussion and analysis at the industrial, national, and international levels.

Chapters 2, 3, and 4 serve as theoretical building blocks for the development of the theoretical framework. The aim here is to align, in terms of human resource management, resources and institutions. Chapter 2 highlights the relevance of the corporate/business strategy in terms of the link between HRM and performance. To this end, I present an overview of the various approaches. Starting with the classic approaches based on a top-down, rationally planned concept of strategy, I proceed to the importance of factors such as power, politics, culture, and environment, which represent a far more emergent and interactive concept of strategy. The chapter ends by drawing attention to the implications that these different approaches have for the development of HRM.

The aim of Chapter 3 is to examine the context of HRM in more detail. I begin by analysing whether the different classical approaches to HRM give sufficient recognition to the context within which HRM is played out. Because of the close relationship between HRM and industrial relations, I explore the contribution made by this association and conclude that institutional theory offers a thorough theoretical base for the inclusion of context in the study of HRM. Chapter 4 is the last of the 'building blocks' and focuses on the very concept of performance itself. I start with an assessment of the impressive amount of research that has been conducted in the area of HRM and performance. Following this overview, I focus on what is the fundamental concern of this book: the missing elements in the present debate on HRM and performance, and the need to develop a more encompassing concept of performance by distinguishing between its strategic, professional, and societal dimensions.

The three building blocks provide the design criteria for the core of the book (Chapter 5), which outlines a contextually based human resource theory. This framework aligns both the strategic dimension and the institutional context and takes into account the interplay between added value and moral values. It encompasses different rationalities, both economic and relational, resulting in a multiple perspective on performance emphasizing goals like profitability, fairness, legitimacy, and viability. The model includes different theoretical perspectives—for example strategic management, systems theory, resource-based view, institutional theory, and social action theory—and is capable of analysing the shaping of HRM policies at different levels of analysis, i.e. organizational, industrial, and international.

If the proof of the pudding is in the eating, then the next three chapters provide just that. Chapter 6, using a series of case studies, illustrates analysis at the organizational level. Chapter 7 outlines the importance of the industrial level by presenting work from two contrasting branches of industry (metalworking and information technology). Each of the companies chosen to represent one of the branches is attempting to introduce measures to improve flexibility. Differences in the degree of institutionalization (high in metalworking and low in information technology) suggest that this should have an effect upon whether flexibility is internally or externally regulated. However, as is discussed, even in a low institutionalized setting, with what would seem like ample room for managerial manoeuvre, managers still opt for external regulation, implying the desire to involve workers' representation in order to secure legitimacy. Chapter 8 deals with the comparative international level of analysis, comparing companies whose origins differ (either US or Netherlands based), but who have subsidiaries in both countries. This represents an ideal research context for analysing the impact of the institutional setting on multinational companies faced with the same kinds of global challenges and management fads.

After this empirical tour, in order to demonstrate the applicability of this way of modelling at various levels of analysis of the employment relationship, it remains for me to finish on a practical note. Chapter 9 provides a range of tools for the analysis, design, and monitoring of HRM practices and policies, which, in their own unique way, have the potential to contribute to long-term organizational viability (Figure 1.2).

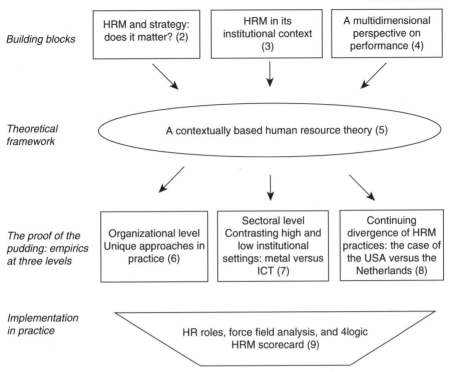

Fig 1.2. Overview of the book

Fellow academics and students with a thorough understanding of strategic management, institutional theory, and the HRM–performance debate need only read the conclusions of Chapters 2, 3, and 4 before proceeding to Chapter 5, where the theoretical framework is developed. Application of my contextually based human resource theory at different levels of analysis (organizational, industrial, and international) can be traced in the empirically oriented Chapters 6, 7, and 8. For practitioners, I recommend that they read Chapters 2, 3, and 4 to get a good overview of the developments in the area of strategic management, institutional theory, and the HRM–performance debate; then, after reading Chapter 5—the core of the book—outlining the theoretical framework and Chapter 6 for a few illustrative vignettes, they should proceed to Chapter 9. Here they will be able to carry out their own force field analysis and, based on the principles of the theoretical framework provided, build up their own 4logic HRM scorecard.

2 HRM and Strategy: Does It Matter?

2.1 Introduction

The title of this chapter refers to the well-known book by Richard Whittington (1993), *What is Strategy, and Does It Matter?* When considering the different approaches to HRM (universalistic, configurational, and contingent: Delery and Doty, 1996), and the rather confusing empirical evidence supporting or rejecting the different perspectives, it is necessary to clarify the issue of whether strategy matters (either at corporate or business level), and if so in what sense it matters, with respect to the linkage between HRM and performance. In order to do this, we need first to understand what strategy is all about. Section 2.2 presents an overview of the various approaches in strategic management that have evolved since the term 'strategy' was first introduced into the study of management and organization. Starting with the classic approaches, based on a top-down, rationally planned concept of strategy, I end with the importance of factors such as power, politics, culture, and environment, which represent a far more emergent and interactive concept of strategy. The implications of all these different approaches for the area of HRM are then highlighted in Section 2.3. The variety of different approaches to strategy and strategic management (for example, Mintzberg *et al.*, 1998, distinguish ten different schools) has given rise to fragmentation. It is not surprising therefore that academics have begun a search for synthesis, which is the topic of Section 2.4. From the developments in strategic management thinking, I draw a clear parallel with the developments in HRM, the classic models of which attempted to present planned and prescriptive approaches with a close fit between HRM policies and practices and the kind of strategy to be aligned with (Section 2.5). More recent insights (and empirical evidence!) present a far less clear linkage between HRM and strategy. These different linkages (Section 2.6) both substantiate and complicate the interaction between HRM and strategy. As has already been done in the area of strategic management, I have luckily been able to synthesize the different linkages (based on Guest, 1997). Finally, in Section 2.7 I summarize my main findings in the area of strategy and strategic management, which are of relevance to the field of HRM and performance.

2.2 What is strategy?

In the impressive amount of literature on strategy the roots of the concept of strategy are linked to military strategy. For example Bracker (1980) relates it to the Greek word *Strategos*, a general, which in turn comes from roots meaning 'army' and 'lead' (Whittington, 1993: 14). Generally speaking, strategy is about achieving a fit between organization and environment, or developing a course of action for achieving an organization's purpose (de Wit and Meyer, 1998). Since its conception different kinds of approaches have been developed. The best known of these, and the one that still dominates all the strategic management textbooks, is the rational planned approach, also referred to as the so-called classical approach. Its main characteristics still bear a strong connotation of the military setting:

- a controlled and conscious process of thought derived directly from the notion of rational economic man,
- for which the prime responsibility rests with the chief executive officer,
- who is in charge of a fully formulated, explicit, and articulated decision-making process,
- in which there is a strict distinction between formulation and implementation.

(based on Mintzberg, 1990 and Whittington, 1993).

In sum, the classical approach to strategy places great confidence in the readiness and capacity of managers to adopt profit-maximizing strategies through rational long-term planning, as Whittington (1993: 17) critically remarks. In the early notions on HRM we find a striking similarity with the above-mentioned premises of the classical approach. For example, Hendry and Pettigrew (1986) state that the call or plea for strategic HRM implies:

- the use of planning;
- a coherent approach to the design and management of personnel systems based on an employment policy and manpower strategy, often underpinned by a philosophy;
- that HRM activities are matched to some explicit strategy;
- that the people of the organization are seen as a strategic resource for achieving competitive advantage.

In reality, however the concept of strategy has many appearances. One of the first to demonstrate this in a clear way was Mintzberg, who distinguishes five meanings of the strategy concept:

1. strategy as a plan (intended); a direction, a guide, or course of action into the future—which implies looking ahead;
2. strategy as a pattern (realized); consistency in behaviour over time—which implies looking at past behaviour;
3. strategy as a ploy; a specific manoeuvre intended to outwit an opponent or competitor;
4. strategy as a position; the way in which the organization positions its products and or services in particular markets in order to achieve a competitive advantage;
5. strategy as a perspective; an organization's fundamental way of doing things, the way in which members of the organization perceive their environment, their customers, etc.

(based on Mintzberg, 1987; see also Mintzberg et al., 1998)

The different meanings of the concept of strategy are representative of the enormous variety of approaches to strategy, approaches such as incrementalism, entrepreneurial, bounded rationality, learning, and co-evolution. No wonder several authors have tried to synthesize and integrate the enormous diversity in this field of academic enquiry (Whittington, 1993; Mintzberg, 1998; Volberda and Elfring, 2001). Using the jungle analogue, Mintzberg et al., (1998) offer a guided tour through the wilds of strategic management by giving a clear overview of the whole field in ten 'schools'. Table 2.1 schematically represents the first three of these, which are prescriptive in nature.

1. The design school sees the process of strategy formation as a deliberate process of conscious thought (MacMillan and Tampoe, 2000). The well-known and often applied SWOT analysis is part of this school.

TABLE 2.1 Three prescriptive schools of strategy

School	Characteristic of the process	Key player	Environment	Strategy	Dominant discipline
Design	Conception	CEO	Opportunities/threats	Explicit perspective	None
Planning	Formal planning	Planners	Stable and controlled	Explicit plan	System theory/cybernetics
Positioning	Analysis	Analysts	Can be analysed	Explicit generic position	Economics

Source: Meerveld (2001), based on Mintzberg et al. (1998)

2. The *planning school* sees strategy as a formal process and entails a stepwise approach to an all-encompassing strategy. This school can be considered a more formalized and more detailed version of the design school.

3. Finally, the *positioning school* perceives strategy mainly from the industrial economics perspective. The competitive position of the organization in its industry/market is analysed with the use of economic methods and techniques. Porter, especially, has made important contributions to this school, which dominated the strategic management field in the 1980s. Well-known concepts developed by Porter (1980, 1985) are his Five Forces model for competitive analysis, the value chain, and generic strategies (cost leadership, differentiation, focus). Consultants also contributed to this school with, for example, the BCG growth share matrix and the experience or learning curve.

The underlying assumption of all three schools is that the environment is more or less stable and can be studied objectively in order to distil changes and opportunities for an all-encompassing strategy. Recently, this kind of approach towards strategy and strategy development has been labelled an *outside-in* approach (Baden-Fuller and Stopford, 1994). The environment, i.e. the market-place, is the starting point for analysis and for the subsequent development of appropriate strategic responses in order to achieve the desired strategic positioning.

The positioning school in particular has stimulated researchers in the field of HRM to link HRM policies and practices to a certain strategic positioning in order to achieve the required (role) behaviours that are expected to contribute to the desired positioning. For example, Schuler and Jackson (1987) link employee role behaviours to the three generic strategies of Porter, and authors like Ackerman (1983), Storey (1995), and Guest (1997) discuss the applicability of Miles and Snow's (1984) typology (prospectors, defenders, analysers and reactors) in the area of strategic HRM. Even Guest's 1997 model for linking HRM to performance continues to make use of the generic strategy types developed by Porter in the 1980s.

The next group of schools (depicted in Table 2.2) are more descriptive in nature.

4. The *entrepreneurial school* emphasizes the important role of a visionary leader who is actively engaged in a search for new opportunities in order to speed the growth of the company. Schumpeter (1934) is often referred to as a source of inspiration to this school.

5. The *cognitive school* considers the strategy formation process as a cognitive process that takes place in the mind of the strategist. In this way strategies emerge as perspectives (frames, mental maps, schemes) that shape how people deal with inputs from the environment. These inputs are subject to all kinds of distorting filters before they are decoded by cognitive maps

TABLE 2.2 Six descriptive schools of strategy

School	Characteristic of the process	Key player	Environment	Strategy	Dominant discipline
Entrepreneural	Vision	Leader	Can be influenced	Implicit perspective	None
Cognitive	Mental process	Mind	Hard to understand	Mental perspective	Psychology
Learning	Emergent	Everyone who learns	Demanding	Implicit patterns	Psychology
Power	Negotiation	Everyone with power	Can be moulded but difficult	Positions, ploys	Politics
Cultural	Collective process	Collectivistic	Incidental	Collective perspective	Anthropology
Environmental	Reactive process	Environment, stakeholders	Dominant and deterministic	Specific position	Biology

Source: Meerveld (2001), based on Mintzberg *et al.* (1998)

(Mintzberg *et al.*, 1998: 170). Simon (1947; 1957) has made an important contribution to this school with his notion of 'bounded rationality' (see also March and Simon, 1958).

6. The starting point for the *learning school* relates back to Lindblom (1959) with his disjointed incrementalism, better known as the science of 'muddling through'. The strategy formation process is seen as a stepwise incremental process. Change and direction is seen as the result of mutual adjustment between the different actors involved and between outside events and internal decisions. Strategy making is above all a collective learning process over time, in which it is hard to distinguish between formulation and implementation (Mintzberg *et al.*, 1998: 208). In addition to contributors like Quinn (1980— logical incrementalism), people like Argyris and Schön (1978—single and double loop learning), Senge (1990—the fifth discipline), and Prahalad and Hamel (1990—dynamic capabilities) are also considered to be part of the so-called learning school.

7. The *power or political school* regards the formation of strategy as a bargaining process between power blocks both within and between organizations. It emphasizes the use of power and politics to negotiate strategies, which favour particular interests (Mintzberg *et al.*, 1998: 234).

8. The *cultural school* considers the process of strategy formation as a process of social interaction, based on the beliefs and shared understandings of the members of the organization. This results in a perspective that is reflected in

the patterns by which the deeply embedded resources (capabilities) are protected and used for achieving competitive advantage (Mintzberg *et al.*, 1998: 267–8).

9. The *environmental school* focuses on the environment as the central actor to the strategy-making process. The organization must respond to the forces of the environment, otherwise it will be 'selected out' (Mintzberg *et al.*, 1998: 288). This school has its roots in contingency theory, but it gained popularity above all through the writings of Hannan and Freeman (1977) on the population ecology of organizations using a biological analogy.

2.3 Implications for HRM and performance

What do these nine schools tell us about the relationship between strategy, HRM, and performance? First of all, there does not seem to be any one best way of strategy making and subsequent organizing, including the shaping of HRM policies. The field of strategic management is characterized by different streams and approaches. However, this pluriformity of the field enables us to draw some important lessons for shedding light on the relationship between strategy, HRM, and performance. The different schools point to the importance of taking into account a number of factors.

The role of the entrepreneur (very often the founder and owner of the company). We can imagine that this person, as part of the dominant coalition, plays an important role in shaping HRM policies and creating a culture that is also quite influential in subsequent shaping of HRM policies. For example, at one of the companies, we studied (see Flood *et al.*, 1996: 220) the role of the founder (still active as CEO) was omnipresent. He disliked specialist staff departments; so, apart from the accounting department (which arose out of the necessity to comply with accounting standards and principles), there was no specialist department whatsoever. In small companies this is no surprise, but in a large shipyard company (employing 450 people!) it was indeed surprising. In the area of human resource management, this meant a lack of drawn-up HRM practices and a subsequent lack of rigidity allowing for flexibility, but it also left ample room for favouritism (Flood *et al.*, 1996: 215–16).

Cognitive processes. Owing to bounded rationality, distorting filters and all kinds of (de)coding processes, these can result in differences in mental maps of the participants involved and might give rise to diverging opinions on the shape of HRM strategies, policies, and practices. For example, in the event of an economic slowdown, the threat of dismissals or factory closure might arise and would undoubtedly lead to diverging opinions among the main stakeholders concerning the severity of the economic slowdown and the kind of measures to be taken (See also Chapter 5 on the dominant coalition).

Incrementalism. Thanks to the different parties involved (both inside and outside the organizational boundaries), HRM strategy can be considered an emergent and stepwise, iterative approach, with feedback loops making it increasingly difficult to understand cause and effect linkages. In order to understand the shaping of HRM strategy and how it affects performance, research can best be aimed at describing change processes in a longitudinal way (see Paauwe, 1989, 1991; Purcell, 1999).

Power and resources. The power positions of the parties involved are often neglected in existing HRM–performance research. Also, the kinds of resources they can mobilize through their networks in order to enforce and strengthen their demands in the HRM area (see resource dependency perspective by Pfeffer and Salancik, 1978) are often neglected. This is strange, because in the related academic field of industrial relations these issues belong to the very core of the matter, and everybody knows how crucial power positions and resources such as unionization rates and work-force positions related to the core work processes (e.g. process operators in the chemical industry, air traffic flight controllers) are in shaping both collective bargaining agreement outcomes and HRM policies (see also Chapter 7).

Culture/ideology. The way in which collective perspectives and intentions develop over time will undoubtedly have an (albeit often unconscious) effect on the shaping of HRM policies and also on the way in which effectiveness of both HRM and the human resources themselves are being perceived by the members of the organization and the degree to which related values and perceptions are being shared. For example, the top management of a large financial service company that opts for value-based management and share-holders' value as the ultimate criterion for judging effectiveness might encounter fierce resistance among its employees. This would especially be true of employees whose values are based upon a stakeholders' conception of the company, in which the interests of customers, employees, and shareholders are being balanced in a careful way.

Environmental and institutional forces. Environmental forces, stemming from trade unions and tripartite (governments, employers federations, trade unions) and bipartite consultative bodies at the national level and subsequent guidelines, can have a large impact upon an organization's HRM strategy and policies, because its management will want to respond to societal pressures in order to achieve legitimacy (see also Chapter 3).

2.4 In search of a synthesis and an overview

The above nine schools are a rich source of inspiration, and they demonstrate quite clearly the different perspectives in the field of strategic management. At the same time, they also demonstrate the apparently increasing degree of fragmentation and ongoing diversity among academics representing different sub-disciplines.

Mintzberg *et al.* (1998) themselves offer their tenth school, the *configurational* one, as a kind of approach that synthesizes the previous nine. The configurational school emphasizes that there is no one best way of organizing and strategy making, but that it depends on the specific circumstances, which will make a certain configuration of context, strategy, structure, and process effective. Periods of stability for a certain configuration will be interrupted occasionally by some transformation process, which can be considered a quantum leap to another configuration. Volberda and Elfring (2001: 11–12), after discussing the causes of fragmentation, also present a synthesis by distinguishing three schools. For each school one can identify a related set of theories, a cluster of problem areas, and accompanying problem-solving tools (Volberda and Elfring, 2001: 17).[1] Mintzberg admits that his own integrative approach (the configurational school) is one among many. And that is indeed true, because, in addition to the above-mentioned modes of integration and synthesis, we also have the approach put forward by Whittington (1993), who distinguishes on the one hand the kind of *outcomes of strategy* and on the other hand the *processes* by which the strategy has been made. Figure 2.1 gives a schematic representation of these two dimensions.

The vertical axis indicates whether a strategy is aimed at producing profit-maximizing outcomes or also allows for more diverse/pluralist outcomes. The horizontal axis focuses on the way in which the strategy process takes place, with, on the one hand, deliberate calculation and reasoning and, on the other

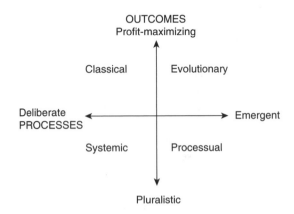

Fig 2.1. Generic perspectives on strategy

Source: Whittington (1993). Reprinted with permission of Thomson Publishing Services.

hand, a more emergent approach based on coincidence, muddling through, etc. (Whittington, 1993: 2).

The *classic approach* (which resembles Mintzberg *et al.*'s (1998) design, planning, and positioning schools) considers strategy as a rational process of deliberate calculation and analysis, designed to maximize long-term advantage. In the HRM area this approach simply implies that the role of the HR function is to maximize the contribution of human assets in order to achieve corporate goals. It encompasses approaches by which we attempt to link individual attitude and role behaviour to organizational performance in a logical and rational manner (see e.g. Huselid, 1995; Koch and McGrath, 1996). This approach is especially popular in the United States in order to justify that the chief HRM officer should have a seat on the board, by demonstrating that people make a difference to profit and can generate added value.

The *evolutionary approach* (which resembles Mintzberg *et al.*'s environmental school) considers businesses 'like the species of biological evolution: competitive processes ruthlessly select out the fittest for survival' (Whittington, 1993: 3–4). It is the market that decides and not the manager. The only thing the manager can do is to adapt the organization as optimally as possible to the demands of the market place. If this is not done, the organization will not survive. In the field of HRM we recognize this approach, this perspective by HR managers who want to keep their human resources as flexible as possible, embarking on core–ring strategies (Atkinson, 1984) and making use of transaction cost economics in order to decide on make-or-buy issues—both with respect to the employees themselves, and also in connection with the kind of HRM activities that should take place in-house or be outsourced and/or delegated to line management or to autonomous work groups (see also Paauwe, 1996).

In the *processual approach*, strategy emerges in small steps based on a process of learning and adaptation (see Mintzberg *et al.*'s cognitive, learning, and political schools). In relation to HRM, this approach refers to the incremental way in which strategic assets (such as patents, knowledge, culture, organizational routines) gradually develop over time into core competences. The main role of the HRM function is to develop and maintain people-related competences over time. The HRM function can also be seen as responsible for contributing to the social fabric, which builds up over the long term, encompassing the less planned and less intentional processes of skill formation, tacit knowledge, willingness to change, and spontaneous co-operation among the members of the organization.

In the *systemic approach* strategies reflect the social system in which they are enacted (see also Mintzberg *et al.*'s cultural school). Emphasizing the social embeddedness of economic activity, the objectives and practices depend on the particular social system in which strategy making takes place, according to

17

HRM and Performance

Whittington (1993: 4). Social systems can be found both at the national, branch or industry level, and in a certain region. Networks in which economic activity is embedded may include families, the state, professional and educational background, religion, and ethnicity, and these very networks influence the means and ends of action.

The systemic perspective is very important, especially from an HRM point of view. It refers to the wider social context of the organization and how this influences and shapes HRM policies and practices, which differ by country, by branch of industry, and even by organization. This perspective implies a plea for embracing the context of the organization, not only with respect to culture, legislation, institutions, etc., but also with respect to its technological and knowledge context (e.g. Silicon Valley or web-based companies; see also Paauwe and Boselie, 2003).

Finally, there is the overview by de Wit and Meyer (1998). In contrast to the aforementioned authors, de Wit and Meyer do not search for a synthesis. Their main goal is to present an overview of all the inherent tensions in the field of strategic management theory and practice, which give rise to different perspectives (see de Wit and Meyer, 1998: 15). For example, the strategy tension between logic *v.* creativity is related to the strategic perspectives of rational thinking *v.* generative thinking. And the strategy tension between deliberate and emergent leads to discussion of the strategy perspectives of planning and incrementalism, perspectives that we have encountered as schools in the overview by Mintzberg *et al.* (1998). De Wit and Meyer (1998) use the overview of strategy tension (in total they distinguish ten tensions[2]) as a framework for their book. For our purposes, I have selected those tensions that add new insights to the previously discussed contributions and that are relevant to the issue of the relationship between HRM and performance.

The first one in this respect is the strategy tension between markets and resources, which gives rise to the strategy perspectives of *outside-in v. inside-out*. We have already encountered these terms when discussing, among others, Porter's contribution and the resource-based view of the firm. In strategic HRM the more classic models are dominated by the outside-in perspective, whereas currently the inside-out perspective using the resource-based view is dominantly visible. In Table 2.3 de Wit and Meyer present an overview of these two related and apparently opposing perspectives.

These two perspectives can be considered a paradox, as a situation in which two seemingly contradictory, or even mutually exclusive, factors appear to be true at the same time. If we accept that both are true, then it has implications for HRM. On the one hand, HRM is dependent on the strategic positioning of the firm as it attempts to fit with the market environment; on the other hand, (human) resources can be cultivated and developed in order to formulate strategies that will result in a sustainable competitive advantage. In Chapter 5

TABLE 2.3 Outside-in versus inside-out perspective

	Outside-in perspective	Inside-out perspective
Emphasis on	Markets over resources	Resources over markets
Orientation	Market/industry-driven	Resource-driven
Starting point	Market/industry structure	Firm's resource infrastructure
Fit through	Adaptation to environment	Adaptation of environment
Strategic focus	Attaining advantageous position	Attaining distinctive resources
Strategic moves	Market/industry positioning	Developing resource base
Tactical moves	Attaining necessary resources	Industry entry and positioning
Competitive weapons	Bargaining power and mobility barriers	Superior resources and imitation barriers

Source: Wit and Meyer (1998). Reprinted with permission of Thomson Publishing Services.

we will pick up this intriguing paradox again and see how we can reconcile these two opposing views in order to generate unique approaches to HRM.

The other related tension I would like to discuss in greater depth is that between profitability and responsibility, which gives rise to the perspectives of *shareholder value v. stakeholder values*. In US-based HRM models the shareholders' perspective dominates (see also Chapter 4): all HRM strategies, tactics, policies, and practices serve only one goal, which is to increase shareholders' value. In contrast, in European (especially mainland European) based models we will encounter more stakeholder-oriented approaches, balancing the needs, interests, and aspirations of the various stakeholders both inside and outside the organization. In Table 2.4 de Wit and Meyer (1998) present an overview of the characteristics of these two opposing perspectives.

It is interesting to note that both tensions and related perspectives (outside-in and inside-out and shareholders *v.* stakeholders) also relate to what has become known as a new stream in organizational theorizing, i.e. *coevolution* (e.g. Futuyama and Slatkin, 1983; Aldrich, 1999). In an excellent overview, Aldrich (1999) describes the origins of evolutionary theory and the related concept of coevolution. Referring to authors such as Baum and Singh (1994) and Roughgarden (1983), he states 'Evolutionary theorists have coined the term coevolution to describe situations in which organizations and populations not only respond to influence from their environments, but also affect their

TABLE 2.4 Shareholder value versus stakeholder value perspectives

	Shareholder value perspective	Stakeholder values perspective
Emphasis on	Profitability over responsibility	Responsibility over profitability
Organizations seen as	Instruments	Joint ventures
Organizational purpose	To serve owner	To serve all parties involved
Measure of success	Share price and dividends (shareholder value)	Satisfaction among stakeholders
Major difficulty	Getting agent to pursue principal's interest	Balancing interest of various stakeholders
Corporate governance through	Independent outside directors with shares	Stakeholders representation
Stakeholder management	Means	End and means
Social responsibility	Individual, not organizational matter	Both individual and organizational
Society best served by	Pursuing self-interest (economic efficiency)	Pursuing joint-interests (economic symbiosis)

Source: Wit and Meyer (1998). Reprinted with permission of Thomson Publishing Service.

environments' (Aldrich, 1999: 38). In a special issue of *Organization Science*, Lewin and Volberda (1999) sketch the contours of this framework for research in the area of strategy and new organizational forms. Normally the environment is considered as the exogenous variable, but they focus on the way in which organizations systematically influence their environments and on how organizational environments (including the populations of organizations) influence those organizations in turn (Lewin and Volberda, 1999: 520). The origins of this issue of *adaptation and selection* can be found in a range of disciplines, including sociology, economics, strategy, and organization theory. Following an excellent review of these sources of inspiration, they define coevolution as

the joint outcome of managerial intentionality, environment and institutional effects. Coevolution assumes that change may occur in all interacting populations of organizations. Change can be driven by direct interaction and feedback from the rest of the system. In other words, change can be recursive and need not be an outcome of either managerial adaptation or environmental selection but rather the outcome of manager-ial intentionality and environmental effects. (Lewin and Volberda, 1999: 526)

The relevance of these authors' remarks can easily be related to the way in which changes in HRM come about. For example, an expected shortage in the labour market arising from an ageing population might give rise to the abolishment of early retirement schemes at the branch or industry level and subsequently to more attention being given to career management for elderly workers within companies.

So the overview of schools and syntheses by Mintzberg *et al.*, Whittington, and de Wit and Meyer offers important clues for the relationship between strategy, HRM, and performance. Before drawing conclusions with respect to my own stance and way of modelling this relationship, I present an overview of the classical HRM approaches in this field.

2.5 Classical strategic approaches in the HRM area

In describing the traditional strategic approaches in the area of HRM, it is necessary to distinguish between process and content models. The *process* of strategy refers to the way a strategy comes about, whereas the *content* is concerned with the 'what' of a strategy. In addition to this well-known distinc-tion, de Wit and Meyer (1998: 5–6) also distinguish the *context* of strategy, which refers to the set of circumstances in which both the process and content of strategy are shaped, developed or simply emerge. Both Mintzberg (in his environmental school) and Whittington (in his systemic perspective) have taken this into account.

One of the classic examples of a process approach to HRM is the one developed by Dyer (1983) and represented in Figure 2.2. This not only repre-sents a process approach (answering questions like how, who, when, and in what ranking order), but is also reminiscent of the rational planning approach that was quite popular in the 1980s.

From the basis of a certain strategic alternative (at business or corporate level), the consequences are analysed/outlined with respect to cost constraints and staff requirements. The next step is to monitor the external environment and to analyse the current human resources with respect to both quantity and quality. The present and required human resources are compared with respect to issues such as:

- Do we have the talents/competences to carry out the selected strategic alternative, or can we obtain them?

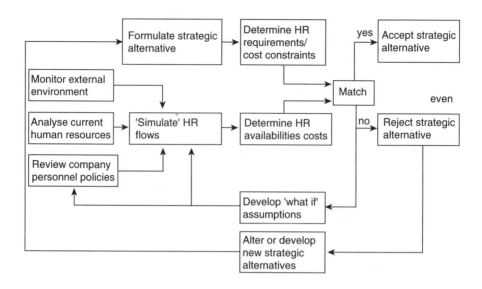

Fig 2.2. The process model of Dyer

Source: Dyer (1983). Reprinted with permission of John Wiley & Sons Inc.

- Are the costs involved in recruiting, retaining, and/or developing the needed talents in line with the assessment of the cost constraints?

If the answers are positive, than the selected alternative can be accepted; if negative, than another strategic option has to be selected and the whole process starts again. Another process-oriented model, by Paauwe (1989; 1991), analyses the forces that are determinative in shaping HRM policies and practices. Based on paired longitudinal case studies, and inspired by both Dunlop (1958) and Mintzberg (1979), Paauwe's approach is typical for an industrial relations orientation towards personnel management as was quite common in, for example, the Netherlands during the 1980s. Academics seemed to be more interested then in the factors shaping HRM than in its proclaimed effectiveness *vis-à-vis* the performance of the firm. Paauwe develops and empirically explores a model (see Figure 2.3) that outlines the forces influencing the process and outcomes of HRM policies and practices, and at the same time unravels the conditions that are influential in creating a certain amount of leeway for the parties involved to pursue their own strategic (Child, 1972) and idiosyncratic (Hollander, 1964) choices.

Paauwe's model is based, on the one hand, on the environmental factors as outlined by Dunlop (1958), and on the other on the organizational characteristics as distinguished by Mintzberg (1979), and is grouped into so-called ideal-types of organizational configurations. These two groups of variables act

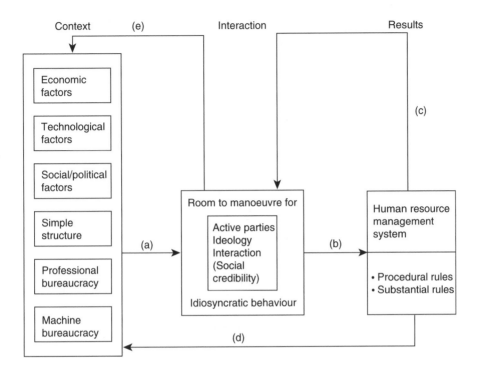

Fig 2.3. Modified conceptual framework

Source: Paauwe (1991).

as independent variables having an effect (arrow a) on the active parties involved in the shaping of HRM policies and practices. The contextual and organizational characteristics allow some leeway for the parties involved to make their choice with respect to the HRM system (arrow b). So the behaviour of the parties involved can be described as active on the one hand and as idiosyncratic and innovative on the other. The actual outcomes (in the next stage) of the HRM system have an effect both on the leeway for the parties involved and on the context (see feedback loops c, d, and e); and then the whole process starts again. The conditions governing the degree of leeway are depicted in Table 2.5.

It is interesting to note that, whereas the process model of Dyer (1983) is prescriptive in nature, the model by Paauwe is purely descriptive. A conceptual model, which also focuses strongly on both the outer and internal context, is the model of the Warwick Business School by Hendry and Pettigrew (1990). They have used their model (Figure 2.4) to describe and analyse the interaction between context and the content of change, also with respect to HRM policies

TABLE 2.5 Conditions governing the degree of leeway

Conditions	Room for manoeuvre	
	Large	Small
Market structure	Monopoly	Polypoly
Competitive strategy	Differentiation/focus	Price
Ratio labour cost/total costs	Towards 0	Towards 1
Financial leeway	Present	Absent

Source: Paauwe (1991: 11)

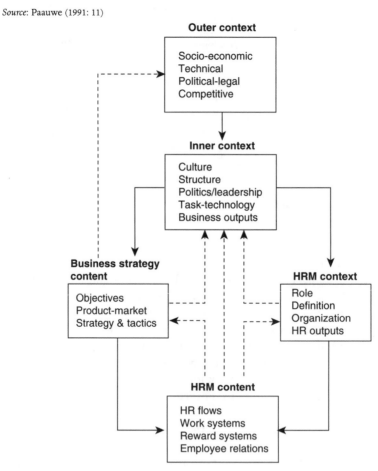

Fig 2.4. Strategic change and human resource management

Source: Hendry and Pettigrew (1990). Reprinted with permission of Taylor and Francis Ltd.

and practices, in more than twenty leading companies in the UK. One of their important research findings is that a purely mechanistic way of achieving fit between strategic changes and HRM policies is out of the question. Based on the influence of both the outer context (including economic, technical, and socio-political factors) and the inner context (including culture, structure, and politics/leadership), the interaction between strategic change and HRM is far more complex.

In discussing the linkage between corporate strategy and HRM, Bamberger and Philips (1991) also point to the importance of environmental factors such as government regulation, labour market conditions, and union strength. Their modelling considers the environment as a mediating variable for human resource management strategies. I shall refer to these findings again in Section 2.6.

A mixture of both process and content is the so-called Harvard model by Beer *et al.* (1984), one of the best known models in HRM theorizing, which starts from a situational perspective (Figure 2.5). Next to market and strategic considerations, it purposively takes into account the interests of the various

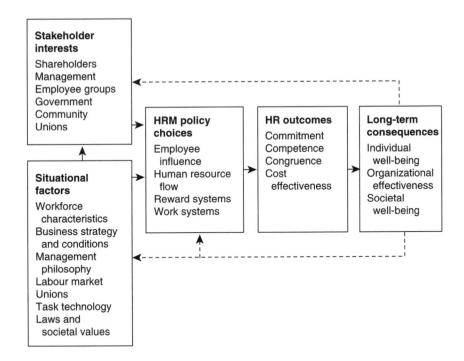

Fig 2.5. The Harvard approach

Source: Beer *et al.* (1984). Reprinted with permission of B. Spector.

HRM and Performance

stakeholders in both the external and internal environment. The emphasized outcomes include not only performance in its strict economic sense, but also individual well-being and societal consequences. The framework is both descriptive and prescriptive. It gives a good overview of the factors that are important in shaping HRM policies, but at the same time is quite conclusive in prescribing the kind of outcomes to which these choices, once made, should lead.

Fombrun *et al.* (1984) (the competition from Michigan Business School) published their approach in the same year as their Harvard counterparts. In their model, achieving a tight fit between strategy, structure, and HRM policies takes place amidst economic, political, and cultural forces. Focused more on the functional level of HRM itself, they emphasize the so-called human resource cycle, which can be considered as one of the first content models. In their cycle, performance is dependent upon selection, appraisal, rewards, and development (Figure 2.6).

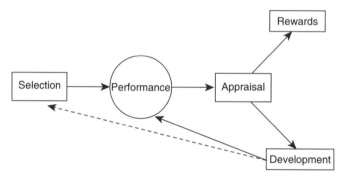

Fig 2.6. The human resource cycle

Source: Fombrun *et al.* (1984). Reprinted with permission of John Wiley & Sons Inc.

The final classic model (if we are allowed to use the word 'classic' in the still rather young discipline of HRM) to be presented here is the model by Schuler and Jackson (1987). Using Porter's generic strategies as a point of departure, they develop a repertoire of role behaviours for every type of strategy (cost effectiveness, innovation, and quality). Subsequently HRM policies and practices are used to stimulate or even enforce the required role behaviours. Table 2.6 presents an overview of the range of possible role behaviours.

The role behaviours required for every distinct competitive strategy differ, and these can be stimulated by a consistent set of HRM practices. For example, in the case of a firm pursuing an innovation strategy, the profile of employee behaviour includes (Schuler and Jackson, 1987: 209):

- A high degree of creative behaviour
- A longer-term focus

TABLE 2.6 Employee role behaviour for competitive strategies

Non-competitive strategy	Competitive strategy
1. Highly repetitive predictable behaviour	Highly creative, innovative behaviour
2. Very short-term focus	Very long-term behaviour
3. Highly co-operative, interdependent behaviour	Highly independent, autonomous behaviour
4. Very low concern for quality	Very high concern for quality
5. Very low concern for quantity	Very high concern for quantity
6. Very low risk taking	Very high-risk taking
7. Very high concern for process	Very high concern for results
8. High preference to avoid responsibility	High preference to assume responsibility
9. Very inflexible to change	Very flexible to change
10. Very comfortable with stability	Very tolerant to ambiguity and unpredictability
11. Narrow skill application	Broad skill application
12. Low job (firm) involvement	High job (firm) involvement

Source: Schuler and Jackson (1987); reprinted with permission from the Academy of Management.

- A relatively high level of co-operative, interdependent behaviour
- A moderate degree of concern for quality
- A moderate concern for quantity
- An equal degree of concern for process and change
- A greater degree of risk taking
- A high tolerance of ambiguity and unpredictability

On the basis of the required types of role behaviour, the following HRM practices can be used to stimulate the employee's behaviour in the case of an innovation strategy (Schuler and Jackson, 1987: 213):

- Job designs that stimulate close interaction and co-ordination among groups of individuals
- Performance appraisals that are more likely to reflect longer-term and group-based achievements

- Jobs that allow employees to develop skills that can be used in other positions in the firm
- Compensation systems that emphasize internal equity rather than external or market based equity
- Pay rates that tend to be low, but allow employees to be stockholders and have more freedom to choose the mix of components (salary, bonus, stock options) that make up their pay package
- Broad career paths to reinforce the development of a broad range of skills

According to Schuler and Jackson (1987), these practices are aimed at facilitating co-operative interdependent behaviour that is oriented towards the longer term and fosters an exchange of ideas and risk taking. The authors follow the same kind of reasoning for the quality and low cost strategy, and in this way are able to present three hypotheses concerning the relationship between competitive strategy, required role behaviours, and related HRM policies and practices (1987: 213). In this respect, one could say that Schuler and Jackson were among the first to describe in a clear-cut way how strategy and HRM policies could be related. They offer a concrete insight into the possible linkages between the content of a certain strategy and the kind of HRM policies that would help to implement that strategy. However, in reality, distinctive competitive strategies are not really that clear-cut. Moreover, one company or one business can have more than one strategic orientation related to a variety of product market combinations, as Vloeberghs (1997: 77) correctly notices. In such a case the required role behaviours are highly mixed. Actual company practice has overtaken this way of modelling. Since the early 1980s we have experienced an enormous rise of so-called high performance, high involvement work systems, which have been applied successfully in a range of industries and do not distinguish between different strategies. This touches on the issue of the universalistic approach of 'best practices' versus the contingent approach of 'best fit', an issue that will be discussed in more detail in Chapter 4 on HRM and performance.

2.6 HRM and strategy: a multitude of linkages

The above overview of models in the area of HRM and strategy is just a selection of all available models. Instead of extensively summarizing a range of models, I have opted for an overview at a more abstract level by discussing how the thinking on the kind of linkages between strategy and HRM has evolved since the early 1980s. As with strategy models, this overview begins in a clear-cut and simple form. Golden and Ramanujam (1985; see also Kluytmans and Paauwe, 1991) distinguish four different kinds of linkages, which represent an increasingly closer relationship with corporate or business strategy.

1. *Administrative linkage.* This kind of linkage (more accurately—hardly any linkage!) reflects the traditional and administrative role of the personnel management function (e.g. Tyson's 'clerk of works' model, 1987), in which there is little interest in establishing a relationship between the strategic orientation of the company and HRM policies and practices.

2. *One way linkage.* Once the strategy has been formulated, the specialist personnel function will be involved in order to design policies and practices that will help to implement the strategy. The personnel management function itself does not participate in the process of strategy formulation. Some authors label this as the reactive role for HRM (Kydd and Oppenheim, 1990).

3. *Two-way linkage.* The relationship between corporate strategy and HRM is a balanced and reciprocal one. Each influences the other, and the personnel management function really contributes to the process of strategy formulation.

4. *Integrative linkage.* The relationship between corporate strategy and HRM is characterized by a strong degree of interaction, both in a formal and an informal way. Both managers and the staff specialists involved operate in the same networks. They have a mutual influence on one another, and responsibility for human resource management is intricately interwoven with responsibility for overall corporate strategy and policies.

Lengnick-Hall and Lengnick-Hall (1988: 455–6) are strongly in favour of developing reciprocal interdependence between strategy and HRM, for the following reasons. First, an integrated approach offers a broader range of solutions to complex organizational problems. Second, integration assures that human, financial, and technological resources are given consideration in setting goals and assessing capabilities for implementation. Third, integration forces organizations explicitly to take into account the individuals who compromise them and who have to implement the strategies. Fourth, reciprocity and integration limits the subordination of human resource preferences to strategic considerations and also limits the neglect of human resources as a vital source of organizational competence and competitive advantage. Here we catch a first glimpse of what will eventually become a very important element in HRM thinking, i.e. the so-called resource-based view.

With a special focus on strategic decision making in the multi-divisional company, Purcell and Ahlstrand (1994) distinguish between *first-order strategies*, concerned with the enterprise's basic goals and the range of businesses and markets served; *second-order strategies*, which focus on the decisions on internal operating procedures; and *third-order strategies*, focusing on employee relations and human resource strategies. Their modelling includes both downstream (from first to third order) and upstream patterns of decision making, but they admit that the dominant mode in the empirical reality is still the downstream pattern. This is why they state conclusively: 'Thus an understanding of human resource strategy can only come about by looking at the opportunities and constraints imposed by first and second order strategies' (Purcell and Ahlstrand, 1994: 48). Human resource management, whatever the rhetoric, is now seen as a third-order activity, shaped largely by the bigger decisions of strategy and structure (Purcell and Ahlstrand, 1994: 80).

More recent research by Gratton *et al.* (1999) indicates the different linkages between what they call 'people processes' and 'business strategy'. Their findings are based on in-depth case-study research among seven large companies (among others, Hewlett-Packard, Glaxo Welcome, and Citibank) in the UK, belonging to the so-called 'Leading Edge Research Consortium'. This was a research project aimed at creating a deeper understanding of those processes that link business strategy to the performance of individuals and the organization. Apart from the well-known distinction between *vertical* linkage (the relationship between business strategy and HRM strategy) and *horizontal* linkage (the consistency and coherence among the various HRM policies and practices), they also mention so-called temporal linkages and—more importantly—point to the difference between the short-term and the long-term and how these relate to the varying strengths of the linkages between people processes and overall corporate strategy.

Temporal linkages

Especially where major organizational restructuring (extreme change and transformation) may be in progress, it is important to balance the need for continuity and consistency in the long run with the challenge of momentary change. In particular, where HRM strategies are concerned, it is important to emphasize the long-term perspective, because the time cycle for people resources is longer than that for financial or technological resources. There must be a vision of the future and a focus on concerns (for example building up leadership, skills, and competences) that are broader, more long-term-oriented, and less problem-centred than the short-term delivery of business goals (Gratton *et al.*, 1999: 21–2). In this respect, it is also important to pay attention to the differences in time cycles between Europe and the Anglo Saxon countries. Chapter 8 below, dealing with the introduction of self-managing teams and flexibility in subsidiaries of the same company in both the USA and the Netherlands, is illustrative in this respect.

Varying strengths of linkages

Closely related to the whole issue of short term versus long term are the varying strengths of linkages between business strategy and HRM strategy and how they affect individual, team, and firm performance. Referring to the short-term linkages, the research outcomes of Gratton *et al.* indicate strong linkages in the areas of:

- the process of *objective-setting*—how to relate required business results to individual and team behaviour and outputs;
- *training*: substantial investments in training in order to meet immediate skill needs;
- *rewards*, especially strong in the American multinationals.

A more medium, moderate linkage is found in the area of performance metrics. Linkages with financial performance are strongly present, but those related to the 'softer' people elements are much weaker.

With respect to the long-term linkages, Gratton *et al.* (1999: 25) find a strong linkage only in the area of leadership development and high-potential cadres. At shop-floor level the development of the workforce lacks a long-term perspective and is highly focused on the actual needs of the moment, which has implications for career planning and psychological contract. This section of the workforce is perceived as problematic in many companies.

Looking back at the overview of linkages, we can safely conclude that they represent different perspectives. Purcell and Ahlstrand (1994) focus on a more or less sequential pattern of decision-making and how it affects HRM strategy. Golden and Ramanujam (1985) and Gratton *et al.* (1999), discuss the strengths of the linkage between corporate strategy and HRM strategy.

I will finalize this section by presenting the overview developed by Guest (1997), inspired by Vektramanan (1989). In the area of strategic management research Guest distinguishes four different types of fit, each representing a different perspective on the linkage between corporate strategy and HRM policies and practices. Compared with the previous authors, and reflecting the progress in research in the 1990s, Guest's four forms of fit represent four different perspectives on how the linkage (or non-linkage) affects performance. This topic will be discussed extensively in Chapter 4. Figure 2.7 presents Guest's overview.

Fit as strategic interaction represents the well-known vertical linkage between corporate strategy and HRM. The hypothesis is that those organizations with the appropriate response and the right match will report superior performance (Guest, 1997: 270). The most usual way of testing this is by using one of the well

	Criterion-specific	Criterion-free
Internal	Fit as an ideal set of practices	Fit as gestalt; Fit as bundles
External	Fit as strategic interaction	Fit as contingency

Fig 2.7. Forms of HRM fit

Source: Guest (1997). Reprinted with permission of Taylor and Francis Ltd.

known typologies of Porter or Miles and Snow, relating it to an associated set of HRM practices, as has been done for example by Schuler and Jackson (1987), and hoping that the combination has a positive effect on some measure of performance.

Fit as contingency reflects the traditional contingency approach and suggests that those organizations whose HRM policies and practices are more responsive to external factors will report superior performance (Guest, 1997: 271). External factors in this case encompass more than just the product market combination and related corporate or business strategy and may also include labour market, legislation, and the specifics of the branch of industry.

Irrespective of external factors or the kind of strategy used, *fit as an ideal set of best practices* implies that there would exist a set of universally applicable so-called best practices. The closer the HRM strategy resembles this ideal set, the better the performance of the company.

The last fit distinguished by Guest is the *fit as gestalt or bundles*. 'Fit as gestalt' indicates an appropriate combination of practices to bring about effective HRM. The sum is greater than the parts, so it is either a synergistic combination of practices or the specific organizational architecture or culture, that binds them together. 'Fit as bundles' is closely related to this approach and implies the existence of a distinctive pattern or configuration (called 'bundles') of practices, that brings about superior performance.

Baron and Kreps (1999: 39; see also Buitendam, 2001) have developed a more extensive treatment of synergy and consistency among HRM practices. First, they distinguish *single-employee consistency*, emphasizing that the different elements of HRM policies and practices that bear on a single employee should be consistent with each other. Second, they distinguish *among-employee consistency*, which implies that employees belonging to the same skill or professional group and doing more or less the same work should be treated similarly. Finally, they distinguish *temporal consistency*, which implies that the way in which employee A is treated today should not differ too much from how he or she was treated yesterday.

Taking internal fit or consistency as described above seriously will result in a situation where the whole (of HRM practices) can be more than the sum of the parts.

2.7 HRM and strategy: lessons learned

The overview of the strategy concept and the different approaches to it in both strategic management and HRM has generated a number of insights, which are useful and which will be helpful in modelling the relationship between strategy, HRM, and performance in the following chapters.

First of all, it is important to accept the fact that simplistic reasoning based on distinguishing a range of strategy types and subsequent HRM policies and practices is out of the question. Becker and Huselid (in Wood, 1999: 377) rightly state that 'The HRM system should be highly idiosyncratic and tailored to each firms' individual situation.' Yet, even in unique situations, it is important to be able to map the various factors and variables that play a role in shaping HRM policies and practices. So it is important to harvest the insights, the clues, that have been generated in the previous sections of this chapter. A summary of these is as follows.

1. Both process and content approaches are important in establishing the relationship between HRM and strategy.

2. Both outside-in (Porter like) and inside-out (resource-based view) approaches are of relevance and can be combined on the basis of a coevolutionary perspective.

3. In addition to rationally planned strategies, (disturbing) cognitive processes, politics, and related power positions and resources also play a role, which leads to an emergent and interactive approach of strategy development. The process of strategy formation itself will be characterized by an interactive, iterative, and thus incremental nature, especially in the field of HRM, where a range of stakeholders (with their ideology and—to a certain degree—shared values) have an interest in the outcomes.

4. The entrepreneur him/herself—as part of the dominant coalition—can play an important role in shaping HRM policies and bringing about an ideology and culture, which is quite determinative in the subsequent shaping of HRM policies.

5. As well as competitive market forces, the social, legal, and cultural environment is important. Legislation, social partnership (between employers federations and trade unions) agreements, and directives can and will guide the shaping of HRM policies and practices in companies.

6. Shareholders are not the only stakeholders who are interested in the outcomes of strategic HRM: customers, employees, and their representative

bodies also have an important voice (whether one likes it or not) in all matters related to HRM.

Related to these last two points is the societal context of HRM. This will be discussed in the next chapter in greater depth. Institutional theory is especially important in this respect because it offers a range of useful concepts and insightful theorizing for discussing and highlighting the interactive relationship between managerial intentionality, organizational design (both with respect to strategy as well as HRM), and institutional context.

Notes

1. Volberda and Elfring (2001), after discussing the causes of fragmentation (pp. 11–12), present a synthesis by distinguishing three schools. For each school one can identify a related set of theories, a cluster of problem areas, and accompanying problem-solving tools (Volberda and Elfring, 2001: 17). Subsequently they present the following schools.

   The *boundary school* focuses on issues of make, buy, and co-operate, which implies that the boundaries of the firm become increasingly vague and difficult to define.

   The *dynamic capabilities* view considers strategic management as a collective learning process aimed at developing distinctive capabilities that are difficult to imitate. In contrast to the outside-in approach, this approach can be labelled inside-out. The starting point for strategic analysis and strategy development are the resources of the organization, which can be developed into distinctive capabilities.

   The *configurational school* equals the description given above as the synthesizing (tenth) school in Mintzberg *et al.*'s approach.

   Mintzberg himself does not seem to be very impressed by this new synthesis. In a short commentary, he simply relegates the boundary school to the environmental school and regards the dynamic capabilities view as a kind of hybrid of the design and learning schools (Volberda and Elfring, 2001: 42).

2. According to de Wit and Meyer (1998: 15) these ten strategy tensions are: logic *v.* creativity; deliberateness *v.* emergentness; revolution *v.* evolution; markets *v.* resources; responsiveness *v.* synergy; competition *v.* co-operation; compliance *v.* choice; control *v.* chaos; globalization *v.* localization; and profitability *v.* responsibility.

3 HRM in its Context: An Institutional Perspective

3.1 Introduction

In the preceding chapter, I showed how using 'outside-in' and 'inside-out' perspectives can facilitate a better understanding of the relationship between HRM, strategy, and subsequent performance. This chapter aims to examine the context of HRM in more detail.

I start by taking a closer look at the field of HRM itself (Section 3.2). Do different HRM models take into account the importance of context? Researchers in the field of industrial relations have a lot of experience with HRM. Dunlop's (1958) modelling is an example of a method that takes economic, technological, and social-political contexts into account.[1] The field of industrial relations (Section 3.3) motivated me to use institutional theory to construct a sound theoretical base that could encompass context in a study of HRM (Section 3.4). Institutional theory has often been criticized for putting too much emphasis on stability, for being deterministic and placing too much emphasis on the conservative and conserving nature of institutions. In response to these criticisms, I show how institutional theory is able to encompass change as well as the role of agency and the processes of deinstitutionalization (Section 3.5). Finally, I summarize my main findings and indicate how they can be used to build a more integrated perspective on HRM (in Section 3.6).

3.2 HRM modelling: is context taken into account?

Looking back at the classic HRM models of Beer *et al.* (1984) and Fombrun *et al.* (1984), we see that they were interested in the impact of context on HRM policies and practices. Fombrun's model (the so-called Michigan approach) refers to context in terms of economic, political, and cultural forces. Beer's model (the so-called Harvard model) is more explicit in that it recognizes a wide range of contextual factors ranging from stakeholder interests to situational factors. In addition to shareholders and management, they consider stakeholders such as employee groups, government, community, and unions. Situational factors that have an impact on the stakeholders include the labour market, task technology, laws, and societal values.

Since Fombrun *et al.* (1984) and Beer *et al.* (1984), research has continued in the field of HRM and performance. At present the main discussion is centred on specific aspects of building a model. The present state of the art focuses on how many boxes (sets of variables) should there be between, on the one hand, *strategic HRM* and on the other, *performance* (see Guest, 1997; Becker *et al.*, 1997; see also chapter 4) in order to account properly for the relationship between strategy, HRM, and performance. It seems that there is less explicit attention to context in current research. Nevertheless, almost every piece of empirical research incorporates control variables, which include contextual features such as the degree of unionization, industry/sector, education level, gender, and nationality. (For a summary of a number of research projects and the kind of control variables used, see Paauwe and Richardson, 1997: 260.) Delery and Doty (1996) distinguish the HRM theories of the last two decades under the headings of universalistic, configurational, and contingent. The latter in particular is interesting for our purposes. Contingency theory states that the relationship between the relevant independent variables (e.g. HRM policies and practices) and the dependent variable (performance) will vary according to influences such as company size, age and technology, capital intensity, degree of unionization, industry/sector ownership, and location.

The concept of 'fit' is also used in HRM theorizing to come to a better understanding of the impact of context. Traditionally, we distinguish only two kinds of fit: *horizontal (internal) fit*, which relates to the coherence and consistency among a set of related HRM practices, and *vertical (strategic) fit*, which relates to the relationship between business strategy and HRM strategies. Wood (1999), however, goes even further in his review article on HRM and performance, in that next to strategic fit and internal fit he distinguishes two more types:

1. *'Organizational fit'* is the coherent fit between sets of HRM practices (HRM systems/bundles) and other systems within the organization. This kind of fit will be dealt with in more detail in Chapter 4.
2. *'Environmental fit'* is the fit between HRM strategies and the organization's environment. This is the kind of fit we shall concentrate on in this chapter.

However, indicating and labelling it is not enough. We need theory to assess the relationship between a set of HRM policies and practices, and to explore how these relate, interact, or are influenced by the context. Moreover, how do we define 'context'? How can we develop a theory that will make it possible to generate hypotheses about the relationship between HRM and its wider context?

In comparing US-based HRM approaches to the real situation in Europe, Brewster (1993) discusses a range of differences and concludes with a plea to develop a 'European' model of HRM. According to Brewster (and many others, e.g. Guest, 1990), in the United States the HRM concept is based on notions of organizational independence and autonomy. However, in most European countries organizational autonomy is constrained at the national level by culture and legislation, at the organizational level by patterns of ownership/corporate governance, and at the HRM level by trade union involvement and consultative arrangements such as works councils (Brewster, 1993: 766). Therefore, what is needed is a model of HRM that can detect the influence of the above-mentioned factors. Brewster puts forward a European model, but with certain reservations, because Europe cannot be conflated into a single entity. The differences between the European countries are sometimes greater than the difference between, say, Germany and Japan, or between the UK and the USA (see Harzing and Sorge, 2003).

What we really need is a universally applicable model, a way of theorizing that can be applied, to every country; a theory that can accommodate the enormous variety in HRM policies and practices as well as the various contextual factors involved. Poole (1990) criticizes a number of HRM models, Beer's model among them, and suggests adding globalization, power, and strategic choice. Hendry and Pettigrew (1990) want to broaden HRM models by including economic, technical, and socio-political topics, including a range of factors that influence strategic decision making in HRM. Of course, all these authors emphasize that they do not want to fall into the trap of contingent determinism. There is, and should be, leeway for the actors involved to make strategic choices. These kinds of notions are current in the field of industrial relations, which has a tradition and a well developed range of theoretical models for carrying out internationally orientated comparative research. For this reason, we now take a closer look at the field of industrial relations.

3.3 The interaction between HRM and industrial relations

From its early inception, the concept of HRM and its relationship with and implications for the area of industrial relations (IR) has received a lot of attention (see Guest, 1987; Storey, 1989; Poole, 1986; Storey and Sisson, 1993; de Nijs, 1996). We are especially interested in what we can learn from industrial relations theory, and from modelling in particular, for the development of an integrated HRM framework that can take context into account explicitly. The classic Dunlop IR model is based on systems thinking and distinguishes not only context, but also actors and shared ideologies. Context, which according to Dunlop (1958: 48) is decisive in shaping the rules established by the actors in an industrial relations system, is subdivided into the following three domains:

1. Technological characteristics of the workplace and community
2. Product and factor markets and/or budgetary constraints
3. Political domain or the locus and distribution of power in society

The term 'actors' refers to hierarchies of managers (and their representatives), hierarchies of workers (and their representatives), and specialized governmental agencies. Shared ideology is defined as a set of ideas and beliefs commonly held by the actors to bind or integrate the system together as an identity (Dunlop, 1958: 53). According to Dunlop (1958: ix), the task of a theory in IR is 'to explain why particular rules are established in particular industrial relations systems and how and why they change in response to changes affecting the systems'. The roles of actors and of the ideology are limited to how they adapt the rules to changes that occur within the three aforementioned domains. The model can be applied at different levels of industrial relations: national, industry branch, and organizational.

Constructive criticism

Over the years, Dunlop's model of industrial relations has served as a focal point, both in practice and in terms of the criticism and suggestions for modification that it has provoked. In particular, the assumptions on which Dunlop's model is based (e.g. pluralism, positivism, and functionalism) have aroused much criticism. From the basis of an overview by Schilstra (1998: 20), the following main criticisms of Dunlop's systems thinking can be listed.

- Behavioural factors are virtually absent from Dunlop's framework. Although he emphasizes actors and their interactions, he neglects to analyse behavioural factors and treats interaction as a black box.
- Dunlop concentrates on rules and procedures as output, as dependent variables of the system. He does not explain the dynamic interactions, the process of how and when actors determine the rules (Schilstra, 1998: 20; see also Bain and Clegg, 1974: 92 and Blain and Gennard 1970: 403). This means that the emphasis is on the product, the web of rules and not on the process of rule-making itself

- Behaviour is mainly considered to be adaptive. It almost exclusively results from the context and changes therein (Schilstra, 1998: 22).
- Dunlop's focus on rules implies a focus on the output of the system. The idea of a 'web of rules' and the subsequent focus on job regulation seems to reflect a conservative bias. The approach only concentrates on accommodation and equilibrium, not on conflict and change (Schilstra, 1998: 23).

The notion of strategic choice

In his search for comparative frameworks within which to analyse industrial relations in different contexts, Poole (1986: 11) states that the main thrust of his theoretical position is that variations in industrial relations institutions and practices have their roots in the strategic choices of the parties in the employment relationship. The first application of the concept of strategic choice (Child, 1972) to the field of industrial relations can be traced back to, among others, Walker (1969), Poole (1986), and Kochan et al. (1984). Kochan and his colleagues extensively adapted and added to Dunlop's original framework. Their amendments included the following.

1. They saw a more active, as opposed to merely adaptive, role for management arising from the introduction of strategic choice. Of course, all parties involved can make strategic decisions, but Kochan et al. (1984: 17) consider management to be the dominant party in this respect.

2. They included more and interrelated levels of industrial relations. Next to the functional level of collective bargaining itself, they also included strategic and workplace levels in their analysis. The strategic level, by definition, concerns long-term and high-level planning and encompasses, from a management point of view, the strategic role of human resources. In much of their work, the strategic level is considered on a par with the corporate level. Kochan et al. (1984: 21) explicitly stress that theory should allow an exploration of both content and the process of strategy formation. The workplace level relates to factors such as supervisory style, worker participation, job design, and work organization (Kochan et al. 1986: 17).

3. They consider that the concept of strategy in industrial relations is useful only if actors have some discretion over decisions. As this is usually the case, there is no place for environmental determinism of the kind suggested by Dunlop (1958).

4. They say that the various levels interact and, because different ideologies dominate each level, instability and conflict are inevitable. However, it is only at the functional level, i.e. the level of collective bargaining, that there is a need for a common ideology to bind the system together.

Different rationalities

According to Poole (1986: 13), the concept of strategy encapsulates, at a more abstract level, the idea of overall design within social action, a design based upon rationality and calculus in the patterning of decisions. Following this line of reasoning, he associates the concept of strategy with the general categories of social action as follows.

- 'Instrumental-rational' refers to the means to utilitarian ends (reflecting material interests and the will to power). Weber (1946) labels this '*zweck-rationalität*'.
- 'Value-rational' refers to ethical, aesthetic, religious, political, or other ideals (involving identification and commitment). Weber (1946) labels this '*wertrationalität*'.
- 'Affectual/emotional' refers to the actor's specific affects and feelings (sentiments and emotions can enhance value-rational commitments).
- 'Traditional' refers to ingrained habits (the institutionalization of previous strategic decisions of either a utilitarian or an idealistic character).

In the field of human resource management, these four kinds of social action and their related rationalities and values are particularly relevant in shaping HRM policies and practices. From an economic and managerial perspective, very often only the instrumental-rational perspective is taken into account. Yet, especially when being involved in the shaping of the employment relationships, other categories of social action, based on values, affections, and traditions, are at stake.

Kochan *et al.* (1986) also attach importance to the role of values, which stem from different rationalities, and to the role of history and the processes of institutionalization. The framework presented in Figure 3.1 summarizes their conceptualization.

Summarizing, we can conclude that the related field of IR has a lot to offer. What have we learned so far?

- The importance of the context subdivided into the economic, technological and political domain
- The notion of strategic choice and discretion
- Different levels of analysis, levels that interact and do not necessarily share the same kind of ideology
- Different types of rationality
- The importance of values and ideology
- Actors and a social action perspective next to a systems perspective
- The importance of history and processes of institutionalization

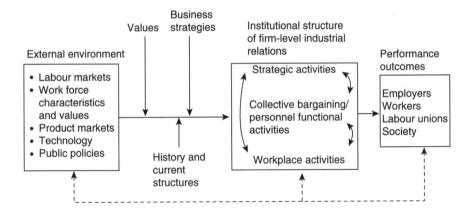

Fig 3.1. General framework for analysing industrial relations issues

Source: Kochan *et al.* (1986). Reprinted with permission of the Academy of Management.

This final point brings us into the realm of (new) institutionalism. This in turn gives us a sound theoretical basis for the inclusion of context in the study of HRM and a way to explore the effect of context on HRM practices, HRM policies, and performance.

3.4 Institutionalism and HRM

According to Powell (1998: 301), the idea that organizations are deeply embedded in wider institutional environments suggests, that organizational practices are often either direct reflections of, or responses to, rules and structures built into their larger environments (Meyer and Rowan, 1977). Jaffee (2001: 227), in a clear introduction to institutional theory, states that:

viewing organisations as institutions means that organisations have a history, a culture, a set of values, traditions, habits, routines and interests. This contrasts with the economic or bureaucratic view of organisations that views organisations as formally rational instruments for the realization of clearly defined objectives. Calling organisations 'institutions' means that they are not simply black boxes that produce goods and services, but human organisations driven by emotion and tradition. . . .

Thus, institutional theory combines a rejection of the optimization assumptions of the rational actor models popular in economics with an interest in institutions as independent variables (Powell, 1998: 301). The process of institutionalization itself can be defined as 'the processes by which societal expectations of appropriate organizational action influence the structuring and behaviour of organizations in given ways' (Dacin, 1997: 48). Selznick, one of the founders of institutional theory, used the term 'institutionalization' to refer to the organizational policies and practices that become 'infused with value beyond the technical requirements of the task at hand' (Jaffee, 2001: 227).

In general, institutional theory shows how the behaviour of organizations is a response not solely to market pressures, but also to institutional pressures e.g. from regulatory agencies, such as the state and the professions, and from general social expectations and the actions of leading organizations (Greenwood and Hinings, 1996).

At the beginning of the 1980s, a group of US-based sociologists presented themselves as *new* institutionalists. Academics such as Selznick, Meyer, Rowan, Scott, DiMaggio, Powell, and Zucker can be considered the founding fathers (and mother—Lynne Zucker) of new institutionalism. According to Greenwood and Hinings (1996), new institutionalism assumes that organizations conform to contextual expectations in order to gain legitimacy and increase their probability of survival. For an extensive treatment of the differences between old and new institutionalism, we refer to DiMaggio and Powell (1991).

With respect to the embeddedness of the relationship between HRM and performance, the contribution from DiMaggio and Powell (1983) is important. They state that rational actors make their organizations increasingly similar as they try to change them (homogenization). The concept that best captures the process of homogenization is isomorphism. DiMaggio and Powell (1983) say that *isomorphism* is a constraining process that forces one unit in a population to resemble other units that are exposed to the same set of environmental conditions. There are two types of isomorphism: competitive and institutional. *Competitive isomorphism* assumes a system of rationality, which emphasizes market competition, niche change, and 'fit', and is most relevant where free and open competition exists. However, for a more complete understanding of organizational change, DiMaggio and Powell (1983) focus more on an alternative perspective, namely *institutional isomorphism*. Three institutional mechanisms are said to influence decision-making in organizations: *coercive mechanisms,* which stem from political influence and the problem of legitimacy; *mimetic mechanisms,* which result from standard responses to uncertainty; and *normative mechanisms,* which are associated with professionalization. Coercive influence refers to the formal and informal pressures exerted by other organizations upon which a firm is dependent, as well as to the cultural expectations held by society. No wonder new institutionalism is linked to the resource dependency theory (e.g. Pfeffer and Salancik, 1978; Oliver, 1991; Zucker, 1977) and population ecology theory (e.g. Trist, 1977; Hannan and Freeman, 1977).

Lammers *et al.* (2000) state that new institutionalism criticizes the 'functionalistic contingency approaches' of the 1960s, which assumed that actors are rational. According to the authors, new institutionalists believe in the 'non-rationality' of processes at all levels in society, i.e. the micro (individual and organizational), meso (branch or industry), and macro levels (national or international). The central theme in new institutionalist approaches is the study of processes of cognitive and normative institutionalism, whereby people and organizations conform *without thinking* to social and cultural influences (Lammers *et al.*, 2000)—without thinking in the sense that these normative influences are *taken-for-granted* assumptions (Zucker, 1977) which actors perceive as being part of their objective reality.

Coercive mechanisms in our field of enquiry (human resource management) include the influence of social partners (trade unions and works councils), labour legislation, and government. Mimetic mechanisms refer to imitations of the strategies and practices of competitors as a result of uncertainty or fashionable hypes in the field of management. Organizations' current interest in developing and implementing HR scorecards (e.g. Becker *et al.* 2001) could be a typical example of a mimetic mechanism in the field of HRM. Normative mechanisms refer to the relationship between management policies and the background of employees in terms of educational level, job experience, and professional networks. According to DiMaggio and Powell (1991), it is these networks, in particular, that encourage isomorphism. Professional networks consist of, for example, universities and professional training institutes that develop and reproduce (taken-for-granted) organizational norms among professional managers and staff specialists in the different functional areas of finance, marketing, accounting, and HRM. To illustrate, everyone currently maintains that human resource management should be business oriented and should contribute to the process of adding value, whereas in the 1970s— in the Netherlands at least—HRM was all about supporting organizational democracy. An acknowledgement of the importance of distinguishing between different employee groups in organizations can be found in Mintzberg (1979) on organizational structures and in Snell (1992) on management control. Figure 3.2 gives a schematic overview of the way in which the three mechanisms identified by DiMaggio and Powell (1991) impact upon human resource management.

3.5 Institutional theory and change

Institutional theory has often been criticized as only being able to explain the persistence and the homogeneity of phenomena. Another critique is that it does not explain the role of interest and agency in shaping action (Dacin *et al.*, 2002: 45–7). Research by people such as Greenwood and Hinings, Oliver, and contributors to the special issue of the *Academy of Management Journal* (edited by Dacin *et al.*, 2002) convincingly demonstrate the opposite: i.e. that institutional

HRM and Performance

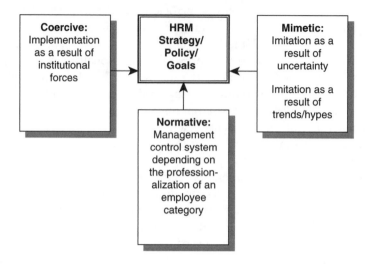

Fig 3.2. HRM and New Institutionalism

Source: Paauwe and Boselie (2003a). Reproduced with permission from *Human Resource Management Journal*.

theory can also account for change. The work by DiMaggio and Powell (1991), discussed in the preceding section, demonstrates how organizations change as a result of the influence of coercive mechanisms, mimetic forces, and normative pressures. However, these pressures imply that organizations in a specific organizational field (sector) will become more alike (i.e. via isomorphism, homogeneity). Therefore, although DiMaggio and Powell are able to account for change, it is change in the same direction, and their approach does not take into account the possibility of uniqueness arising from specific interests and human agency. Greenwood and Hinings (1996) do look at this problem. They start from the premise that a major source of organizational resistance to change derives from the normative embeddedness of an organization within its institutional context. In order to be able to account for change, they explore the interaction between context and (strategic) choice. More specifically, they focus on the link between organizational context, intra-organizational dynamics, and the role of individuals in making choices. They state that change, unique change, can occur only if an organization decouples itself from the institutional context and reformulates its internal interpretive scheme. An organization's interpretative scheme consists of

- assumptions about the appropriate domain in which the organization should operate;

- beliefs and values about the principles of organizing;
- defined performance criteria to assess success.

Decoupling from the institutional context depends on an organization's internal dynamics, which include

- the kind and degree of commitment to change;
- the power structures and coalitions favouring or opposing organizational change;
- the capacity to implement change. Greenwood and Hinings (1996: 1039) define this capacity as the ability to manage the transition process from one template to another.

Oliver (1991) complements this dynamic perspective and makes it possible to account for change in the institutional framework by showing how organizations can respond to institutional processes and by discussing the antecedents of de-institutionalization.

Organizations use different strategies (options) to respond to institutional processes ranging from acquiescence to manipulation. The scheme shown in Table 3.1, taken from Oliver (1991: 152), gives a full overview of the range of strategies/options.

The problem with this overview is that the responses are formulated either in a conforming way ('acquiesce'/'compromise') or in a negative way ('avoid'/'defy'/'manipulate'). If Oliver had also formulated positive and more constructive strategic responses, such as 'lead', 'initiate', and 'develop', the scheme would provide a more complete overview of strategic responses.

Oliver went on to introduce the idea of de-institutionalization (1992: 564), which she defined as the process by which the legitimacy of an established or institutionalized practice erodes or discontinues. In identifying the various factors that contribute to this process of de-institutionalization, and thus to change, she distinguishes two different groups of determinants. Based on a summary by Jaffee (2001), these two groups can be described as follows:

- *Intra-organizational determinants*: 'Pressures may arise within the organization as new members are recruited, performance declines, power alignments shift, goals are more clearly defined or the organizational structure is transformed owing to diversification or mergers. These rather common events can conceivably threaten, or at least call into question, institutionalised patterns of organization and behaviour and stimulate change' (Jaffee, 2001: 235; Oliver, 1992: 579).
- *External environmental forces*: 'These might include increasing competition or environmental turbulence, changes in government regulations, shifts in

TABLE 3.1 Strategic responses to institutional processes

Strategies	Tactics	Examples
	Habit	Following invisible, taken-for-granted norms
Acquiesce	Imitate	Mimicking institutional models
	Comply	Obeying rules and accepting norms
	Balance	Balancing the expectations of multiple constituents
Compromise	Pacify	Placating and accommodating institutional elements
	Bargain	Negotiating with institutional stakeholders
	Conceal	Disguising non-conformity
Avoid	Buffer	Loosening institutional attachments
	Escape	Changing goals, activities, or domains
	Dismiss	Ignoring explicit norms and values
Defy	Challenge	Contesting rules and requirements
	Attack	Assaulting the sources of institutional pressure
	Co-opt	Importing influential constituents
Manipulate	Influence	Shaping values and criteria
	Control	Dominating institutional constituents and process

Source: Oliver (1991). Reprinted with permission of the Academy of Management.

public opinion, dramatic events or crises and changes in task environment relationships' (Jaffee, 2001: 235; Oliver, 1992: 579).

Colomy (1998) introduced human agency and interests into the debate on institutionalism and change. He rightly drew attention to the role of human agency in transforming the normative, cognitive, and regulative aspects of institutions (see also Jaffee, 2001: 236). Moreover, Dacin *et al.* (2002) summarize a range of studies (e.g. Kraatz and Moore, 2002; Sherer and Lee, 2002; Townley, 2002; Zilber, 2002) that explicitly pay attention to the role of power, interests, and agency in determining how organizations interpret and respond to institutions: actors are not passive—they make choices in the interpretation of the meaning put forth (Dacin *et al.*, 2002: 47).

Towards a synthesis

Above, I outlined:

- The process of institutionalization that is aimed at bringing about stability, legitimacy and homogeneity
- The range of strategic responses open to organizations in reacting to institutional pressures
- The process of de-institutionalization (owing to environmental and/or intra-organizational forces)
- The role of human agency in changing institutions

The great variety of aspects of institutional theory put forward by different authors requires some kind of synthesis. Scott (1994) produced such a synthesis, and this is presented in the schematic overview of the cyclical and iterative processes by which institutions develop, reinforce, and change (see Figure 3.3).

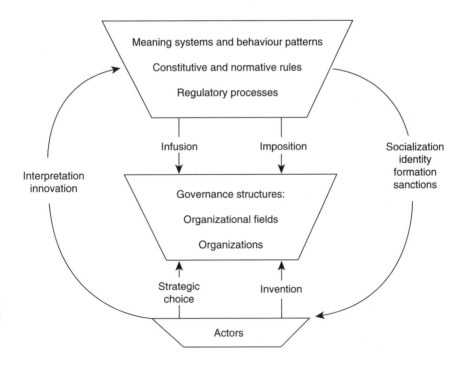

Fig 3.3. Institutions: a layered model

Source: Scott (1994). Reprinted by permission of Sage Publications, Inc.

As can be seen, institutions are made up of three components:

1. meaning systems and related behaviour patterns, which contain
2. symbolic elements, including representational, constitutive, and normative components, which are
3. enforced by regulatory processes.

'Meaning systems' refer to shared meaning, which is indispensable in collective activity. Meaning systems give rise to organizations as well as to distinctive fields of organizations. As meanings arise, they are preserved and modified by human behaviour, making related actions and patterns of behaviour equally important. The importance of human agents is illustrated in Figure 3.3 by the arrows linking institutional elements with actors. A meaning system must incorporate different kinds of rules in order to qualify as an institution. Representational rules are used to formulate the collection of knowledge claims, including empirically based observations and fundamental assumptions—for example that water flows downhill, and that foxes chase rabbits (Scott, 1994: 60). Constitutive rules describe the nature of actors and their capacity for action, defining their interests, rights, and capacities. Normative rules, finally, exist in the expectations that others have of our behaviour, and they become internalized through socialization processes. Examples are that as a citizen one should vote, or that one should not throw any waste out of the car window.

The regulatory processes are the enforcement mechanisms that back the institutional rules, either in formally designed and centralized form or in informally administered and decentralized shape. The regulatory processes can be defined on the basis of DiMaggio and Powell's (1983, 1991) contribution, distinguishing three mechanisms (coercive, mimetic, and normative) for enforcing organizations to become more alike (institutional isomorphism), as outlined in Section 3.4.

Having defined institutions and regulatory processes, Scott moves on to the level of organizational fields, as can be seen in Figure 3.3. He states that institutional arguments are applied logically, at the level of analysis of the organizational field, and not at the societal or individual organizational level. DiMaggio and Powell (1991: 64–5) define the concept of organizational field as 'those organizations that in the aggregate, constitute a recognised area of institutional life: key suppliers, resource and product consumers, regulatory agencies, and other organizations that produce similar services and products'.

Having described how institutional arrangements might influence organizations, Scott discusses what organizational structures result from the influence. From the basis of different assumptions regarding the role of rationality and intentional action in organization design, he distinguishes two camps of authors and researchers. One camp builds on a bounded rationality model to describe how actors deal with economic choices and their known and assumed effects in designing organizational forms; the second camp sums up a number of reasons why this line of thought is incorrect. Current choices are constrained by existing structures, information is imperfect, outcomes are often unanticipated, environments may change more quickly and more abruptly than expected, and dominant organizations may suppress the development of more efficient forms. In relation to HRM, Scott rightly draws our attention to the fact that both camps tell their part of the story and that we are in need of both.

3.6 Summary and conclusions

In the previous sections we have examined the context of HRM in more detail. Our quest focused especially on finding the right theoretical frameworks for including the context of HRM, since this is considered to be of importance when discussing the relationship between HRM and performance, at least so long as we have a debate between 'best practices' versus 'best fit'. The best fit assumes a fit between HRM and a range of contingencies including the context.

HRM theorizing itself provided us with a range of clues. In the first place, there are more fits than just the vertical and the horizontal—I have referred to organizational and environmental fit as well. The IR field has a reputation for explaining differences in industrial relations across countries on the basis of differences in context, be they political, historical, or economic.

The comparative aspect has always been very important in the field of industrial relations. Models can account for different systems of industrial relations per country, but also per branch or industry. A short overview led to the following findings, which are relevant for the relationship between strategy, HRM, and performance.

- The context can be subdivided into the economic, technological, and political domains.
- Leeway, strategic choice, and discretion counteract a too deterministic perspective.
- National, industry branch, and corporate levels interact and do not necessarily share the same kind of ideology.
- Different types of rationality affect decisions in the field of industrial relations and HRM.
- Next to a systems perspective, empirical reality demands an actors' and social action perspective as well.
- History and processes of institutionalization are important.

HRM and Performance

Our quest/search ended in the realm of institutional theory, especially new institutionalism. In considering the contributions of a range of academics, I emphasized the fact that, on the one hand, processes of institutionalization bring about stability, legitimacy, and homogeneity; however, on the other hand organizations are subject to change, owing to processes of de-institutionalization and human agency, in selecting a range of strategic responses that are open to organizations when reacting to institutional pressures.

In the next chapter we focus on the third building block, i.e. the concept of performance.

Note

1. 'Economic' includes ownership and control, organizational size and structure, the growth path of an organization, industry structure, and markets. 'Technological' includes skills, work organization, and labour force requirements of technologies. 'Socio-political' includes the institutional framework, particularly the national education and training systems.

4   A Multidimensional Perspective on Performance

4.1 Introduction[1]

This chapter sets out to develop a more encompassing perspective on the concept of performance. Very often the debate on HRM and performance is confined to the concept of business performance in financial economic terms. Such a narrow-minded definition does not do full justice to the concept of performance, especially in the area of HRM and performance. The preceding chapters on strategy and on institutional context have resulted in insights enabling us to develop a more encompassing concept of performance, which is based not only on economic rationality but also on other types of rationality.

In this chapter I begin with an overview of the background of the interest, both among academics and practitioners, in how HRM can contribute to performance (Section 4.2). Section 4.3 presents the different theories and conceptual models in this area, providing the platform for summarizing, in Section 4.4, the impressive amount of empirical research that has been carried out in the last two decades on both sides of the Atlantic. On the basis of that overview, I then present in a somewhat challenging way the missing elements in the present debate on HRM and performance in Section 4.5. These give rise to a more encompassing perspective on the concept of performance, in which a strategic dimension, a professional dimension, and finally a societal dimension are distinguished. In this way the balance is restored between economic and relational rationality, between 'zweck-' and 'wertrationalität'.

4.2 Reasons for the increased interest in HRM and performance

Why are academics in the field of HRM and business managers interested in HRM and performance? Is it just the profit factor, or is there another reason? Academics as well as managers seem to give particular attention to critical success factors and sustained competitive advantage of an organization.

HRM and Performance

In both this largely theoretical literature and the emerging conventional wisdom among human resource professionals there is a growing consensus that organizational human resource policies can, if properly configured, provide a direct and economically significant contribution to firm performance. ... literature, although largely conceptual, concludes that human resource management practices can help create a source of sustained competitive advantage ... (Huselid, 1995)

Pfeffer (1995) sees sustainable competitive advantage as something that

- distinguishes an organization from its competitors;
- provides positive economic benefits; and
- is not readily duplicated.

Both Huselid (1995) and Pfeffer (1995) use principles of *the resource-based theory of the firm* (RBV) (Wernerfelt, 1984; Barney, 1991, 1995; Grant, 1991; Mahoney and Pandian, 1992). In the resource-based view, the emphasis is on gaining sustainable competitive advantage by means of effective and efficient utilization of the resources of an organization. In this perspective the firm is seen as a bundle of tangible and intangible resources and capabilities required for product/market competition (Kamoche, 1996). MacDuffie states that

human resources can be a primary source of sustainable competitive advantage for a firm. Employee knowledge about products, processes and customers that is embedded in routines and social interaction patterns can create organizational capabilities more difficult to imitate than readily purchased technological capabilities. (MacDuffie, 1995: 198)

So it is no wonder that, in the area of HRM, the resource-based view has been widely applied by authors such as Wright *et al.* (1994); Paauwe (1994); Lado and Wilson (1994); Boxall (1996); Coff (1997, 1999); Barney and Wright (1998); Boxall and Steeneveld (1999); and Paauwe and Boselie (2000). In the contextually based human resource theory, Paauwe, inspired by Barney (1991), states that competitive advantage through people can be achieved/created only by human resource capabilities/competences that are valuable, rare, imperfectly imitable, and imperfectly substitutable (Paauwe, 1996). And of course these capabilities and competences need to be embedded in the right organizational structures, culture, and management systems.

The aspects 'valuable', 'rare', 'imperfectly imitable', and 'imperfectly substitutable' of the (human) resources of an organization determine whether the organization has the power/strength to develop a sustained competitive advantage.

4.3 Categorizing theories

The relationship between HRM and organizational performance has been widely debated over the last decade (Wright and Snell, 1998; Guest, 1999a, b; Purcell, 1999; Gerhart, 1999, Gerhart et al., 2000; Boselie et al., 2001; Delery and Shaw, 2001; Wright and Gardner, 2001).

Delery and Doty (1996) distinguish three dominant modes of theorizing in the literature on strategic human resource management and organizational performance: the universalistic, the contingent, and the configuration mode.

The universalistic mode is associated with the terms 'best practice' and 'high performance work systems' (HPWS), and its underlying assumptions or arguments may seem somewhat simplistic:

1. that there is a linear relationship between HRM practices or systems and organizational performance;
2. that 'best practices' are universally applicable and successful;
3. that organizational success is best measured in terms of financial performance: indicators such as profit, market share, and sales levels.

Osterman (1994), Pfeffer (1994), and Huselid (1995) may be taken to represent those who take a universalistic perspective. For example, Pfeffer (1994) argues that greater use of 16 specific practices, including participation and empowerment, incentive pay, employment security, promotion from within, and training and skill development, will result in higher productivity and profit across all types of organization.

Delery and Doty's *contingency mode* says that the relationship between the relevant independent variable and the dependent variable will vary according to such influences as company size, company age, technology, capital intensity, the degree of unionization, industry / sector, ownership, and location. Contingency arguments imply potentially complex interactions between HRM variables, between HRM variables and performance indicators, between HRM variables and contingency factors, and between performance and contingency factors. Delery and Doty (1996) cite Schuler and Jackson (1987) and Gomez-Meija and Balkin (1992) as mainstream contingency theorists, but the tradition goes back much further and includes the work of Woodward (1965), Pugh and Hickson (1976), Pugh and Hinings (1976), Pugh and Payne (1977), and Mintzberg (1979).

The *configurational mode* of Delery and Doty (1996) is rather more complex. Arthur's (1992; 1994) control and commitment HRM systems are based on the idea that 'the closer an organization's HR practices resemble the correct prototypical system [for its business strategy], the greater the performance gains' (Delery and Doty, 1996). MacDuffie's (1995) research findings in the automobile industry are seen as representative of the configurational perspective, where the holistic principle identifies a unique pattern of factors. This means that HRM practices affect performance not individually, but as inter-related elements in an internally consistent bundle or system of HRM practices. Also, the assumption of equifinality holds, which means that multiple unique configurations can result in the same kind of maximum performance (Ichniowski et al., 1997; Delery and Doty, 1996; see also Lowe et al., 1997; Appelbaum et al., 2000). The configurations used in this kind of research are very often ideal types rather than empirically observable phenomena. Another characteristic of the configurational mode is the internal fit, or consistency with other organizational systems (management control, budgeting) and organizational culture.

Guest (1997) takes a somewhat different approach. He recognizes three broad categories of general-level theory on HRM: strategic theories, descriptive theories, and normative theories. *Strategic theories* are concerned primarily with the relationship between a range of external contingencies and HRM policy and practice. The central theme here is that 'a good fit (strategy, policy and practices with the context) will be associated with superior performance' (Guest, 1997). The work of Miles and Snow (1981), Schuler and Jackson (1987), and Hendry and Pettigrew (1990) are examples of this type of HRM theory. Guest (1997) concludes that strategic theories are simplistic in characterizing HRM and are weak in specifying the process that links HRM to organizational performance and adopt a limited view of performance (concentrating too heavily on measures like profits and sales).

Guest's *descriptive theories* of HRM set out to describe the field in a comprehensive way. They map the field and classify inputs and outcomes, placing the emphasis on an open systems approach. Researchers using descriptive theories try to particularize the field under investigation and address some of the relationships within it (e.g. Beer et al., 1985; Kochan et al., 1986; Paauwe, 1989). This perspective could be considered realistic, but, as Guest says (1997), it fails to provide a clear focus for any test of the relationship between HRM and performance.

His *normative theories* of HRM are more prescriptive, taking the view either that a sufficient body of knowledge exists to provide a basis for prescribed best practices, or that a set of values indicates best practice (Guest, 1997). Research by Walton (1985), Lawler (1986), Guest (1987), and Pfeffer (1994) is representative of this approach. According to Guest (1997), normative theories are predominantly focused on the internal characteristics of HRM at the expense of broader strategic issues, while leaving unclear the basis for specifying the list of HRM practices.

Existing conceptual models

The first conceptual models explicating the relationship between HRM and performance are probably the classic models of Beer *et al.* (1984) and of Fombrun *et al.* (1984), as discussed in Chapter 2. Beer *et al.* link HRM policy choices (with respect to employee influence, human resource flows, reward systems, etc.) first of all to HRM outcomes, which in turn have an effect upon long-term consequences. HRM outcomes are the '4 Cs': commitment, competence, congruence, and cost effectiveness. Long-term consequences are subdivided into individual well-being, organizational effectiveness, and societal well-being.

Fombrun *et al.* (1984) develop the so-called HR cycle, in which four crucial HRM practices (selection, rewards, appraisal, and training/development) contribute to performance at both individual and organizational level.

Guest (1987) develops a normative model, identifying four policy goals: integration, employee commitment, flexibility/adaptability, and quality. In his model these goals serve as human resource outcomes; goals and policies together generate a range of organizational outcomes such as high job performance and low turnover. Table 4.1 presents a full overview of the model based on Guest (1987).

Since then a lot of empirical research has been carried out. This has been summarized by Paauwe and Richardson (1997), using the framework presented in Figure 4.1. In the next section I give a full overview of this framework. The latest developments in building theoretical frameworks focuses on the discussion of how many boxes should there be in between HRM and firm performance, and on the crucial links between independent variables like business and/or HRM strategy and financial performance indicators.

Becker *et al.* (1997) present a conceptual model of the HR–shareholder value relationship (see Figure 4.2). In this model the authors assume that business and strategic initiatives affect the design of HRM systems. The HRM systems in their conceptual model affect: (1) employee skills, (2) employee motivation, and (3) job design and work structures. These factors are presumed to have an impact on productivity, creativity, discretionary effort, and so on. In total, this conceptual model contains seven 'boxes' and, in effect, represents a chain of excellence. The final 'box', and thus the ultimate outcome of this chain, represents the market value of the firm.

To date there is very little research that 'peels back the onion' and describes the processes through which HRM systems influence the principal intermediate variables that ultimately affect firm performance as described in Figure 4.2.

HRM and Performance

TABLE 4.1 Policies for identifying human resource and organizational
outcomes

Policies	Human resource outcomes	Organizational outcomes
Organizational and job design		High job performance
Policy formulation and implementation/ management of change	Strategic planning/ implementation	High problem solving
Recruitment, selection, and socialization	Commitment	Successful change
Appraisal, training, and development	Flexibility/adaptability	Low turnover
Manpower flows— through, up, and out of the organization		Low absence
Reward systems	Quality	Low grievance level
Communication systems		High cost-effectiveness, i.e. full utilization of human resources

Source: Guest (1997); reprinted with permission of Blackwell Publishing.

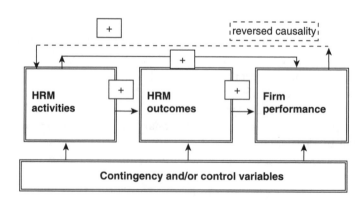

Fig 4.1. General overview of the linkage between HRM activities, outcomes, and performance

Source: Paauwe and Richardson (1997).

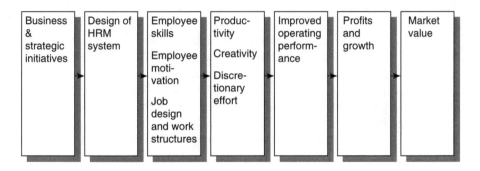

Fig 4.2. A model of the HR–shareholder value relationship

Source: Becker *et al.* (1997). Reprinted with permission of John Wiley & Sons Inc.

At about the same time, Guest (1997) presented his conceptual model for 'linking HRM and performance' (see Figure 4.3). In contrast to that of Becker *et al.* (1997), Guest's model focuses on HRM practices (instead of HRM systems). In it the HRM outcome, 'high commitment', represents the desire to belong to the organization and the willingness to do things for the organization; 'high quality' refers to the capabilities and to the knowledge and skills of staff; and 'flexibility' stands for the functional (rather than numerical) flexibility of the employees of the firm. Guest assumes that 'only when all three

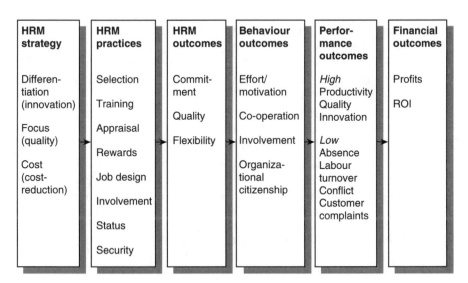

Fig 4.3. Linking HRM and performance

Source: Guest (1997). Reprinted with permission of Taylor and Francis Ltd.

HRM outcomes are achieved can we expect behaviour change and higher performance'.

Wright and Gardner (2001) observe two fundamental questions with respect to this type of conceptual modelling: How many boxes should be in the black box? And what should be in each box (or, how may items should be put in each box)? To open the black box with respect to the relationship between HRM and performance, boxes can be added to the existing conceptual models. In addition, more items can be added to each (main) box, thus creating what the authors call 'sub-boxes'. According to Wright and Gardner (2001), such an approach creates complexity, and the phenomena in the end will become unmanageable. Until now there has been no consensus in the field of HRM with respect to this problem. Another very important notion is related to the linearity of the models: 'The similarity among all of these models is that they all have their basis in a linear causal process' (Wright and Gardner, 2001).

Evidence for non-linear relationships in empirical research (e.g. Arthur, 1994) suggests that the reality is more complex than most of the existing conceptual models we tend to apply. A second notion of Wright and Gardner (2001) deals with the question: What is the causal direction? It can very well be the case that positive financial results also generate improvements in a range of HRM practices.

The models of Becker *et al.* (1997) and Guest (1997) both reveal a number of 'hidden' assumptions, relevant for further research on the relationship between HRM and performance:

1. Vertical 'fit' is a necessary condition for success, represented by the link between strategy and design of HRM systems or HRM practices.
2. The relationship between HRM and performance is linear. (See also the majority of previous research on HRM and performance—among others Arthur, 1994; Huselid, 1995.)
3. There is a sequential link between HRM ('design of HRM system' or 'HRM practices') and market value / financial performance. In other words, there is a chain of interrelated boxes.
4. Financial performance, represented by profits, growth, and market value, is the final outcome of the transformation process and therefore is representative of organizational performance and subsequent success.

4.4 HRM and performance: what has been achieved up to now?

Empirical results on HRM and performance have been presented in a range of special issues of international academic journals like the *Academy of Management*

Journal (39/4, 1996), *Industrial Relations* (35/3, 1996), the *International Journal of Human Resource Management* (8/3, 1997; 12/7, 2001), *Human Resource Management* (Fall, 1997), *Human Resource Management Review* (8, 1998), the *Human Resource Management Journal* (Fall, 1999), *Personnel Psychology* (53, 2000) and again the *Human Resource Management Journal* (13/3, 2003). Continued interest in the topic is evident from international seminars and conferences, which have been and continue to be organized.

The framework devised by Paauwe and Richardson (1997) synthesizes the results of prior research (see Figure 4.4). HRM activities give rise to HRM outcomes, which influence the performance of the firm. Some HRM activities, however, influence the performance of the firm directly (see upper arrow). The dashed reverse arrow indicates the possibility of reverse causality (Hendry *et al.*, 1989; Hiltrop, 1999; Laroche, 2001), i.e. that firm performance itself will give rise to a change (very often perceived as an improvement) in HRM practices. The appendices to this chapter summarize the results of a large number of empirical papers. Appendix 4.1 presents an overview of empirical research, specifying the relationships between HRM activities, HRM outcomes, and subsequent effects upon firm performance, as depicted in Figure 4.4.

Comparing US, UK, and Dutch approaches

Quantitative research on the links between HRM and performance has been carried out mainly by US and UK academics (in the US or UK context), although worldwide research on HRM and performance is gaining popularity; for example, Boselie (2002) presents an overview of studies carried out in a number of other countries (see Table 4.2).

Appendix 4.2 provides an overview of some notable papers from the USA and the UK. These articles draw on a variety of theories such as contingency theory, socio-technics, and resource-based theory. The majority of US-based academics explicitly base the use of bundles on strategic human resource management principles and adopt a shareholder perspective, paying little or no attention to other stakeholders such as employees, trade unions, and society at large. They therefore focus on productivity or financial performance indicators such as the return on investment or assets or equity, or Tobin's q.

In contrast, UK research projects (e.g. Guest and Peccei, 1994; McNabb and Whitfield, 1997) apply a stakeholder perspective, or at least some sort of pluralist framework, and include such outcomes as absenteeism, employee turnover, commitment, motivation, satisfaction, trust, conflict, and social climate. Also, most UK academics are sceptical of the 'American Dream' view, which maintains that 'best practice' will emerge from universal or normative modelling (Guest, 1992; Purcell, 1999; Tyson, 1999).

HRM and Performance

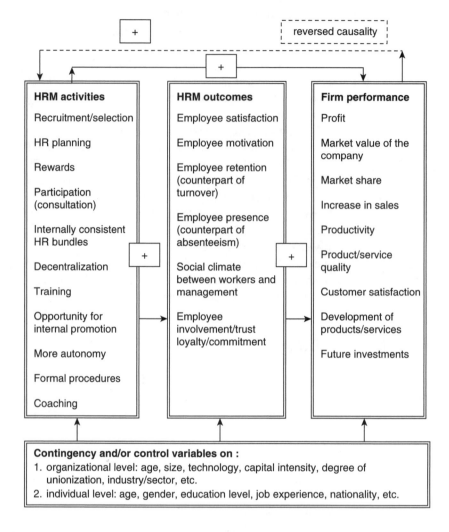

Fig 4.4. HRM activities in relation to HRM outcomes and firm performance

Note: adapted version of Paauwe and Richardson (1997).

One of the problems in nearly all the existing literature (for an overview see Gerhart, 1999) is a reliance on cross-sectional work that makes it virtually impossible to be confident about the causal relationships linking HRM to outcomes. As Arthur (1994: 684) expresses it, 'although the findings of this study are consistent with a conceptual model in which the choice of human resource system leads to changes in manufacturing performance, the cross-

TABLE 4.2 Overview of studies of HRM and performance outside the
UK and USA

Country	Studies
Australia	Gollan and Davis (1999)
Canada	Godard (1998)
China	Mitsuhashi *et al.* (2000).
Finland	Lahteenmaki *et al.* (1998)
France	d'Arcimoles (1997); Laroche (2001)
Germany	Backes-Gellner *et al.* (1997)
Greece	Panayotopoulou (2001)
Ireland	Flood *et al.* (1999); Monks and Schuster (2001)
Japan	Ichniowski and Shaw (1999); Kato and Morishima (2002)
Korea, Taiwan, Singapore, and Thailand	Bae and Lawler (2000); Bae *et al.* (2001); Huang (2001)
Netherlands	Leijten (1992); Leget (1997); Verburg (1998); Biemans (1999); Meihuizen (1999); Doorewaard and Meihuizen (2000); Boselie *et al.* (2001a); Den Hartog and Verburg (2001); Boselie (2002)
New Zealand	Guthrie (2001)
Russia	Fey *et al.* (2000); Fey and Björkman (2001)
Spain	De Saa Perez and Garcia Falcon (2001)

Source: Boselie (2002).

sectional data used here did not permit any tests of the causal ordering between effects of system and performance'.

Some studies, e.g. Banker *et al.* (1996), Lazear (1996), Pil and MacDuffie (1996), and d'Arcimoles (1997), do use a longitudinal research approach. Nevertheless, data collection on management issues over a long time period is still difficult and may be too expensive if traditional survey methods are used. A possible solution may be to analyse existing databases of business organizations, specialist research institutions, or branch organizations. One of the few studies using both cross-sectional and longitudinal data is the one by Guest *et al.*

(2003). Using subjective performance indicators, they establish a range of associations between HRM and both productivity and financial performance, but their study fails to show that HRM causes higher performance. Their analysis of longitudinal data lends stronger support to the view that profitability creates scope for more HRM, rather than vice versa (Guest *et al.*, 2003: 309).

The literature mentioned in Appendix 4.2 pays relatively little attention to contingency variables such as the age, size, technology, and unionization of firms. Although such variables are sometimes included in the model, the researchers tend to downplay, or even ignore, their relevance. Control variables such as the size and technology level of firm normally account for a great deal of the variance in statistical analyses of organization studies. (Evidence for this statement is provided in Appendix 4.1.) Together with organizational factors (size, sector, trade union presence, age, R&D intensity, and capital intensity), Guest (1999b) also emphasizes the potential importance of the personal characteristics of personnel, such as age, gender, qualifications, income, and position in the organization. From an overview of 60 empirically based papers, Boselie and Dietz (2003) conclude that the above-mentioned contingency factors were those most frequently mentioned. In the conceptual model by Paauwe and Richardson (1997) these items are represented as contingencies or control variables on an organizational and individual level (see Figure 4.4).

Empirical results from the Netherlands

Appendix 4.3 gives a summary of empirical research carried out in the Netherlands. The work of Leijten (1992), Leget (1997), and Verburg (1998) closely follows the tradition of the US research. They tend to use HRM typologies, or clusters (bundles), to focus on financial performance indicators, to analyse at the organizational level, to use quantitative cross-sectional surveys, and to adopt a 'hard' HRM approach.

Another line of Dutch research focuses more on the way human resource management is shaped within organizations. The approaches used by Paauwe (1989, 1998), ten Have (1993), Kluytmans and van Sluijs (1995), Looise (1996), Looise and Paauwe (1998), Schilstra (1998), and Kluytmans (1999) do not fit either Delery and Doty's (1996) categories or Guest's typology (1997). Their research was aimed not primarily at the relationship between HRM and performance (as independent and dependent variables respectively), but at the determining factors influencing the shape and formation of HRM policies and practices. In general, a variety of exogenous influences are seen to restrict the management's room to manoeuvre. Notably, in the Netherlands collective bargaining agreements and labour laws prescribe, prohibit, and influence the HRM policies and practices of organizations. Ten Have (1993) investigated 600 industrial companies and found that larger companies tend to retain their own individual methods of personnel management and hardly ever relate this to wider corporate strategy. He also concluded that a lack of 'fit' between corporate strategy and personnel management had no effect on company performance. It is striking that Huselid's (1995) US study on the role of 'external fit as matching' (fit between HRM and strategy) revolves around the same discussion; as yet there is no conclusive empirical proof that a fit between HRM and organizational strategy is necessary in order to create a better performance than competitors. This problem could be a reflection of measurement errors in this type of empirical research and may be difficult to overcome using 'conventional' survey methods. It could also be the result of a more serious theoretical issue: that the strategic HRM (SHRM) assumption of necessary fit between HRM and strategy to create a competitive advantage does not hold and therefore should be rejected. However, until now the data presented so far is inconclusive with respect to this point.

Paauwe's (1989) main conclusion, foreshadowing that of ten Have (1993), was that contingency factors affect the leeway of both organization and management. More recently, Paauwe (1998) has argued that between 10 and 12 of Pfeffer's (1994) 16 'best practices' had been in place in almost every Dutch company from the 1970s onwards via legislation, works councils, and trade unions (see Table 4.3). For example, the Dutch trade unions (FNV, CNV, etc.) have been influential in shaping HRM arrangements at the national level (SER, Stichting van de Arbeid, media, etc.), at the industry/sector level (via the collective bargaining agreement), at the company level, and at the business unit level (e.g. in the case of reorganizations).

In the Dutch context, trade unions work closely with the works councils, and every organization in the Netherlands with more than 50 employees is legally obliged to instal a works council. Dutch law equips the representatives of the employees with a number of rights towards the employer/management. Therefore, the institutional context has a profound influence on the shape of human resource management in Dutch organizations, and alternative theory (e.g. institutional theory) is needed to supplement existing frameworks in order to come to a more comprehensive understanding of the link between HRM and performance. The managers responsible for HR management are mainly engaged in applying labour legislation (conditions of employment, collective bargaining agreements, etc.) to their specific business organizations. It is a matter not just of 'seeking strategic HRM opportunities for sustained

TABLE 4.3 Pfeffer's 'best practices' and Paauwe's comments

Best practices (Pfeffer, 1994)	HRM practices that are common in the Netherlands (Paauwe, 1998)
1. Employment security	Yes
2. Selectivity in recruiting	No
3. High wages	Yes
4. Incentive pay	No
5. Employee ownership	Yes
6. Information sharing	Yes
7. Participation and empowerment	Yes
8. Self-managed teams	Yes
9. Training and skill development	Yes
10. Cross-utilization and cross-training	No
11. Symbolic egalitarianism	No
12. Wage compression	Yes
13. Promotion from within	Yes
14. Long-term perspectives	Yes
15. Monitoring of practices	No
16. All-embracing philosophy	No

Source: based on Pfeffer (1994) and Paauwe (1998).

competitive advantage', but also of 'implementing the labour regulations and agreements'. We can wonder whether, in such an institutionalized context, companies are still able to achieve a competitive advantage, because all companies have to meet the same requirements.

Two remarks have to be made in this respect. First, the effect on performance depends also on the specific application in a company and how it will be accepted and used by line management and employees. Truss and Gratton (2003) label this 'enactment'. A second remark refers to the level to which competitive advantage refers. One could say that at company level legislation and the influence of trade unions hinder the achievement/realization of a competitive advantage. However, at a national level the Dutch might be considered to be so-called 'early Pfefferites'; so at the level of nations competing for economic prosperity the Netherlands might have a competitive advantage. And indeed, in a list of top performing countries, the Netherlands is in the top four of the most competitive nations, after the United States, Finland, and Luxembourg (Institute for Management Development, 2002).

So the claim that externally imposed institutions will automatically have a negative impact on performance is too extreme. Even at company level some organizations succeed in creating competitive advantage in an institutionalized context, through a proactive and innovative attitude towards the regulations and institutions. Mirvis (1997) calls these types of organizations 'leaders' (i.e. HRM innovators), in contrast to 'laggards', which have difficulty in following and adapting to new rules. 'Leaders' possess organizational competences to 'overcome institutional obstacles', while 'laggards' perceive institutional mechanisms as restraining and threatening. An institutional requirement might be that a firm is obliged to hire a fixed percentage of non-natives, for example 10 per cent of the total workforce. An example of how a 'leader' company deals with this would be a fast-food chain which responds by employing a larger proportion of workers from ethnic minority groups in districts where the population is mainly made up of non-natives. The strategic consideration for the company is to 'match the cultural background of employees with the sphere of the neighbourhood and its potential consumers' (managing diversity), so creating competitive advantage through people; but the institutional requirements (the obligation to employ 10 per cent non-natives) provides the trigger.

The above mentioned review of papers from the USA, the UK, and a number of mainland European countries put a lot of flesh on the general skeleton (Guest, 1997) stating that HRM practices have an effect upon HRM outcomes, which in turn have an impact on the performance of the firm. However, do all these results and hypotheses tested also imply that we have thoroughly responded to Guests' call (1997) for a theory about HRM, about performance, and about the linkages between HRM and performance? Taking into account all the papers referred to, would it be safe to conclude that the gaps in theory are about to be filled in and that we are nearing the point at which we can allow ourselves to feel justifiably complacent? It could be argued that the key research issue of HRM and performance seems to be on track. There are methodological difficulties, which are readily acknowledged, but there is still a lot of research going on and we can expect many more interesting findings. However, there are other methodological, which imply more profound, problems with the current approaches. The use of cross-sectional data collected through preformatted questionnaires leads to an *imposed* reality upon the research subjects. This ignores the existence of an *emergent* reality. Once we accept the existence of such a reality, the difficulties of the previous approaches become apparent and a whole range of new issues and conceptual refinements arise. So it might be necessary to exchange the emerging feeling of complacency for a feeling of unease. The next section is meant to induce that feeling.

4.5 HRM and performance: missing elements

The notion of HRM and performance is based heavily upon the organizational imperative (Kamoche, 1994) and has a momentum for profitability, productivity, and cost efficiency. The prevailing dominance of the organizational imperative seems to be paralleled by neglect of a number of elements that are also extremely relevant. The following sub-sections describe these missing elements and the incomplete images of HRM and performance resulting from them.[2]

Human resources are not just resources. They are active individuals with a past, internalized values, and norms (not necessarily those of the employing organization). They belong to different groups inside and outside the organization, groups whose behaviour is governed partially by institutions. It's quite remarkable in this respect that many models used by HRM academics simply lack a clarification of the kind of view/image of mankind that they take as their point of reference.

Human resource management is more than being strategic and performance oriented. The HRM function as one of the organizational functions is also involved in the process of rendering professional services and establishing a sense of corporate citizenship. Taking a closer look at the HRM function and the different activities involved in it, we see that many of the activities carried out simply have to do with the rendering of services, preferably in a professional way. Many of these activities (for example complying with the regulations for health and safety, taking care of jubilees, early retirement schemes) are by no means strategic and do not (or not much) relate to the performance of the firm. They must be carried out, however, in a proper way because of all kinds of legislation, collective bargaining agreement regulations, and administrative/accounting practices. Especially from a Dutch/western European perspective, personnel management activities to meet the demands arising out of corporate social responsibility and related legislation and institutions are abundantly present, for example the employment of a set minimum percentage of people belonging to minority groups or handicapped, etc. This calls for a plea to include the professional rendering of services and the meeting of societal expectations as well as aspects of HRM performance.

Human resource research should imply more than just input/output systems reasoning. Many of the models and approaches utilized in research into HRM and performance employ a systems-based approach, which involves HRM practices and policies as input variables, HRM outcomes as intermediate variables, and firm performance indicators as the dependent variables. Contingency variables such as age, size, and technology are used as control variables. So there is a substantial negligence of the actual process itself (Tyson, 1996), the various actors and stakeholders involved, the administrative heritage, the values and institutions involved (Brewster, 1993; Paauwe, 1991).

The yardstick of human resource outcomes is not just economic rationality. At the beginning of this section I referred to the dominance of the organizational imperative with its emphasis on efficiency, effectiveness, etc. (Kamoche, 1994: 32). From the stakeholders' perspective, however, and recognizing the importance of values and institutions in the employment relationship, we should not focus exclusively on economic rationality. We need to adopt a broader perspective of business performance, which is also based on relational rationality (Eelens, 1995; Schipper, 1993). This concept relates to *the development and maintenance of sustainable relations with all the relevant stakeholders, not just customers and shareholders.* Maintaining relationships should be an end in itself. If the firm's relationship with, say, employees, works councils, and trade unions were seen as a means to an end, it would mean very little to the people involved. Trust and integrity are crucial in this respect. HRM should therefore include relational rationality as one of its objectives. Moreover, the very interplay between those two forms of rationality and the underlying processes of the various parties involved can generate unique possibilities for achieving competitive advantage (see Chapters 5 and 6).

HRM can be very effective by operating on a reactive short-term basis and just reducing the level of employment should the need for this suddenly arise. I have deliberately emphasized a number of perspectives that can be considered to be the opposite of HRM in order to contrast the so-called strategic and pro-active nature of the latter concept. Not everything can be planned for (see also Mintzberg, 1994), and sometimes the most effective form of HRM is the one that allows for a change in policies and practices quite flexibly on short notice. One of our case studies below involves a shipyard company—which has been among the most profitable in the Netherlands for many years—that simply refuses to put its personnel policies in writing because that would imply an inherent standardization which would impede flexibility and the ability to benefit from sudden market opportunities that might arise. Another example would be the need for an abrupt turnaround—because of a collapse in export markets, a political boycott of products (e.g. US import levies on steel), or the aftermath of an attack by terrorists (e.g. US airline companies being forced to reduce the level of employment after the drastic fall in air traffic passengers following the terrorist attack in September 2001.

HRM is not just about optimizing/maximizing performance. It's more about satisfying the different aspiration levels of the various stakeholders involved, such as employees, shareholders, works council members, and trade union activists. We sometimes have the impression that research in the area of HRM and performance is all about generating added value, generating profits; but an important aspect of HRM—especially if we focus on the employment relation-ship—is not so much the 'generating', but rather, bringing about a system of 'distributive justice' with respect to work, time, rewards, information, oppor-tunities for training and (career) development, and—finally—participation.

HRM is not just geared towards fulfilling/meeting strategic objectives. It's geared towards meeting a number of conditions that need to be fulfilled before we can start working on the realization of strategic objectives and the resulting performance. Research evidence from the Netherlands gives the following indications. A survey by Scheurer *et al.* (1993), based on 58 medium-sized organizations in industry, trade, and services, show that in 40 per cent of the cases there is no linkage at all between corporate strategy and personnel management. Another survey, by ten Have (1993), based on 600 industrial companies, draws the conclusion that personnel management in larger com-panies tends to follow its own leads and is hardly related to corporate strategy. In addition, ten Have notes that the lack of fit (i.e. linkage between corporate strategy and personnel management) does not seem to affect company per-formance (either negatively or positively). Also, Huselid (1995) finds no evi-dence for 'strategic fit' (which he labels 'external fit') between corporate strategy and HRM as a necessary condition for organizational success.

Are these findings disappointing? Or do they simply reflect that the policies and practices of personnel management are typically embedded in the system of institutional labour relations as it has evolved? An important role in this falls on the industrial relations parties via collective bargaining and collective measures. The role of the works council, which has legal competency in matters relating to personnel, might be even more important. The limited room to manoeuvre means that, apart from strategic objectives, HRM is shaped partially by the power relations among the parties concerned, each with their own objectives, interests, and claims vis-à-vis personnel management policies and practices.

Looking back at these missing elements, we can conclude that the initial overview of the research progress up to now is based on limited or unrefined assumptions, assumptions that do not take into account the underlying pro-cesses, the interaction patterns between parties concerned, and the institutional context, and are based upon a narrow-minded definition of performance. These unrefined assumptions imply the usage of limited analytical frameworks for analysing performance based on simple input/output reasoning. Needless to say, as a consequence people resort to/take refuge in a narrow research methodology, very often based on a cross-sectional research design and the use of pre-formatted questionnaires with as many closed questions as possible. The result is—albeit in itself quite impressive—the discovery of an imposed and limited reality.

So, we first need a more encompassing and sophisticated definition of performance, one that takes into account the pluralistic/multidimensional nature of the concept. Second, we need theoretical models and accompanying research designs that take into account the institutional setting and allow reality to emerge and enable us to analyse the underlying processes. One way of achieving this is to opt for models that combine different theoretical perspectives, such as systems theory, interactive models, a resource-based perspective, and organizational behavioural theory (see also Guest, 1997; Wright and McMahan, 1992). Before proceeding to that kind of model in the next chapter, I will sketch in the next section the contours of the concept of performance from a multidimensional perspective.

4.6. A multidimensional perspective on performance

On the basis of the core characteristics of strategic HRM, a number of authors and practitioners would argue that its *strategic contribution*, its closer alignment to business, is at the heart of HRM as a concept and as a normative model for a distinct type of personnel management. A consequence of this dominant characteristic of HRM is the emphasis in empirical research (see Appendix 4.1) on establishing the relationship (preferably a causal one) between a number of HRM policies and practices and the performance of the firm, for which very often financial–economic indicators are used. However, from our stakeholders' perspective, which incorporates both economic and relational rationality, we need a more multidimensional model of performance, because of the interaction between the need for HRM to contribute to business performance, to the professional rendering of services, and to the societal accountability of the firm.

The seminal writings by Beer *et al.* (1984) already included a multi-faceted approach to the concept of organizational effectiveness, using a stakeholders' perspective, which encompassed the interests of stakeholders such as employees, customers, shareholders, suppliers, works councils, and trade unions.

HRM and Performance

Many other academics also prefer to use stakeholder approach, including Kamoche (1994: 41); Paauwe (1994; 1996); Guest and Peccei (1994); Martell and Carroll (1995: 502); Backes-Gellner, Frick and Sadowski (1997); Looise (1996); Looise and Paauwe (1998); Boselie (1999); and Tyson (1999). All these authors are in favour of a more multidimensional concept of performance.

One of the most recent contributions in this area is from Boxall and Purcell (2003), who focus on labour productivity, organizational flexibility, and social legitimacy as goals of HRM. All these approaches are in contrast with the present practice in the USA, where *shareholder* models tend to be used for the most part.

Societal performance

As stated earlier in this chapter, financial performance indicators are too narrow to be reliable pointers to long-term organizational success. In the Rhineland models (typically in Germany and the Netherlands), stakeholders other than shareholders play a crucial role. Employees get support from works councils and trade unions. Their appraisal of an organization's performance is focused on topics such as:

- Productivity, continuity, and profits
- Health and safety conditions for employees
- Employment security (job security, insurances for sickness and/or unemployment)
- Development of employees (training and education)
- Wages
- Employee satisfaction
- Work pressure

Next to works councils and trade unions, the government and tri-or bipartite advisory bodies are important stakeholders representing society at large. Many governments issue legislation and guidelines (very often in close co-operation with associations of employers and trade union federations) concerning topics such as improving conditions for part-time work, combining work with care, and creating employment opportunities for ethnic minorities, disabled people, young unemployed people, and those who have been unemployed for long periods. Companies that adhere to this kind of legislation and guidelines thereby meet criteria of fairness and legitimacy. 'Fairness' in this respect refers to the principle of equity in the exchange relationship between individual and organization. 'Legitimacy' refers to the relationship between the organization and society at large. In the eyes of the main stakeholders, the way in which the company manifests itself in society should be perceived as legitimate. Meeting the criteria of fairness and legitimacy, and thus achieving relational rationality, contributes to the societal performance of an organization.

Professional performance

Focusing on HRM activities as carried out by a specialist staff department, we can use the concept of professional performance. With respect to the professional rendering of services by the specialist personnel function, both Tsui and Gomez (1988) and Guest and Peccei (1994) emphasize the link between the performance of the HRM function and the overall effectiveness or performance of HRM policies and practices. For this reason, they develop a range of indicators to measure the effectiveness of the HRM specialist staff department. (See the more practitioners' oriented Chapter 9 for an overview.)

On the topic of integration, Guest and Peccei (1994) distinguish four different types of integration or fit. The first two are the well-known vertical/strategic fit[3] and the fit among HRM policies and practices itself (horizontal fit).[4] However, in relation to the professional rendering of services, they also distinguish the following:

- *Functional integration*, focuses on the importance of a high-quality personnel department in order to realize the effective management of human resources. Indicators for this kind of integration are the staffing (quality) of the department and the location of it in the organization.
- *Process integration* refers to the delivery processes of the HRM department. It encompasses both the efficiency of personnel processes and also the degree of quality level and customer service as manifested in the behaviour of personnel specialists.

Both functional and process integration are crucial for the professional rendering of services by the specialist HRM department and are included in our notion of the so-called professional dimension of performance.

In summary, I present the following framework for a multidimensional perspective on performance (see Figure 4.5, based on Sangers and Paauwe, 1996):

1. *Strategic dimension*, focused on board of directors, CEO, shareholders, and financial institutions
2. *Professional dimension*, focused on line managers, employees, and personnel department
3. *Societal dimension*, focused on works councils, trade unions, government, and other interest groups

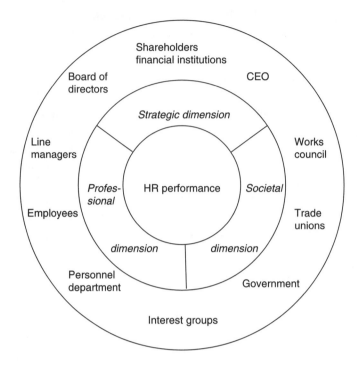

Fig 4.5. Strategic, professional, and societal human resource dimensions

Source: Sangers and Paauwe (1996).

This framework highlights the different dimensions and stakeholders. It is important to note that all three dimensions are applicable to different HRM policies and practices. So, for example, training and development can have simultaneous effects on strategic, societal, and professional performance. However, there can be a difference in emphasis. For example, improving working conditions will in the first instance appeal to the societal dimension. Needless to say, however, safer working conditions will result in fewer disturbances by accidents and hence will improve productivity. As far as the different stakeholders are concerned, I have linked them to the different dimensions, only suggesting that their dominant concern might be in that direction. So the framework does not imply that the CEO is interested only in the strategic dimension.

The next chapter emphasizes that the interaction between the various stakeholders, all of whom take into account the different perspectives on performance (and more importantly who share a 'sense' of acceptance *vis-à-vis* each other's role), is one of the essential characteristics of creating unique approaches to the management of human resources and of their potential effects (whether positive or negative!) on performance. Related to this is the blending of strategic market objectives and institutional claims.

4.7 Summary and conclusions

In this chapter we have developed a more encompassing perspective on performance related to HRM, a multidimensional perspective based on the following premises.

- Both economic rationality and relational rationality are important in achieving organizational effectiveness in the long run.
- Human resources are not just aimed at contributing to added value. They also appreciate moral values such as fairness and legitimacy. HRM should recognize this dimension of performance.
- Human resource management should be oriented towards more than just strategic and (financial) performance. It should also be involved in the process of professionally rendering services.
- The very essence of managing human resources exceeds the boundaries of the organization and is influenced by stakeholders and institutional arrangements both inside and outside the organization.

From these premises we have unravelled the concept of performance into three dimensions: *strategic, professional and societal*. This implies that we are in need of a more integrative theoretical model, based on different theoretical perspectives such as social action theory, systems thinking, contingency theory, institutional approaches, and a resource-based theory of the firm. The latter in particular seems to offer a fruitful perspective, as we have seen in the chapter on strategy, and this will form a substantial element of the integrative model in the next chapter.

Appendix 4.1 Overview Results of Prior Research on HRM and Performance

Impact of HRM activities on HRM Outcomes and Performance

Recruitment and selection

- HRM activities that are involved in getting the right person on the right spot (employee skill and organizational structures) contribute to higher productivity and increased market value of the company. Moreover, they have a slight negative impact on turnover (Huselid, 1995).

HRM and Performance

- Staffing selectivity is positively related to perceived market performance (Delaney and Huselid, 1996).
- Evaluation and investment in recruitment and selection are positively related to labour productivity (Koch and McGrath, 1996).
- Selective selection is negatively related to employee turnover (Verburg, 1998).
- Selective selection is positively related with perceived profit, market share, and investments in the near future (Verburg, 1998).

HR planning

- Sophisticated human resource planning activities are positively related to labour productivity (Koch and McGrath, 1996).

Rewards

- Reward is positively correlated to the different dimensions of the performance of the firm: product quality, product development, profit, market share, customer satisfaction, and growth in sales (Kalleberg and Moody, 1994).
- Higher rewards contribute to a better social climate between management and the other employees (Kalleberg and Moody, 1994; Fernie *et al.* 1994).
- Higher rewards contribute to a decrease in turnover (Arthur, 1994).
- Incentive compensation has a positive impact on perceived organizational performance (Delaney and Huselid, 1996).
- Performance-related pay affects productivity positively (Lazear, 1996).
- Outcome-based incentives on sales, customer satisfaction, and profit increases with the intensity of competition and the proportion of upscale customers and decreases with the level of supervisory monitoring (Banker *et al.* 1996).
- Performance-related pay affects employee motivation positively (Dowling and Richardson, 1997).
- Flexible rewarding is positively related to profit (Leget, 1997).
- Excellent reward systems are positively related to perceived profit, market share, and investments in the near future (Verburg, 1998).
- Employee share ownership schemes, profit-related pay, and performance-related pay are positively related to financial performance (McNabb and Whitfield, 1997).
- Employee stock option plans affect productivity positively (Meihuizen, 1999).
- Pay for performance is positively related to employee trust and organizational commitment (Appelbaum *et al.* 2000).
- Perceived high wages are positively related to trust in decision making and perceived employee job security (Boselie *et al.* 2001b).

- Perceived excellent secondary work conditions are positively related to employee satisfaction and negatively related to intention to leave the organization (Boselie and van der Wiele, 2001).
- Perceived high wages are positively related to employee satisfaction and negatively related to intention to leave the organization (Boselie and van der Wiele, 2001).

Participation (consultation)

- Employee involvement practices (aimed at generating commitment) have a positive influence on productivity and product quality (Fernie *et al.*, 1995).
- Employee involvement results in better social climate (Fernie *et al.*, 1995).
- Commitment (*v.* control)-oriented HR systems have a positive impact on productivity and result in a lower degree of turnover (Arthur, 1994).
- Participation in decisions is positively related with organizational commitment (Wallace, 1995).
- Quality and labour productivity improve over time after the formation of teams (Banker *et al.* 1996).
- Employee participation is positively related to trust in decision making and perceived employee job security (Boselie *et al.*, 2001*b*).

Internally consistent HR bundles

- Stimulating personnel management has a positive impact on employee commitment, organizational support, training and education facilities, level of education, and expectations with respect to wage increases (Leijten, 1992).
- Stimulating personnel management has a negative effect on illness (Leijten, 1992).
- Bundles of internally consistent HRM practices are associated with higher productivity and quality (MacDuffie, 1995).
- High-performance work systems are positively related to productivity (Appelbaum *et al.*, 2000).
- High-involvement work practices are positively related to employee retention and firm productivity (Guthrie, 2001).

Decentralization

- Decentralization of authority will result in a lower degree of turnover (Arthur, 1994).

Training

- Training has a positive impact on the different dimensions of the performance of the firm: product quality, product development, market share, and growth of sales (Kalleberg and Moody, 1994).

HRM and Performance

- More investment in training results in higher profit (Kalleberg and Moody, 1994; d'Arcimoles, 1997).
- More investment in training results in a lower degree of turnover (Arthur, 1994).
- Training has a positive impact on the relationship between management and the other employees (Kalleberg and Moody, 1994).
- Training has a positive impact on received organizational performance (Delaney and Huselid, 1996).
- Management development is positively related to profit (Leget, 1997).
- Focus on training is positively related to perceived profit, market share, and investments in the near future (Verburg, 1998).
- Training practices affect perceived organizational performance positively (Harel and Tzafrir, 1999).
- Formal and informal training are positively related to employee trust and intrinsic motivation (Appelbaum *et al.*, 2000).
- Training and development are positively related to trust in decision making and perceived employee job security (Boselie *et al.*, 2001b).

Opportunities for internal promotion

- Internal promotion opportunities are positively related to perceived profit, market share, and investments in the near future (Verburg, 1998).
- Promotion opportunities are positively related to organizational commitment and job satisfaction (Appelbaum *et al.*, 2000).

More autonomy

- Autonomy is positively related to job satisfaction (Wallace, 1995).
- Autonomy is positively related to employee trust and intrinsic motivation (Appelbaum *et al.*, 2000).

Formal procedures

- Formal procedures (with respect to downsizing) are positively related to the number of dismissals/lay-offs (Fernie *et al.*, 1995).

Coaching

- Coaching is positively related to profit (Leget, 1997).
- Support of direct supervisor is positively related to trust in decision making and perceived employee job security (Boselie *et al.*, 2001b).
- Support of direct supervisor is positively related to employee satisfaction and negatively related to intention to leave the organization (Boselie and van der Wiele, 2001).

Information sharing

- Information sharing is positively related to trust in decision making and perceived employee job security (Boselie *et al.*, 2001*b*).
- Information sharing is positively related to employee satisfaction and negatively related to intention to leave the organization (Boselie and van der Wiele, 2001).

Employment security

- Employment security is positively related to productivity, employee trust, and organizational commitment (Appelbaum *et al.*, 2000).

Impact of HRM outcomes on performance

Employee satisfaction

- Job satisfaction is positively related to organizational commitment (Wallace, 1995).
- Employee satisfaction has a negative effect on employee absence due to illness (Boselie *et al.*, 1998).
- Employee satisfaction is positively related to comparative productivity and reduced labour costs (Guest, 2001).
- Employee satisfaction is negatively related to intention to leave the organization (Boselie and van der Wiele, 2001).

Employee motivation

- Motivation by means of reward systems contributes to an increase in productivity (Arthur, 1994; Fernie *et al.*, 1995; Huselid, 1995).
- Motivation through rewards contributes to a higher market value of the company (Huselid, 1995).
- Motivation is positively related to employee commitment (Guest, 2001).

Employee retention (the reverse of employee turnover)

- Turnover results in decreased productivity (Katz *et al.*, 1985; Arthur, 1994).
- Voluntary dismissals have a negative impact on profit (d'Arcimoles, 1997).
- Tenure (of employees) has a negative effect on employee absence due to illness (Boselie *et al.*, 1998).
- Company tenure is positively related to employee trust in decision making (Boselie *et al.*, 2001).

HRM and Performance

Employee presence

- Absenteeism results in decreased productivity (Katz *et al.*, 1985; Arthur, 1994).
- Absenteeism has a negative impact on profit (d'Arcimoles, 1997).

Social climate between workers and management

- Improved social climate and commitment of employees have a positive impact on productivity and product quality (Katz *et al.*, 1985).
- Co-worker conflict is positively related to overall job stress (Appelbaum *et al.*, 2000).

Employee involvement/trust/loyalty/commitment

- Employee trust is negatively related to overall job stress (Appelbaum *et al.*, 2000).
- Intrinsic motivation is positively related to overall job stress (Appelbaum *et al.*, 2000).
- Employee trust in decision making is positively related to perceived job security (Boselie *et al.*, 2001b).
- Employee quality/commitment is positively related to labour productivity and quality of goods/services (Guest, 2001).
- Employee commitment is positively related to comparative productivity, quality, and financial performance (Guest, 2001).

Impact of contingencies on HRM outcomes and performance

Organizational level

- Degree of unionization is positively related to productivity (Arthur, 1994; Huselid, 1995).
- Union presence is negatively related to employee satisfaction with the amount of influence over job (Delbridge and Whitfield, 1999).
- Firm size (number of employees) has a positive effect on training and development facilities and on absence due to illness (Leijten, 1992).
- Size of the organization has a positive relationship with profit and a negative relationship with employee turnover (Huselid, 1995).
- Size is positively related to net profit (Koene *et al.*, 1998).
- Size is negatively related to employee satisfaction with the amount of influence over job (Delbridge and Whitfield, 1999).
- Establishment size is positively related to financial performance (Scholarios *et al.*, 1999).

- Size (200–10,000 employees) is positively related to financial performance (McNabb and Whitfield, 1997).
- Establishment age is positively related to commitment (Scholarios *et al.*, 1999).
- Research and Development intensity has a negative impact on employee turnover and profit (Huselid, 1995).
- Capital intensity is positively related to productivity and profit, and is negatively related to employee turnover (Huselid, 1995).
- Working in the public rather than the private sector is positively related to motivation (Guest, 1999*a*).
- Working in the public sector is negatively related to employee satisfaction with the amount of influence over job (Delbridge and Whitfield, 1999).
- Production sectors are negatively related to commitment (Scholarios *et al.*, 1999).
- Deep economic recession results in poor company performance and poor HRM (Lahteenmaki *et al.*, 1998).

Individual (employee) level

- Employee age is positively related to motivation (Guest, 1999*a*).
- Employee age is positively related to commitment (Scholarios *et al.*, 1999).
- Employee age is positively related to propensity to remain with the company (Flood *et al.*, 1999).
- Employee age is positively related to employee satisfaction (Boselie and van der Wiele, 2001).
- Working on fixed term is positively related to motivation (Guest, 1999*a*).
- Having a lower income is positively related to motivation (Guest, 1999*a*).
- Being more senior in the organization is positively related to motivation (Guest, 1999*a*).
- Gender (female) is positively related to employee satisfaction with the amount of influence over job (Delbridge and Whitfield, 1999).
- Gender (female) is positively related to employee satisfaction (Boselie and van der Wiele, 2001).
- Having a full time contract or an 80 per cent contract is negatively related to intention to leave the organization (Boselie and van der Wiele, 2001).
- Having children at home is positively related to employee satisfaction (Boselie and van der Wiele, 2001).

'Reversed causality'

- Increasing profit results in higher investments in training ↔ 'reversed causality' (Hendry *et al.*, 1989).
- High-performance organizations use advanced human resource management strategies and techniques to attract and retain talent (Hiltrop, 1999).

HRM and Performance

- A (financially) better firm performance leads to investment in HRM practices (Laroche, 2001).

Appendix 4.2 Overview of Empirical Research, USA and UK

	Arthur (1994)	Huselid (1995)	MacDuffie (1995)	Guest and Peccei (1994)	McNabb and Whitfield (1997)
Country	USA	USA	USA	UK	UK
Theory	Contingency behaviour control	Resource-based behaviour	Resource-based socio-technics	Stakeholder	Stakeholder
Use of HR clusters	HR systems	HR systems	HR bundles	HR bundles	No
Performance indicators	Productivity, quality, employee turnover	Productivity, employee turnover, Tobin's q	Productivity, quality	Employee turnover, HRM, professional and administrative effectiveness	Recognized union, closed shop, flexibility, team working, financial performance
Sample	Single sector, steels minimills	Major industries, profit & non-profit	Single sector, automotive assembly	Single sector, National Health National Health	Multiple sectors
No. of observations	$N = 30$	$N = 968$	$N = 57$	$N = 303$	$N = 274$
Response rate	56%	28%	63%	51%	83%
Research method[*]	Quantitative (survey)	Quantitative (survey)	Quantitative (survey)	Quantitative (survey)	Quantitative (survey)
Input method	HR managers	HR managers	Departmental managers, staff group	HR managers, general managers	HR managers, financial managers, union representatives

[*]All studies are cross-sectional.
Source: Boselie (2002).

Appendix 4.3 Illustrative Overview of Dutch Empirical Research

	Leijten (1992)	Leget (1997)	Verburg (1998)	Paauwe (1989)	Ten Have (1993)	Schilstra (1998)
Country	NL	NL	NL	NL	NL	NL
Theory	Contingency, stakeholder	Cybernetics, socio-technics	Contingency, configuration	Contingency, stakeholder, industrial relations systems	Contingency, transaction, socio-technics	Industrial relations, stakeholder network
Use of HR clusters	HR typologies	No	HR clusters	n.r.*	n.r.	n.r.
Performance indicators	Absence, employee turnover, commitment, profit, conflicts	Profit	Employee turnover, commitment, profit, market share	n.r.	n.r.	n.r.

(*Continued*)

Appendix 4.3 (*Contd*)

	Leijten (1992)	Leget (1997)	Verburg (1998)	Paauwe (1989)	Ten Have (1993)	Schilstra (1998)
Sample	Single sector, metal industry	Multiple sectors	Multiple sectors	3 sectors: furniture, architecture, and insurance	Multiple sectors	2 sectors: metal and computer industries
No. of observations	N = 58	N = 91	N = 47 (NL) N = 42 (China)	N = 6	N = 437	N = 14
Response rate	55%	52%	100%	n.r.	73%	n.r.
Research method**	Quantitative (survey)	Quantitative (survey) and qualitative (interviews)	Quantitative (survey)	Qualitative (case study)	Quantitative (survey)	Qualitative (case study)
Input method	HR managers, 10 % employees	HR managers, line managers	HR managers, line managers	HR managers, line managers, works council, trade union	panel data	HR managers, works council, trade union

* n.r. = not relevant
** All studies are cross-sectional except for that of Paauwe, which uses a longitudinal approach.
Source: Boselie (2002).

Notes

1. This chapter is partially based upon two previously published papers:
   - J. Paauwe and J. P. Boselie, 'Human Resource Management en het presenteren van de organisatie', *MAB*, April 2000, pp. 111–12.
   - J. P. Boselie, J. Paauwe, and P. J. Jansen, 'Human Resource Management and performance: Lessons from the Netherlands', *International Journal of Human Resource Management*, 12: 1107–25; (http://www.tandf.co.uk/journals/routledge/09585192.html)
2. I was inspired in this respect by a number of critical authors and their writings, including Keenoy and Antony (1992), Legge (1995), Storey (1989, 1995), Kamoche (1994), Kluytmans and Paauwe (1991).
3. Guest and Peccei (1994) label this 'organizational integration', which emphasizes the fit between business strategy and human resource strategy
4. Guest and Peccei (1994) label this 'policy integration'. This kind of integration is concerned with the content of HRM strategy itself and the extent to which the resulting HRM policies cohere. Later on this kind of integration would become more popular under the heading 'bundles' or 'configurational approach.'

5 A Contextually Based Human Resource Theory

5.1 Introduction

In the preceding chapters I have presented a range of insights derived from the field of strategic management, industrial relations/institutional theory, and the various concepts, approaches, and empirical results with respect to ongoing research in the area of HRM and performance. In this chapter I develop and present my model of the Contextually Based Human Resource Theory (CBHRT). The insights derived from the previous chapters will be used as design parameters for this model. These will be outlined in Section 5.2 (strategy), 5.3 (context), and 5.4 (performance). The main composing theoretical parts of the model and its underlying assumptions will be discussed in section 5.5. Section 5.6 presents the model itself, inclusive an extensive treatment of the various parts of the model. Section 5.7 presents an overview of the various ways in which we can use the model for research, teaching, and consultancy practice. In Section 5.8 I conclude by drawing attention to HRM strategy as an enabling device for making a range of strategic options possible. From the base of value-laden HRM (including both economic and relational rationality), a climate of high trust and willingness to change can be created, which serves as a good starting point in dynamic market situations. In this way we revert the triad of 'strategy→HRM→performance' into an alternative, and far more realistic, 'value-laden/ethical HRM→organizational viability→enabling strategic options'.

5.2 Strategic design criteria

Chapter 2 presented an overview of the various approaches in strategic management and considered the kind of syntheses pursued by authors such as Mintzberg *et al.*, (1998), Whittington (1993), de Wit and Meyer (1998), and Volberda and Elfring (2001). Relating this more specifically to the issue of strategic HRM and performance, we are able to infer the following design criteria.

1. Both the process of strategy and the content of strategy are of relevance.
2. Both the 'outside-in' perspective (Porter-like approaches) and the 'inside-out' perspective (RBV) should be included.
3. In addition to (bounded) rationally planned strategies, politics and related power positions and resources play a role, which leads to an emergent and interactive approach of strategy development.
4. In addition to competitive market forces, the social, legal, and cultural environments are important.
5. Shareholders are not the only stakeholders interested in the outcomes of strategic HRM: customers, employees, and their representative bodies also have an important say.

5.3 Institutional context

Chapter 3 considered the context of HRM in more detail. First I discussed the various types of fit as distinguished in the field of strategic HRM modelling and theorizing itself. I then looked at the interaction between HRM and industrial relations. A closer examination of the field of industrial relations and the kind of models that have been developed since the seminal work of Dunlop (1958) has generated a range of insights, of which we can make good use. Finally, I explored the field of new institutionalism—a promising area because of its focus on the embeddedness of organizations (inclusive HRM) in its wider institutional environment. Summarizing, the following design criteria can be inferred.

1. In addition to the well-known distinction between vertical (or strategic) fit and horizontal (fit), it is important to take into account organizational and environmental fit.
2. The external environment can be subdivided into economic, technological, and political (based on Dunlop, 1958).
3. Strategic choice and discretion of the actors involved (human agents) counteract a too deterministic point of view with respect to 'environment'.
4. The field of both HRM and industrial relations is characterized by different rationalities (economic and relational).
5. Values and ideology do play a role in the shaping of HRM policies.
6. History and processes of (de)-institutionalization have a major say in the way in which HRM policies come about.

5.4 Performance

Chapter 4 presented an overview of the ongoing research in the area of HRM and performance. Discussing and analysing the results, I developed a more encompassing perspective on performance, a multidimensional perspective based on the following premises.

1. Both economic rationality and relational rationality are important in achieving organizational effectiveness in the long run.
2. Human resources are not just resources only aimed at contributing to added value: moral values such as fairness and legitimacy are an integral part of the performance construct.
3. Human resource management entails more than just being strategic and (financial) performance oriented: it also involves the professional rendering of services.
4. The very essence of the management of human resources exceeds the boundaries of the organization and is influenced by stakeholders and by institutional arrangements both inside and outside the organization.

From these premises, I unravelled the concept of performance into three dimensions: strategic, professional, and societal.

5.5 An eclectic approach to theoretical perspectives

The majority of the classic HRM models as discussed in this book are based on open systems theory, which emphasizes that organizations can be described as input, transformation, and output systems involved in transactions with a surrounding environment. This is a way of conceptualizing with a strong emphasis upon functionalism. Also, models such as Guest (1997) and Becker *et al.*, (1997), dealing with how many boxes there should be between strategic impulses and final outcomes, reflect a systems perspective. However, open systems theory is a kind of theorizing at a very abstract level, and thus lacks the specifics to generate hypotheses in the field of strategic HRM. In the 1980s many authors expressed their concern about a lack of proper theorizing (see e.g. Dyer, 1984; Zedeck and Cascio, 1984). Wright and McMahan were among the first to tackle this growing feeling of uneasiness and they offered a range of potentially useful theoretical perspectives in their widely quoted 1992 paper. Subsequently they distinguished

HRM and Performance

- A resource-based view of the firm
- The behavioural perspective
- Cybernetic systems
- Agency and transaction cost theory
- A resource dependence/power model
- Institutionalism

More recently, both Delery and Shaw (2001) and Paauwe and Boselie (2003) have acknowledged the importance of the resource-based view (RBV) in strategic HRM research. From an overview of all ongoing research in the field of HRM and performance, they conclude that RBV is one of the dominant theories in this area. Inspired by Barney (1991), authors like Wright *et al.* (1994), Paauwe (1994), Kamoche (1996), and Boxall (1996) were among the first to introduce the RBV in the area of strategic HRM. All of them explicitly stated that people *par excellence* fit the criteria/assumptions of value, rareness, inimitability, and non-substitution, which according to Barney (1991) are the necessary conditions for organizational success. So, as a first step in building our model, we will make use of the RBV.

In their impressive overview of the field of organization sociology, Lammers *et al.* (2000) discern two main approaches to studying and analysing organizations: the 'systems' perspective and the 'actors' perspective. The 'systems' perspective perceives the organization as a social–cultural whole or 'gestalt', which is kept together by goals, norms, and solidarity. The functionalistic way of analysing organizations acts as a source of inspiration for this perspective. The 'actors' perspective refers to the organization as a conglomerate, a coalition of actors (parties)—actors who are on the one hand willing to co-operate because that will benefit their own interests, but on the other hand compete and hinder each other because of conflicting interests. In this perspective we recognize the conflict-sociological tradition. Why do we pay attention to this distinction? Do we need to opt for one or the other of them? Lammers (1990) is very decisive when he states that, if we look at organizations and organizational phenomena (e.g. HRM), we can't opt for 'either–or'. We will recognize goal-oriented systems by their emphasis on a common purpose and we will discern power and conflict among competing actors. He labels this the so-called 'double character' of organizations: systems and actors. So in the present modelling I too will opt for this double character by explicitly taking into account both the 'systems' and the 'actors' perspective.

The field of strategic management has experienced a paradigm shift from the 'outside-in' perspective of the 1980s (Porter, 1980) to the 'inside-out' and dynamic capabilities (Teece *et al.* 1997) perspective of the 1990s. Of course, we need both. The combining of market conditions and a firm's own resources and capabilities enable a certain strategic positioning on the part of the firm in order to fight competition and to achieve a sustainable competitive advantage. This is an ongoing interaction, which implies continuous renewal and organizational adaptation. Lewin and Volberda (1999), in discussing a framework for research on strategy and new organizational forms, stress the importance of considering the joint outcomes of managerial intentionality, adaptation, and environmental selection. They label their approach *coevolution*, of which the origins can be traced back to, among others, Weber (1978), Chandler (1962), Weick (1979), and Aldrich (1999) (see Lewin and Volberda, 1999: 524–5).

Lewin and Volberda (1999: 526) define coevolution as the joint outcome of managerial intentionality, environment, and institutional effects. So a firm's strategic and organizational adaptations coevolve with changes in the environment—changes that can be of a competitive, dynamic, technological, or institutional nature (Lewin *et al.*, 1999: 535). The authors apply the concept of coevolution to the study of organization populations and new organizational forms, but their ideas are also relevant to the field of strategic HRM, in which the outcomes and changes can also be traced back to the interaction between managerial intentionality, organizational adaptation, and environmental dynamics (market pressures, institutional changes, etc.). The concept of coevolution blends the, until now, distinct and separate approaches of institutionalism and strategic management, of which I shall make use in my modelling.

Finally, Oliver (1997) attempts to combine, in a more explicit way, institutional and resource-based views in the field of strategic management. From the contrasting assumptions of the resource-based view and institutional theory, she distinguishes two types of rationality:

resource-based theorists assume that managers make rational choices bounded by uncertainty, information limitations and heuristic biases, whereas institutional theorists assume that managers commonly make non-rational choices bounded by social judgment, historical limitations and the inertial force of habit. (Oliver, 1997: 10)

As opposed to *economic rationality*, which is motivated by efficiency and profitability, *normative rationality* refers to choices induced by historical precedent and social justification (Oliver, 1997: 701). In the preceding chapter I emphasized the importance of relational rationality, the definition of which parallels that given by Oliver with respect to normative rationality. Both concepts of rationality (economic and relational/normative) are of course also relevant in the field of strategic HRM. For example, in the area of compensation and pay schemes, Gerhart *et al.* (1996) provide interesting venues for future research by combining the perspectives of both the resource-based view and institutional theory.

In this section I have managed to bring together some different sources of inspiration—RBV, institutional theory, systems thinking, actors perspective, and coevolution—in an eclectic but reasoned way, because of the high relevance of all these sources for a better understanding of the relationship between strategic HRM and performance.

5.6 Framework for a contextually based human resource theory

Wright *et al.* (1994) and Paauwe (1994) state that people encompass the general RBV assumptions of value, rareness, inimitability, and non-substitution (Barney, 1991); Wright *et al.* apply resource-based theory more specifically to strategic human resource management. In 1994, Paauwe, inspired by the RBV, developed the so-called Human Resource Based Theory of the firm. However, after discussion with colleagues, the name appeared to be a bit too general and did not effectively distinguish between pure RBV approaches and Paauwe's model, which explicitly incorporates both the strategic market and the institutional context. So in 2003 the name was changed to the Contextually Based Human Resource Theory (CBHRT). Paauwe's framework is depicted in Figure 5.1. This model incorporates elements of the contingency and configurational mode (Delery and Doty, 1996), institutionalism (DiMaggio and Powell, 1983), and RBV, and is inspired by the Harvard approach (Beer *et al.*, 1984).

In Paauwe's model, two dimensions in the environment more or less dominate the crafting of HRM, depending on the degree of leeway. On the one hand, HRM is determined to a certain degree by demands arising from relevant *product market combinations* and *the appropriate technology* (the PMT dimension). These demands are usually expressed in terms of criteria such as efficiency, effectiveness, flexibility, quality, and innovativeness. This dimension represents the tough economic rationality of national and international competition. The domain resembles the concept of competitive isomorphism, which, according to DiMaggio and Powell (1983), refers to a system's rationality in emphasizing market competition, niche change, and fitness measures. In Weber's (1946) terminology, the prominent kind of rationality in the PMT dimension is *'zweckrationalität'*, based on criteria of efficiency and effectiveness.

On the other hand, it is important to emphasize that the so-called free market is embedded in a *socio-political, cultural,* and *legal context* (the SCL dimension). Prevailing values and norms and their institutionalization[1] channel and correct the outcomes of market forces. In this dimension we recognize the concept of institutional isomorphism. For example, more or less widely shared societal values such as fairness (a fair balance in the exchange relationship between organization and individual) and legitimacy (the acceptance of organizations in the wider society in which they operate) will also have an impact on the shaping of HRM policies and practices. Weber (1946) refers to this as *'wertrationalität'*.

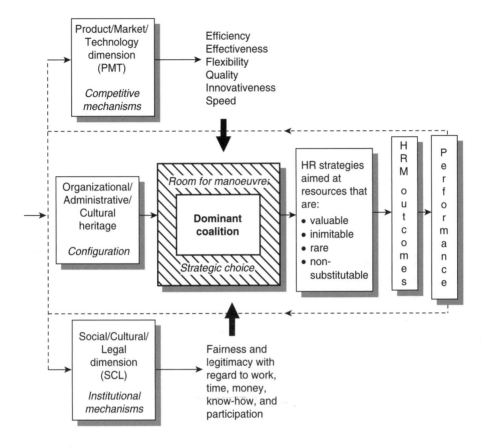

Fig 5.1. The contextually based human resource theory

Source: Paauwe (1994; 1998).

Paauwe (1994) prefers the concept of relational rationality, which refers to establishing sustainable and trustworthy relationships with both internal and external stakeholders (see the criteria of fairness and legitimacy). So the model highlights the intrinsic tension in the shaping of HRM policies between *economic rationality* (added value—see the PMT dimension) on the one hand and *relational rationality* (moral values—see the SCL dimension) on the other.

In addition to these two dimensions, the historical, grown configuration of a firm also has a bearing on shaping and structuring HRM policies and practices. These configurations may be looked upon as the outcome of past choices of strategy in interaction with the way in which structuring issues were originally posed and the kind of organizational culture this has engendered. Bartlett and Ghoshal (1989) use the concept of *administrative heritage* to identify the

HRM and Performance

influence of structures, methods, competences, and values that originated in the past. They consider this heritage an important influential factor (for better or for worse) in continued organization structuring, including HRM. Barney (1991) mentions that one of the reasons why resources (including human resources) are imperfectly imitable are *unique historical conditions*; elsewhere (Barney, 1995) he refers to the concept of *path dependency.* All these writers refer to the unique configuration or 'gestalt' of the organization. Delery and Doty (1996) distinguish the configurational approach, emphasizing a unique fit between HRM policies and practices and other organizational characteristics (e.g. organizational structure, technical system, culture).

At first glance, our conceptual framework might give the impression of being based on general systems modelling. However, this impression is corrected by the introduction of the so-called *dominant coalition,* as it then also includes an actors' perspective, as well as an indication of the degree of leeway for shaping HRM policies and practices. Examples of important actors are top management, the supervisory board, middle and lower management teams (depending on the unit of analysis), works councils, shop stewards, and, of course, the HRM department or human resource manager. All of these actors have their own values, norms, and attitudes, shared with others to a greater or lesser degree. In this respect, it is important to note that the interaction between the actors involved and their shared ideology *vis-à-vis* each other's position and role is an important element in creating understanding and credibility. In contrast, a lack of shared ideology might result in tension and conflict (see Figure 5.2).

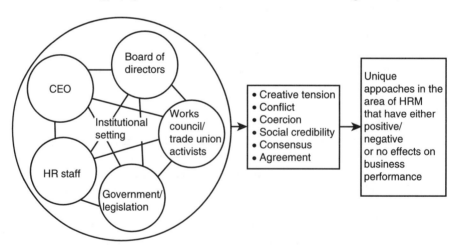

Fig 5.2. The interaction process and outcomes generated by the dominant coalition
Source: Paauwe (1998).

92

The three forces that have an impact on the *dominant coalition* (the PMT dimension, SCL dimension, and configuration) do not imply that actors adapt only to market forces, administrative heritage, or institutional setting. So I do not adhere to a deterministic contingency perspective. On the contrary: the shaded area in Figure 5.1 represents the *degree of leeway/room for manoeuvre* for the dominant coalition in making its own strategic choices (Child, 1972). Conditions, that determine leeway include the labour–capital ratio, the financial health of the company (solvability), the rate of unionization, and market strategy. In the case of an organization with a market monopoly, for instance, the room for manoeuvring is obviously considerable. However, when manufacturers are numerous, competition keen, and financial resilience low, there will be little room for structured HRM activities (Paauwe, 1991).

The dominant coalition is involved in shaping and selecting HRM policies and practices for which different fits are available. Wood (1999) identifies four such fits, based on a review of the various authors in this area.

1. *Strategic fit:*[2] the fit between HRM strategies and the business or competitive strategy of the organization. In the present model this is the fit between PMT dimension and HRM strategies.
2. *Organizational fit:* the fit between a coherent set of HRM practices (HRM systems/bundles) and other systems within the organization. In my model this phenomenon represents the fit between administrative and cultural heritage and HRM strategies.
3. *Environmental fit:* the fit between HRM strategies and the organization's environment. In my model this is represented by the fit between the SCL dimension and HRM strategies.
4. *Internal fit:*[3] the fit between HRM practices as coherent and consistent bundles.

The dominant coalition is challenged to enable HRM to make a genuine contribution to sustainable competitive advantage, aside from the importance of distinguishing different fits. By aiming for uniqueness (unique approaches), this challenge can be met. The 'trade/exchange' between individual and the organization should be structured in such a way that we can speak of *uniqueness* in the company involved. (The literature on the resource-based theory of the firm (Mahoney and Pandian, 1992) refers to the term 'heterogeneity'.) In other words, the arrangement between the individual and the organization should be *firm-specific*. This uniqueness is valuable, scarce, virtually inimitable, and difficult to replace in the short run (Barney, 1991).

The resource-based view focuses on the key success factors of individual firm behaviour in achieving firm-specific advantages by means of a portfolio of differential core skills and routines, coherence across skills, and unique proprietary know-how. Many of these core skills and routines are embedded in the attitudes and behaviours of the people employed or otherwise linked to the company. Linking the resource-based view to institutional theory can contribute to uniqueness by optimally blending environmental factors (which can be both an opportunity and a constraint) with internal resources and capabilities.

The unique shaping of HRM strategies is aimed at generating HRM outcomes,[4] which in their turn contribute to the performance of the firm[5] (see models of Becker *et al.*, 1997; Guest, 1997; Delery and Shaw, 2001). Chapter 4 dealt with this topic extensively from the framework by Paauwe and Richardson (1997), who distinguish the sequence of HRM activities, HRM outcomes, and firm performance. Of course, their framework is far too general to be labelled a conceptual model. The proper question is how many boxes there should be between HRM activities and the performance of the firm[6] (Wright and Gardner, 2001). From the basis of authors like Becker *et al.* (1997), Guest (1997), and Delery and Shaw (2001), I discussed more complex models and depicted them in the appendices to Chapter 4, to which readers should refer for a full overview of that discussion.

It is important to emphasize that all of these conceptual models take HRM strategies and/or policies and practices as a starting point. Therefore, they deal with only the right-hand side of the model. The very elements I emphasize are outlined in the left-hand side of the model and all have to do with the *shaping* of HRM, a process, that in itself has, of course, an effect upon the kind of outcomes it generates. Outcomes aimed at achieving both *economic rationality* (e.g. productivity, increasing shareholders' value) and *relational rationality* (e.g. proper work–life balance, which contributes to fairness or ecologically sound ways of producing in order to avoid depletion of natural resources, and thus contributes to legitimacy).

5.7 Implications, and possibilities for application/ different usages

To date, the present model has been used for

- Teaching purposes
- Academic inquiry/research
- Mental map/force field analysis, to describe the forces that have an impact upon HRM
- Consultancy purposes

Teaching

Students just becoming familiar with the field of HRM very often think of it as a functional area in which a range of related HRM activities (staffing, appraisal, reward, training and development) are meant to control, to manage the in-, through- and outflow of personnel/staff. They do not relate it to performance, to the process of generating added value; nor do they relate it to the specifics of the organization itself, or to the kind of context in which it is operating. When they first start to get a feeling for *strategic* HRM, often, although they do think about its possible performance effects, this is restricted to its financial economic implications alone. And they think about the possible linkages with corporate or business strategy, ignoring all the possible environmental factors—again, a too narrow perspective ignoring all the forces in the environment that have an impact on the shaping of HRM policies and practices. Only when they start to develop a feeling for the uniqueness of the organization in its specific context, the dominant coalition and the degree of leeway, does their learning progress at a deeper and more reflective level. This kind of learning involves an analysis of the various forces that have an impact on HRM and the possibilities for shaping HRM practices and policies that might result in a unique contribution to sustained competitive advantage.

Empirical research

Up to now the framework has been used mainly to carry out a range of case studies aimed at generating insights in the forces and actors that have an impact on HRM and the conditions defining leeway and room for manoeuvre. Chapter 6 gives an overview of the possibilities and findings in this respect. Is the framework capable of generating a set of rectifiable hypotheses—hypotheses that can be tested for in a quantitative research design? In this respect we encounter a problem. The first part of the model (the left-hand side) is descriptive in outlining the forces (PMT dimension, SCL dimension, and administrative heritage) that have an impact upon both the dominant coalition and the kind of leeway available for shaping HRM practices and policies. Just like Beer *et al.*'s famous Harvard model (1984), the framework in this respect is more about mapping relevant factors than a set of related testifiable hypotheses. Descriptive qualitative research of an explorative nature fits naturally with this kind of modelling. However, hypotheses are possible with respect to factors determining leeway. On the basis of exploratory research by Paauwe (1991) and

HRM and Performance

Boselie (2002), the following hypotheses can be formulated with respect to the conditions governing leeway (see also Table 5.1).

TABLE 5.1 Limitations to freedom and leeway

	HRM room for manoeuvre: large	HRM room for manoeuvre: small
Market situation	Market growth	Market decline
Strategy (Porter, 1985)	Differentiation	Cost reduction
Stakeholders: 'coercive mechanisms' (DiMaggio and Powell, 1983)	Limited number of relevant stakeholders	Large number of relevant stakeholders
Rules, procedures, and 'legislation': 'coercive mechanisms' (DiMaggio and Powell, 1983)	Limited	Extensive
Professionalization of employee groups: 'normative mechanisms' (DiMaggio and Powell, 1983)	Low Example: direct supervision (Arthur, 1994) and/or personnel control (Merchant, 1985) in the hotel and catering industry	High Example: the role/position of medical specialists in hospitals
Market structure (Paauwe, 1989, 1991)	Monopoly	Polypoly
Competitive strategy (Porter, 1985; Paauwe, 1989, 1991)	Differentiation/ focus	Price
Ratio of labour/total costs (Paauwe, 1989, 1991)	Towards 0	Towards 1
Financial leeway (Paauwe, 1989, 1991)	Present	Absent

Source: adapted from Paauwe (1989; 1991) and Boselie (2002: 143).

- *Hypothesis 1*: Market growth (in contrast to market decline) is positively related to the freedom and leeway of HRM.

- *Hypothesis 2:* The number of relevant stakeholders (coercive mechanisms) of an organization is negatively related to the freedom and leeway of HRM.
- *Hypothesis 3:* Rules, procedures, and legislation (coercive mechanisms) are negatively related to the freedom and leeway of HRM.
- *Hypothesis 4:* A monopoly market structure offers HRM more freedom and leeway than does a polypoly market structure.
- *Hypothesis 5:* Differentiation strategy (in contrast to cost reduction or price strategy) is positively related to the freedom and leeway of HRM.
- *Hypothesis 6:* The ratio of labour to total costs is negatively related to the freedom and leeway of HRM.
- *Hypothesis 7:* Financial leeway is positively related to the freedom and leeway of HRM.

The second part (the right-hand side) of the model is more normative/prescriptive, stipulating that in order to achieve a sustained competitive advantage we should develop HRM policies and practices that contribute to human resource, and meet the criteria of being valuable, rare, difficult to imitate, and difficult to substitute. Using the value, rareness, imitability, and organization framework (VRIO) by Barney (1997), it is possible to test for the availability and nature of (human) resources meeting the criteria of the RBV (valuable, rare, difficult to imitate, and difficult to substitute), as depicted in Figure 5.3.

From a case-study approach, we can test the full framework by establishing whether companies that have made optimal use of combining the PMT and SCL dimensions do indeed possess a unique competitive

IS A RESOURCE...

Valuable?	Rare?	Difficult to imitate?	Supported by organization?	Competitive implications	Performance
No	—	—		Competitive disadvantage	Below normal
Yes	No	—	↑	Competitive parity	Normal
Yes	Yes	No	│	Temporary competitive advantage	Above normal
Yes	Yes	Yes	↓	Sustained competitive advantage	Above normal

Fig 5.3. The VRIO framework

Source: Barney (1997: 162).

advantage, or do perform better ('performance' of course in its multidimensional meaning).

Force field analysis

During a range of training sessions with HRM managers, I used the model to relate it to their own companies. The left-hand side of the model was used to describe the present situation by outlining both market and institutional forces, taking into account the specifics of the organization (including its administrative heritage) and the present dominant coalition. From this kind of mental framing, and using the model as a force field analysis device, the participants were able to establish a good overview of the present situation ('Ist'), including upcoming challenges and issues. During this exercise the participants worked in pairs and each partner fulfilled, alternately, the roles of consultant and of client. In the consultant's role they helped their client by posing the right questions in order to analyse the different forces (See Appendix 5.1 for an overview of these questions). The systematic overview of forces having an impact on the organization and the relevant actors was used as a stepping stone for the next stage, in which, during a creative process, the contours became visible of the kind of HRM policies and practices that, based on the degree of available leeway, would be possible and, hopefully, would contribute to a sustained competitive advantage. It goes without saying that this was the most difficult part, and very often time was lacking to complete the entire exercise. However, participants were pleased to have had a good analysis and overview of the so-called 'Ist' situation with the present challenges and issues. Appendix 5.2 gives an anonymous example of the force field analysis of a food factory and its subsequent design of HRM policies and practices.

Consultancy

With our help, a number of companies used the CBHRT to develop a clear insight into the specific context and available degree of leeway available to them for generating insights with respect to possible HRM policies and practices that would help to contribute to a sustained competitive advantage ('Soll'). Very often this consultancy track was initiated as a follow-up activity of the force field analysis that people undertook during the previously mentioned training sessions.

5.8 HRM as an enabler for a range of strategic options

The majority of strategic HRM models use the chosen business strategy as a starting point and then try to establish the kind of HRM policies and practices (very often combined in bundles/systems) that contribute to an increased (financial) performance. My own way of modelling, emphasizing both economic and relational rationality, focuses on HRM policies and practices, which meet the criteria of both added value (in its economic meaning) and moral values such as fairness, legitimacy, sustainability. What advantages can we expect from this kind of value laden or ethical HRM? From a manager's point of view, meeting the criteria of relational rationality implies, in essence, 'treating your people well'. What are the associated benefits compared with another company, which treats its people differently? We can expect

- Lower absence
- Higher satisfaction
- Greater willingness to stay with the company
- Higher effort

These outcomes imply that one should be able to run the business on a lower control cost base, compared with companies that operate under a poor HRM system. However, a lower control cost base can also be achieved by outsourcing operations, which is what many companies do nowadays. So the real advantages of ethical HRM must be sought in another direction. The main advantages of ethical HRM will be that employees have

- A greater willingness to trust management
- Greater willingness to change, even at the risk of some personal danger
- A 'they will treat me fairly' feeling
- More room for manoeuvre for management

In a high-change market situation all this can be very important. So neither lower cost nor greater trust in themselves guarantee high performance. But the greater degree of trust and willingness to change implies a better starting point/platform for implementing change and for implementing a range of strategies. In this way, ethical HRM acts as an enabling device for a range of strategic options. Support for this approach is found in the outcomes of exploratory research by Dyer and Shafer (1999), based on a number of case studies they develop a model in which HRM strategy supports organizational agility. An agile organization aims to develop a built-in capacity to shift, flex, and adjust, either alone or with alliance partners, as circumstances change, and to do so as a matter of course (Dyer and Shafer, 1999: 148). In the same way, Boxall and Purcell (2003) include flexibility as one of the main goals (along with labour productivity and legitimacy) of strategic HRM systems. In effect, these organizations aim to optimize adaptability and efficiency simultaneously. In the strategic management literature, this is referred to as meeting simultaneously the demands of exploration and exploitation (see March, 1991; Levinthal and March, 1993; Volberda, 1998; Lewin, Long and Caroll, 1999).

Exploration involves experimenting with ideas, paradigms, technologies, strategies, and knowledge in hope of finding new alternatives that are superior to obsolete practices. In contrast exploitation is associated with systematic reasoning, risk aversion, defining and measuring performance, and explicitly linking activities to these measures. Exploitation involves improving existing capabilities, processes and technologies, as well as rationalizing and reducing costs...(March, 1991; cited in Lewin *et al.*, 1999: 536)

The CBHRT, with its emphasis on achieving a unique combination of both economic and relational rationality, and of both added value and moral values, is able to generate an agile and viable organization that creates room for manoeuvre for the parties involved and enables the pursuit of different strategic options.

5.9 Summary and conclusions

From a basis of the building blocks of strategic management, RBV, and industrial relations/institutional theory, I have outlined a contextually based human resource theory, a theoretical framework that enables a complete overview of the factors influencing the shaping of HRM policies and practices. Moreover, the theory emphasizes different rationalities and resulting outcomes. It also takes into account the various actors involved and their interaction with strategy and the wider societal context. The model can be used for different purposes. Instead of focusing only on the relationship between strategy, HRM, and subsequent performance, it also allows us to discuss the way in which, ethical HRM is an important enabling factor, one that widens the room for manoeuvre and increases the range of possible strategic options. Considered in this way, HRM acts as a starting point, an enabler for a range of strategic options.

This chapter ends the more theoretical part of the book. The remainder of the book consists of chapters reflecting the empirical reality. These chapters demonstrate, at various levels of analysis, insights that can be generated using the kind of theorizing outlined in the chapters above. To start with, Chapter 6 provides examples of case-studies that I have carried out using the framework of the contextually based human resource theory, and shows how the very combination of RBV principles and a more institutional perspective has resulted in a unique shaping of HRM practices contributing to a sustained competitive advantage.

Chapter 7 uses the same framework but at the level of the industry branch, comparing branches with high and low degrees of institutionalization and examining how this has an effect on the shaping of HRM policies and practices and related industrial relations. Chapter 8 takes us one level of analysis higher by presenting a study that compares/contrasts the effects of differences in institutional settings at country level. In this study internationally operating chemical companies—with head offices and subsidiaries in both the USA and the Netherlands—are compared with respect to the introduction of HRM practices such as empowered teams and flexibility. The final chapter combines theory and empirics to develop a more practical and implementation-oriented approach, one that will be attractive from a practitioners' perspective. The different HR roles will be linked to the various aspects of performance (strategic, professional, and societal), and I develop the so-called '4logic HRM scorecard', which will help in the development, monitoring, and measurement of HRM policies and practices, aimed at contributing to a sustained competitive advantage and a viable organization in the long run.

Appendix 5.1 Examples of Questions for Analysing Different Forces

Product–market–technology dimension (PMT)

Which market/competitive mechanisms have a direct impact on the shaping of your organization?

- Product–market combinations
- Technology (e.g. automation, intranet)

Social–cultural–legal dimension (SCL)

Which institutional mechanisms have a direct impact on the shaping of your organization?

- Legislation
- Rules

HRM and Performance

- Procedures
- Convenants
- Influence of social partners (trade unions, works councils, and other relevant stakeholders)

Configuration

What are the key characteristics of the configuration of your organization?

- Organization's age
- Spirit of the times (*zeitgeist*) when organization was founded
- Management philosophy, mission, and strategy of the founders
- Current ownership structure
- Critical incidents in the past (e.g. merger, take-overs, reorganizations)

Dominant coalition

Which actors/stakeholders/groups/parties determine the HRM strategy of your organization?

- Board of directors
- HRM director
- Social partners (works council and/or trade unions)
- Line management
- Employees

HRM policies and practices

Which HRM policies and practices can be applied for the benefit of the HRM strategy of your organization?

- Planning/recruitment/selection/socialization
- Appraisal/rewards
- Training/development
- Participation/decentralization/empowerment/autonomy/teamwork
- Leadership/coaching/mentorship
- Job design/division of labour

Leeway/room for manoeuvre

What is the leeway or room for manoeuvre of the dominant coalition with respect to strategic HR choices in your organization?

- For example caused by legislation, collective bargaining agreements (CBAs), or convenants between social partners
- For example determined by specific (business) knowledge, experiences, or available resources (e.g. financial resources, natural resources)

HRM outcomes

Which HRM outcomes can be used to measure the effects of the HRM strategy in your organization?

- Satisfaction/motivation/commitment/trust/stress/loyalty (subjective data)
- Employee turnover/employee absence/conflicts between management and employees (objective data)

Performance

Which performance indicators can be used to measure the effects of the HRM strategy in your organization?

- Productivity/service and product quality/customer satisfaction/R&D efforts
- Sales/market share/growth/profits/market value

Source: Boselie and Paauwe (2002).

Appendix 5.2: Example of Force Field Analysis of Soup and Sauce Factory

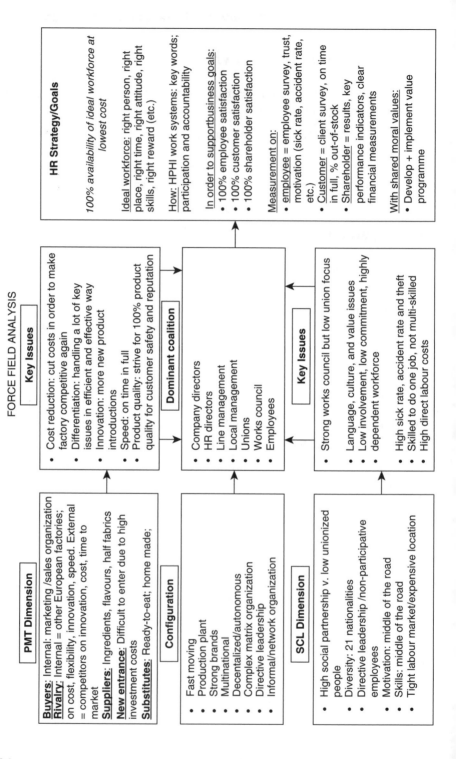

FORCE FIELD ANALYSIS

PMT Dimension

Key Issues

Buyers: Internal: marketing /sales organization **Rivalry:** Internal = other European factories; on cost, flexibility, innovation, speed. External = competitors on innovation, cost, time to market
Suppliers: Ingredients, flavours, half fabrics
New entrance: Difficult to enter due to high investment costs
Substitutes: Ready-to-eat; home made;

- Cost reduction: cut costs in order to make factory competitive again
- Differentiation: handling a lot of key issues in efficient and effective way
- Innovation: more new product introductions
- Speed: on time in full
- Product quality: strive for 100% product quality for customer safety and reputation

Configuration

- Fast moving
- Production plant
- Strong brands
- Multinational
- Decentralized/autonomous
- Complex matrix organization
- Directive leadership
- Informal/network organization

Dominant coalition

- Company directors
- HR directors
- Line management
- Local management
- Unions
- Works council
- Employees

HR Strategy/Goals

100% availability of ideal workforce at lowest cost

Ideal workforce: right person, right place, right time, right attitude, right skills, right reward (etc.)

How: HPHI work systems: key words; participation and accountability

In order to support business goals:
- 100% employee satisfaction
- 100% customer satisfaction
- 100% shareholder satisfaction

Measurement on:
- employee = employee survey, trust, motivation (sick rate, accident rate, etc.)
- Customer = client survey, on time in full, % out-of-stock
- Shareholder = results, key performance indicators, clear financial measurements

With shared moral values:
- Develop + implement value programme

SCL Dimension

Key Issues

- High social partnership v. low unionized people
- Diversity: 21 nationalities
- Directive leadership /non-participative employees
- Motivation: middle of the road
- Skills: middle of the road
- Tight labour market/expensive location

- Strong works council but low union focus
- Language, culture, and value issues
- Low involvement, low commitment, highly dependent workforce
- High sick rate, accident rate and theft
- Skilled to do one job, not multi-skilled
- High direct labour costs

104

Notes

1. Institutionalisation is defined by Selznick (1957) as 'to be infused with value beyond the technical requirements of the task at hand'. Scott (1992) defines it as 'the process by which actions are repeated and given similar meaning by self and others'. Finally, Meyer *et al.* (1987) define it as 'a process by which a given set of units and a pattern of activities come to be normatively and cognitively held in place and practically taken for granted as lawful'.
2. Also known as the vertical fit.
3. Also known as the horizontal fit.
4. HRM outcomes, e.g. employee satisfaction, motivation, commitment, involvement, organizational citizenship, trust, social climate between workers and management, loyalty, retention (the counterpart of employee turnover), and employee presence (the counterpart of employee absence).
5. Performance of the firm, e.g. productivity, product/service quality, customer satisfaction, sales, market share, profits, and market value.
6. Kanfer (1994) and Guest (1997) argue that the distance between HRM practices or systems and financial performance indicators (e.g. sales, profits, and market value) is too large to enable valid and reliable statements to be made on (statistically) significant effects found in empirical research. Those significant relationships found in prior research might be an indication of 'reversed causality'.

6 The Contextually Based Human Resource Theory in Practice

6.1 Introduction

Having outlined the model of the CBHRT in the previous, theoretical, part of the book, the remaining chapters are more empirical in nature.

In this chapter I present a range of case-study vignettes in order to illustrate different aspects of the CBHRT model and explain how organizations are able to make use of it to achieve long-term viability. The two dimensions of the model (the product market technology (PMT) dimension and the social cultural legal (SCL) dimension), have each been able to create a leeway for shaping HRM policies that are uniquely its own and which have helped significantly to build a sustainable competitive advantage. The illustrative cases are part of ongoing research projects. More extensive reports are available; however, in this book I simply present a summary of the main characteristics and findings in order to demonstrate how the CBHRT model can be, and has been, applied.

The first case study draws an illuminating comparison between two furniture factories pursuing different strategies to fight competition. The main difference here is in the PMT dimension. One company relies on a competitive strategy based on price, while the other follows more a focus/differentiation strategy by opting for the upper-end, high-quality, design market segment; in doing so the latter company provides itself with more leeway for shaping its HRM policies and practices (Section 6.2).

The second case study has been selected to illustrate how companies can make use of the SCL dimension. At first sight this dimension might seem only to offer constraints and limitations and to hinder the proper pursuit of achieving organizational success and a sustained competitive position. However, once redefined as an arena of opportunities, the innovative combinations of market and societal dimensions can offer a sustained competitive advantage. We see how one firm in a traditional industry, embedded in a heavily regulated institutional context, did just that (Section 6.3: container transhipment company).

The third example is illustrative of how the fostering of consistency and longevity in the specific characteristics of an organizational configuration, rather than succumbing to pressures for constant organizational change, can help to establish long-term viability. A highly successful Dutch theme/leisure park has purposefully nurtured its unique administrative heritage (i.e. its path dependency) over the course of many years, and this has reaped commercial rewards in the face of stiff competition (Section 6.4: Efteling).

Section 6.5 highlights the experience of the world-famous Heineken Company. When the firm opted for a reorganization and transformation, it managed to do so in line with its administrative heritage and institutional setting, in a manner that strengthened its competitive position in both the product and the labour market.

The previous examples are all based in the profit sector. In section 6.6 I present an example from the public health care sector. I describe the struggle of a specialized eye hospital to remain independent in the face of pressures from central government to become subsumed into a larger entity. The hospital succeeded in large part by making optimal use of its profile in the marketplace for delivering specialist medical care, as well as by implementing the right organizational change processes and HRM policies and practices. In this way it created leeway, became a renowned centre of excellence, and built up legitimacy in the eyes of the relevant stakeholders which eventually led to a successful defence of the hospital's stand to retain its independence.

Finally, Section 6.7 provides an example of a company in the socially sensitive industry of temporary work agencies. The profiled company took the lead in demonstrating its responsibility towards society at large by initiating the industry's first collective bargaining agreement, as well as becoming actively involved in drafting legislation (i.e. creating an institutional setting) to further augment both the legitimacy and security standards of temporary work agencies. In this way it forged a highly respected reputation among the general public, which of course had beneficial consequences for the firm's position in the marketplace.

All of the case studies involved intensive fieldwork using different data collection methods (semi-structured interviews, document analysis, surveys, group interviews). We gathered data and opinions from a wide variety of interviewees, including top management, human resource managers, and officers, plus representatives of the works council and/or shop-floor employees.

6.2 Two furniture companies in search of competitive advantage

There are many furniture companies operating in the eastern part of the Netherlands, part of a long tradition in the region. The two companies highlighted here are both small family-owned firms operating in the same environment: one that is simple (in terms of well-known rival firms and distribution channels), yet dynamic because of fluctuating market demands and fierce competition from rivals in neighbouring Germany. Both firms employ around 40–50 persons, and both are engaged in the production of wall units and the like.

In the early 1990s both firms sought to develop export markets and to scale down series production in order to reduce retailer stock. One company—'ABC Design'—opted for a differentiation/focus strategy by explicitly focusing on the top market segment: high-quality furniture with exclusive designs and a very limited number of units produced per series. In line with this, the design of its furniture is outsourced to specialist agencies and the firm has invested more in the automation of its machinery and, importantly, in upgrading the quality and educational levels of the employees.

The other company—'Furniture Works'—opted instead for a low-cost strategy based on competitive pricing. It too involves external designers and has also intensified its training and development efforts. However, its machinery has stayed more or less the same, owing to a lack of financial resources, which limits new investment.

The two chosen competitive strategies represent varying degrees of leeway for shaping HRM policies and practices (see also Chapter 5). So if we compare the two companies more closely, we discern several key differences. On *training*, ABC Design makes an extremely thorough inventory of the educational and training level of its present staff. The management team then develops a systematic training plan based on the kind of competences needed to realize the chosen strategy (i.e. differentiation). Finally, the firm has a new performance appraisal system. By this approach, ABC Design is in fact heading in the direction of implementing a 'high-performance/high-involvement' work system, to which end it carefully screens its employees' ability, motivation, and opportunity to participate. The other company gives attention to training but in a far less systematic way.

Secondly, both companies implement *quality management*, but ABC Design's approach is to train and involve every employee, whereas Furniture Works has simply appointed somebody to be responsible for quality inspection and control.

Owing to the price premium in the top design and quality market segment, ABC Design protects itself from the fierce *price competition* faced by Furniture Works. In this way ABC Design enjoys more (financial) leeway to improve further its machinery and to upgrade further the competences of its workforce and involve employees more intensively in the implementation of the chosen strategy. ABC Design also pays more attention to the proper alignment between its different HRM practices (e.g. selectivity in recruiting, performance appraisal, training and development) in order to stimulate the implementation of the chosen strategy. Furniture Works does carry out some of these HRM practices, but in a more *ad hoc*, stand-alone fashion.

The greater degree of leeway enables ABC Design to pay more attention to both vertical and horizontal fit and to design in a careful way the proper HRM tools in order to implement the chosen strategy.

6.3 Using your administrative heritage to win prizes

In the leisure market the Dutch firm Efteling has won several prestigious international prizes and is recognized as one of the best theme parks in the world, even in competition with more internationally famous and better-resourced rivals such as Six Flags and Disneyworld Paris.

Its origins in the 1930s was as a playground for local children, but by the early 1950s it had developed into a 'fairytale' park with a design based on the drawings of the famous painter Anton Pieck. Over the years more and more attractions have been added, until it is now a spectacular, fully equipped leisure park complete with hotel, residential bungalows, and a golf course, which attracts more than 2.5 million visitors a year. In the Netherlands there is a well-known saying that everybody will visit the Efteling at least three times in her or his lifetime: once as a child, once as a father or mother with their own children, and once as a grandfather or grandmother.

The secret of the organization's success can be traced back to its origins, and in particular to the way it has managed to preserve its administrative heritage—to such a degree that many people in the Netherlands consider the Efteling a part of their *national* heritage. Comparing it with other theme parks, one notices the differences immediately. Whereas other parks are simply a collection of entertainment 'toys' (like roller coasters), the Efteling park is beautifully situated in its natural environment. The uniform layout throughout the grounds ensures that it remains faithful to Pieck's artistic vision. So visitors who might not appreciate all the attractions—which will make you giddy with either excitement or nausea!—nevertheless like to visit the park to wander through its beautiful setting and admire the lovely scenery.

So the secret of Efteling's success is due in part to the preservation and cultivation of the heritage of its original designer. But it has also to do with the fact that the only shareholder is the Foundation Nature Park for the Efteling, whose main objective is to preserve nature. An expanding company might be expected to consider this kind of corporate governance structure a major hindrance to plans for growth in visitor numbers and sales revenue; but in fact this shareholder is not interested in any kind of dividend on its shares, and so the financial position of the Efteling is very strong. More importantly, the park's management team has 'used' this institutional embeddedness as an opportunity for developing and fostering a formula, which has resulted in a unique commercial advantage for this small player facing stiff competition from nearby multinational corporations.

People management within Efteling reflects the character and culture of the park, which can be compared to a family-owned company. In total the park employs about 1,500 employees, the majority of which can be considered seasonal and holiday workers—permanent employees number only around 280. Many employees have a long-lasting employment relationship with the firm. Even some of the seasonal workers have been members of staff for more than twenty years; during the closed season they are entitled to unemployment benefits based on Dutch social security legislation, and the Efteling organization stays in touch with them by sending them information, newsletters, and Christmas gifts. When the season starts again they are simply re-hired. Last year the park started to experiment with opening hours during the winter season and during evenings, whereas in previous years it was always closed then. All new employees (both permanent and seasonal workers) receive comprehensive training in hospitality, etc.

Not surprisingly, the atmosphere among the workers is very much that of a community, characterized by a warm, easy-going attitude among the employees combined with a high degree of dedication to the Efteling. The advantages of fostering such a 'family'-like culture are a strong sense of loyalty and commitment among employees, albeit sometimes in rather too laid-back a manner.

Management faces the twin challenges of combining the best of two worlds: on the one hand preserving the family atmosphere and employees' and customers' love for the Efteling, while on the other trying to achieve a higher degree of service quality and greater cost effectiveness. The sound financial situation of the park does not constitute a burning platform in this respect, but with the entry into the Dutch market of more global players (such as Six Flags), and still more due to follow, the Efteling will need to remain alert and flexible to stay ahead of competition.

Using the CBHRT perspective, we can see how the present organizational configuration, including the company's HRM strategy, has been clearly influenced—even shaped—by its administrative heritage (encompassing both the artistic values of the original designer and the objectives of the dominant shareholder). More importantly, we can also discern how this heritage has been used deliberately to develop and expand the theme park in a highly consistent way. This has resulted in a very strong competitive position for the complex.

6.4 A container transhipment company making optimal use of its institutional setting

Rotterdam has the largest port in the world and is the market leader in providing transportation and shipment services for goods and containers bound for the Western European economies. But local competition is fierce, from nearby harbour cities such as Antwerp in Belgium and Hamburg in Germany, both of which are eager to take Rotterdam's business and dominate the regional market.

Shipping companies are hugely influential in the market owing to an increasing trend among them to merge or form large alliances. Container shipment companies face powerful clients which demand quality, low prices, flexibility, and speed of delivery and transhipment services at any time of the day or night convenient to them. Ships need to be unloaded and loaded as fast as possible without causing any damage to the containers and goods (PMT dimension). This case study reports how one container shipment company based in Rotterdam aims to deliver the best possible services to its customers at competitive prices.

Normally, introducing new technology as a way to become more cost-effective implies reducing workforce numbers, and resistance to such changes, especially in unionized environments, can usually be expected to be fierce. So when senior managers at the firm wanted to apply technology in order to mechanize and automate the whole process of loading and unloading containers, they knew they would have to deal with the highly institutionalized arrangements in force across the port.

As in most port cities around the world, the trade unions in Rotterdam are in a very strong bargaining position. Union density is almost 80 per cent, and the collective bargaining agreement site contains a number of regulations to safeguard employment, including a harbour-wide labour resource pool and relatively high wages. The terms of the harbour-wide agreement make redundancies and lay-offs almost impossible, so that the Rotterdam dockworkers have had little to fear from any management change programmes. Nevertheless, they share with top management a desire to see their company flourish and achieve a sustained competitive advantage. Put another way, both the trade unions and works council members are willing to be co-operative regarding the introduction of more advanced technology and measures to increase quality and flexibility, largely as a consequence of the near-absolute guarantee to safeguard employment provided by the institutional arrangements (SCL dimension).

The dominant coalition in this company consists of the CEO, the HR manager, and the members of the works council (in which the unions have a strong presence). Together, they have introduced a smart scheme for improving productivity and quality based on developing a highly trained, multi-skilled, and functionally flexible workforce. The firm allows all workers to attend courses in order to familiarize themselves with the various functions relating to the proper handling of containers (ten functions in total). Such workers can then be deployed in a variety of ways, depending upon the nature and intensity of the workload at any one time. The majority of employees are now able to perform more than one function, and to the further benefit of the company they have also gained improved mutual understanding and co-ordination. Management ends up with a highly qualified and agile workforce at its disposal. Employees, meanwhile, are entitled to a pay increase the moment they qualify as fully trained in a new function, irrespective of whether or not they actually carry out that particular task. This whole process of organizational change is accompanied by an abundant flow of information from the side of top management and the HR department, which stimulates participation and the involvement of both unions and works council.

In comparison with other container shipment companies, this firm is far ahead in the development and application of advanced technology, and as a result is able to offer high-quality services, a high degree of flexibility, and a large degree of reliability and commitment to meeting the deadlines of their customers. A pleasing side-effect is that the company's state-of-the-art technology and processes are a source of considerable pride among the employees, enhancing their commitment and loyalty to the firm.

Reflecting on this case, we can conclude that the institutional setting, which forbids the lay-off of workers and thus results in a low level of resistance to the introduction of new technology, has been used to management's advantage in order to implement technology and flexibility measures in a way that has contributed significantly to a sustained competitive advantage. This approach has, among other benefits, resulted in long-term secure contracts, and has led to the provision of a dedicated terminal at the port for several major shipping companies.

6.5 The Heineken model: how to become an employer of choice

Heineken is the second largest brewery company in the world and arguably has the world's best-known beer brand, next to Budweiser. In the mid-1990s it needed to revitalize itself. In spite of still impressive sales/turnover figures and an acceptable return on investment (ROI), the company recognized that it could do better. Innovation was poor, and in Heineken's home base, the

HRM and Performance

Netherlands, small breweries with a carefully cultivated craftsmanship image were threatening to take over the giant's market share. In order to make the company more dynamic, more innovative, and more flexible, the management team opted for a huge transformation project, affecting 2,000 employees working in two large breweries. It went under the slogan, *'It's the people that make Heineken.'*

The phasing-in of more advanced technology necessitated a programme of delayering through voluntary redundancies or relocations within Heineken. This paved the way for a radical overhaul of established production practices, led by the implementation of a system of (autonomous) task groups at the shop-floor level.

Up to that point, employees' experience of Heineken as an employer had been good. As a family-owned company it had always displayed a rather paternalistic attitude towards its employees, taking good care of them and ensuring good pay and a high degree of job security. However, these workers were now confronted with major organizational upheaval, insecurity, and demanding new jobs. The new ways of working demanded a higher level of knowledge and competence from them. Given the twin facts that most people on the shop-floor had worked there for a very long time and that their average age was 41, everyone involved—from management and trade unions to works council members and the workers themselves—realized that not all employees would be able to meet the new requirements. So, what to do?

The managers knew that they would need buy-in from the trade unions, since between 70 and 80 per cent of the affected employees were members of the unions involved in collective bargaining with Heineken. Fortunately, the corporate HR manager and his department were able to build on their already co-operative and constructive relationship with the unions and the works council to devise an initiative that is still widely cited as a fine example of how to manage employee relationships in an innovative way. The deal took into account the institutional setting (i.e. the strong position of the trade unions) and the administrative heritage of the company (i.e. its long tradition of looking after its staff) to produce an accord centring on a five-year guarantee of employment in exchange for a retraining of all employees at the two breweries, either individually or collectively, for the new jobs. Heineken brought in an external agency to test every employee beforehand to check his or her 'trainability' and 'employability'. For those for whom the test indicated that they might not be able to acquire the new job competences, even if properly trained, Heineken management vowed to find them real alternative employment. In the event, the firm succeeded in retraining the majority of workers and found other jobs, either in or outside Heineken, for the remaining 300–400 employees. This agreement became well known in the

Netherlands and was often referred to as the 'Heineken model'. The unions still favour it as an example to be imitated by other firms.

The Heineken Company itself benefited a lot from the deal. It made the reorganization possible; the co-operative relationships with the unions remained intact and were even strengthened; and in the end it gave the company a very good image in the labour market as a preferred employer. Moreover, the whole process of organizational change and the way in which management dealt with the interests of its employees was perceived as being in line with the strong quality reputation of its beer brand.

6.6 The Rotterdam Eye Hospital: the search for legitimacy among its stakeholders[1]

The Rotterdam Eye Hospital was founded in 1874 and specializes in ophthalmology. The organization employs approximately thirty ophthalmology specialists, plus 250 nurses and other personnel. Over 125,000 patients are treated there every year. The majority of these are treated in a day, requiring no overnight stay. It is the only independent eye hospital in the Netherlands. The way in which it retained its independence when faced by the prospect of a merger with a much larger organization is the subject of this case study.

Prior to the 1980s Dutch health care organizations could be characterized by their inward-looking narrow focus. The open-ended funding at the time reinforced and strengthened this internal orientation: health insurers paid all costs incurred by every health care organization. But drastic cuts introduced by the government, which was facing a severe economic recession in 1982, led to major transitions throughout the service, driven by an increased emphasis on cost-effective performance and quality. 'Efficiency' was the magic word in those days, and one way to achieve this, according to the government's Ministry of Health, Welfare, and Sport, was to encourage and even initiate mergers between organizations to achieve economies of scale. One such proposed 'merger' involved the Rotterdam Eye Hospital and the much larger academic hospital, Dijkzigt Rotterdam (at that time ten times bigger in terms of total number of employees and patients), barely one kilometer away.

As soon as the debate on a full merger made it apparent that the Eye Hospital ran the risk of being swallowed up by the 'big brother' Dijkzigt, its separate identity even disappearing eventually, the board of directors and the medical specialists acted in unison to plead for the Eye Hospital to retain its independence. The only way to maintain its independent position was to find ways to legitimate its right for independent existence as a highly specialized hospital, and to convince relevant stakeholders (e.g. government, financiers) of the surplus value of this structure.

The Ministry of Health, Welfare, and Sport indicated that it would approve the eye hospital's independent status only on condition that it develops into an excellent health care centre, with outstanding, efficient, and effective management and a highly ranked research record. Thus, external pressure in the form of a debate on the organization's legitimacy caused a major change in the culture, moving away from the relatively passive attitudes that characterized the period prior to 1982 and towards an active and innovative mind-set with a broad willingness among employees to embrace continuous change. This was essential if the hospital was to deliver on the government's performance demands in terms of efficiency, effectiveness, and high-quality services.

The managing director and financial director took the lead in this process, supported by their staffs and each of the medical specialists. The organization pursued the status of centre of excellence in the following areas:

- Becoming the preferred partner for co-operation with both national and international counterparts
- Achieving technical excellence in medical health care
- Achieving business excellence in, for example, management and logistics
- Achieving academic excellence in both medical and management research
- Offering excellent service quality to clients

Leadership became more visible by its clearly communicating to all staff members the new vision and strategy and by giving them more involvement, participation, and autonomy. It was especially important for the core group of medical specialists to feel that they were part of the new challenge. They improved substantially on research and development, in this way contributing significantly to the realization of the Eye Hospital as a centre of excellence.

To reach a high level of both reliability and efficiency, the principles and practices of business process re-engineering, as well as logistics management, total quality management, and benchmarking—few of which one would expect to encounter in a medical setting—were all applied to the different medical treatments.

The HR department supported the transformation, with practices including more selective recruitment, the improvement of both vertical and horizontal communication systems, and, importantly, involvement of the specialists in the development and implementation of the new strategic reforms.

The results have been dramatic. In the Dutch health care sector the Rotterdam Eye Hospital has become renowned for its innovations and continuous improvement programmes. The following examples illustrate the innovativeness and the passion for change of this organization.

The Contextually Based Human Resource Theory in Practice

1. Within the space of a few years since being granted independent status, the Rotterdam Eye Hospital became the first non-US hospital to be accepted as a member of the elite American Association of Eye and Ear Hospitals, one of only 15 top institutes inducted into the Association. By the end of the 1990s the hospital had taken the lead in founding the European equivalent of the American Association, tasked with a key role in research on benchmarking eye hospitals in Europe.

2. The Eye Hospital co-operates with several Dutch universities, including the Rotterdam School of Economics and Rotterdam School of Management on management issues, the Rotterdam Faculty of Medicine and Health Sciences on medical research, and the technical University of Eindhoven on logistics. This co-operation has resulted in unique benchmarking exercises conducted into different parts of the hospital—learning from, for example, the supply chain management used by Ahold, a large Dutch supermarket chain, and the consumer logistics of Royal Dutch Airlines (KLM). These benchmarks were used to improve the internal business processes and the quality of service to clients.

3. Since 1999 the Rotterdam Eye Hospital has been one of the leading health care organizations in the Netherlands with respect to 'chain of excellence in treatment of patients [*ketenzorg*]', an integrative approach to clients' needs that aims for service quality improvement.

4. A substantial improvement in the hospital's research and development record has allowed medical specialists to contribute in a decisive way to the realization of the Eye Hospital as a centre of excellence.

5. In 2000 the organization received the Cap Gemini Ernst & Young award for best and most innovative website in the Dutch health care sector. The Eye Hospital appeared to be one of the first organizations to present, among other things, information on waiting lists, customer satisfaction (number of complaints), employee absence due to illness, and employee turnover rates.

6. In 2002 the Minister of Health, Welfare, and Sport highlighted the successes of the Rotterdam Eye Hospital as a best practice example for modern health care management in the Netherlands.

In summary, the key to the success of the Rotterdam Eye Hospital appears to have been the organization's culture of continuous improvement and innovation, which emerged in the 1980s as a result of external political mechanisms. Applying state-of-the-art management and control systems, in combination with stimulating HRM practices and excellent leadership, were crucial in the endeavour to gain legitimacy in the eyes of the relevant stakeholders for an independent and viable medical institution.

6.7 A responsible employer providing its customers with economic employment flexibility[2]

In the 1960s and 1970s the rise of temporary agency work (TAW) used to be a sensitive subject in the Netherlands. Operators in the sector faced two major obstacles in their struggle for legitimacy in the eyes of the Dutch public and policy-makers: countering the negative stereotypes surrounding the industry, many of which had arisen from the activities of illegal personnel placement agencies ('koppelbazen'), and, relatedly, having to work within constraining legislative frameworks. As the largest temporary work agency in its home market of the Netherlands, and one of the five largest in the world, the Randstad Corporation is a noteworthy example of a company that relies upon its ability to manage both these socio-cultural/institutional pressures demanded by society and staff *and* the product-efficiency pressures demanded by their clients.

Conscious of the social sensitivities surrounding its services, the Randstad Corporation has been involved in an active search for much-prized legitimacy throughout its history. The firm has been at the forefront of establishing minimum standards for the professional contracting of temporary staff. In the early 1960s it introduced social security insurance for temporary agency employees and took steps to address concerns over working conditions and training possibilities. A decade later, in the early 1970s, Randstad's management actively engaged with the Dutch unions in drawing up the first collective agreements for temporary agency workers. Over twenty years on, Randstad was one of the main architects of the 1999 'flexibility and security' legislation, which brought temporary agency workers under normal Dutch labour law.

Some of these efforts to professionalize their business increased the cost of temporary agency workers. For example, the introduction of social security insurance in the 1960s raised the price of a 'temp' by approximately 30 per cent, but demand for agency work boomed as companies that previously had been wary of having uninsured personnel working on their premises now saw new possibilities for taking advantage of agency work. The more recent 'flexibility and security' legislation, meanwhile, was criticized for both its complexity and its negative impact on the economic attractiveness of using 'temps'. (The new law increased the opportunities for client organizations to hire workers on such contracts directly.)

Nevertheless, most agencies now agree that the various institutional constraints have proved beneficial for their business. The 'flexicurity' legislation did a lot to augment the societal acceptance of the industry as a regular (responsible) employer. It also stimulated the market for relatively high-skill temping and increased market possibilities for so-called 'managed services', where the agency not only provides the temporary employees, but also takes responsibility for their operational human resource management (both markets offering the agencies higher margins). The responsible attitude shown by the company has also helped it to gain major contracts with other large companies that have set their own, similar, standards for corporate social responsibility. It has also facilitated co-operation with the national government, opening markets previously restricted to the nationalized Public Employment Service. In addition, the increasing professionalization of the field and growing standards for consistent trustworthiness and socially responsible behaviour of the agencies themselves also functions—especially for the larger agencies like Randstad—as a form of market protection against the smaller and less organized agencies. It effectively raises the operating standards in the temporary agency workers' market, increasing the benefits to the larger agencies (such as Randstad) of being able to offer long-standing and sophisticated formalized services.

The conviction that the company can contribute to society through its professional experience in employment issues is deeply ingrained in Randstad. Each consultant in the store will reproduce the companies' mantra, 'knowing, serving, trusting'. When the German government presented a plan to organize its own public employment service along the lines of the Dutch business model, most of the temporary work agencies operating in the German market opposed the idea, as they felt it would interfere with free market principles. Randstad offered advisory assistance 'with its extensive experience in the area' (Financieele Dagblad, 2002).

This short case study shows how socially responsible behaviour, in which due and proper attention is paid to the institutional setting, has made good business sense for the Randstad organization. Randstad has developed into the leading Dutch agency for temporary employment with a national market share of almost 40 per cent in 2000 and a worldwide position in the top five of such agencies.

6.8 Conclusions

The selected case studies provide examples of the way in which the theoretical framework of the CBHRT helps to analyse and explain the interaction between, for example, the PMT and the SCL dimensions.

They also demonstrate the importance of taking into account the administrative heritage—its organizational configuration and path dependency—of an enterprise, and of (re-)interpreting it not as a burden from the past but often as an important element to be cultivated and brought up to date to realize consistency between corporate strategy and related HRM policies and practices, as the Efteling and Heineken cases show.

Bringing about legitimacy by taking into account the interests of a variety of stakeholders is also extremely relevant in establishing viability in the long run. The examples from the Rotterdam Eye Hospital and Randstad Company convincingly demonstrate this point.

All of these case-study vignettes are at the level of the individual organization. In the next chapter we proceed to the industrial branch level. On the basis of empirical evidence, the value is again demonstrated of the kind of analysis in which the very interaction between the various dimensions of the contextually based human resource theory helps to explain the shaping of HRM policies and practices, with respect to both content and process.

Notes

1. The data for this case study vignette were provided by Dr Paul Boselie.
2. The data for this case study vignette were provided by Dr Bas Koene.

7 Contrasting Metal and IT Sectors: Internal Versus External Regulation of Flexibility

Keimpe Schilstra, Graham Dietz, and Jaap Paauwe

7.1 Introduction

The previous chapter described and analysed how the contextually based human resource theory (CBHRT) could inform and explain HRM policy decisions inside discrete organizations. This chapter looks at how the theoretical framework can explain the selection of HRM policies with a focus on employment practices enhancing various forms of flexibility of companies responding to institutional constraints imposed at the *sectoral* level. The HRM policies studied focus on flexibility-enhancing employment practices such as numerical, functional, and financial flexibility.

To reiterate, the theory argues that within each organization there is a 'dominant coalition' comprising the principal decision-makers in the areas of business strategy, operational strategy, and, for our purposes, human resource management strategy. The various players in the dominant coalition should therefore base their judgements and decisions on HRM matters on careful assessments of the two contingent dimensions, the PMT dimension and the SCL dimension. The nature of the two dimensions imposes constraints on decision-makers' 'degree of leeway' and may even contain some threats. But, as we shall see, if used judiciously, one or both may offer opportunities and sources of potential competitive advantage.

The chapter presents case study evidence on 13 Dutch firms drawn from two contrasting sectors, the metal industry and the IT industry. These case studies were carried out in the second half of the 1990s and are extensively described and analysed in Schilstra (1998). Specifically, we examine how the firms set about achieving a balance between the internal regulation of their employment relations and the regulation sought, in part, externally (i.e. between companies and/or their representatives and trade unions). Some of the findings are surprising, even counterintuitive, to standard managerial ortho-doxy. But we shall argue that an interpretation of the findings according to the CBHRT offers a compelling explanation for the apparent anomalies.

The chapter is set out as follows. The following section provides a short explanation of the distinction we draw between internal and external regula-tion of the employment relationship. The research is then set in its Dutch context with an overview of the country's system of industrial relations and a sketch of what a typical 'dominant coalition' might be expected to feature. Section 7.4 describes briefly the research methodology, while the following three sections describe the two sectors studied and the 13 firms involved. Sections 7.8 and 7.9 set out the findings, including two short case studies from each sector. In the final section we review and discuss the insights that our theoretical framework can shed on this process.

7.2 Internal and external regulation of the employment relationship

The conditions under which an employer decides to hire labour and an employee decides to sell his or her labour to that employer are determined in an ongoing process between these two parties, with additional input, either indirectly or directly, from several other actors, including the state, plus representatives of the employer (e.g. an employers' association) and the em-ployee (e.g. a trade union or works council). In these interactions each actor is expected to try to best utilize the margin between on the one hand its own autonomy and resources and on the other its interdependence from the other actors and their respective resources. The conflicts of interest that arise must be resolved in order that each actor can achieve its goals.

Huiskamp (1995; 2003) distinguishes between internal regulation and exter-nal regulation. Internal regulation takes place within the organization, with a specific employer, and none of the actors involved plays a serious role in any other organization's regulations. External regulation takes place at levels above the organization, in which actors other than those directly involved in the exchange are able to impose rules; in other words, the regulation involves more than one employer.

There are two main forms of internal regulation, *individual* and *collective*. Our interest here is with the latter.[1] While an employer can impose collectively binding rules unilaterally, in several north-west European contexts a joint process of what might be termed 'internal collective regulation' is undertaken between a single employer and a small group of employees representing the interests of their work colleagues as a whole. The employees' representative constituency may come from the firm's works council or may be a company-specific union (as is also the case in Japan, of course).[2]

External regulation meanwhile comes from two main sources. The first is the government, which sets substantive rules constraining the employment relationship at the workplace level (e.g. a minimum wage or health and safety legislation) and procedural rules governing formal negotiations or consultations among different parties (e.g. the legal underpinnings of various industrial relations institutions at the national, sectoral, and company levels). The second source of external regulation—and our interest here—stems from representatives of employers and employees negotiating sectoral or company-level collective bargaining agreements.

The managerial decision on which of the two types of regulation, or a combination of both, to adopt is not as straightforward as the orthodox assumption—that managers should pursue economically rational HRM policy (i.e. internal regulation wherever possible)—might have us expect. Employers must weigh up the perceived drawbacks of both options. For external regulation, management concerns centre principally on inflexible curbs to substantive rules, as well as on the procedural implications of trade union involvement and whether they can be responsive to company-specific concerns. The main drawback of relying on internal regulation is that, according to Dutch law in the absence of collective arrangements applied to the entire workforce, any modifications to the employment relationship might have to be negotiated with each employee individually, increasing transaction costs and wasting management time and resources, or require a lengthy, costly and unsettling change management programme. A second unwanted byproduct of an internal approach to the distributional aspects of the employment relationship is that managerial contingency and opportunism on such matters might accentuate conflicts of interest between employer and employee, debilitating efforts to promote unity of purpose and the pursuit of joint gains (Kochan and Katz, 1988: 7), while at the same time 'politicizing' the employment relationship (Bolweg, 1989: 9). So, while management may perceive internal regulation as leaving more leeway for company-specific fine-tuning, external regulation can reduce the cost of regulation and administration. Generally, the conventional wisdom views these twin advantages as insufficient to outweigh the supposed lower responsiveness of external regulation. But is this correct?

7.3 The Dutch balance[3]

The typical decision-making process on almost any matter of significance in the Netherlands involves an extensive process of multi-party consensus-building and the pursuit of mutually beneficial compromise. The Dutch view this distinctive approach as a cherished national characteristic; it is the Dutch 'way of doing things'. This cultural norm is manifested in the extensive deliberations on the country's social and economic policy conducted on a tripartite basis at the national level, between the government (itself invariably a coalition of several political parties), employers' associations, and trade unions.

This shared decision-making process is replicated at the sectoral level as well, with bipartite collective bargaining between employers' associations and trade unions in each industry. These collective agreements cover approximately 85 per cent of the entire Dutch workforce, and their terms automatically override any inserted into an individual employment contract. At the level of the individual enterprise, company-level bargaining can further supplement the sectoral agreement, while the Works Councils Act of 1979 requires all enterprises with a headcount exceeding 100 to have a works council which meets a minimum of six times a year 'for the purpose of consultations with and representation of the persons employed in the enterprise'.[4] Trade union density in the Netherlands is around 25 per cent; union membership in works councils averages around 65 per cent.

Thus, at the risk of simplification, we can construct a basic diagram of who might feature as potential actors in the 'dominant coalition' of a Dutch firm employing more than 100 staff (see Figure 7.1). A management team with this size of workforce will engage with its works council over a wide range of HRM-related concerns. In addition, should a significant proportion of the workforce be members of a trade union, sufficient demand may exist for the union(s) to represent employees' interests, whether on the works council or in company-level collective bargaining. Then, depending on which sector the firm operates within, its employees' primary terms and conditions of labour may be covered

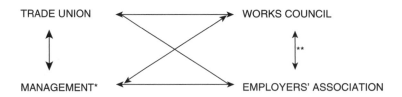

Fig 7.1. Dutch 'dominant coalitions'

  * Within the management constituency the personnel manager is a special actor. (S)he is the buffer between the business-oriented management team and the workforce, although ultimately is obliged to represent the interests of owners/managers.

  ** Although we included this relationship in the research design, we found virtually no evidence of formal contact between works council members and regional representatives of the employers' association, though they may meet incidentally.

by a collective agreement concluded between the national trade unions and the relevant employers' association for that sector.

In sum, neither the Netherlands' social norms nor its labour laws favour internal regulation of the employment relationship; rather, external regulation is enshrined in both. Indeed, a striking aspect of the Dutch system is that the terms and conditions governing the relationship between an employer and an employee can be determined 'far away from the place where the work is actually being performed' (Huiskamp, 1995: 30).

That said, two trends have emerged in Dutch industrial relations in the period beginning in the early 1980s and extending up to the late 1990s. The first has seen a tendency toward decentralization, characterized by a movement away from national and sectoral agreements and towards the level of the individual enterprise. The scale of the shift has been modest; however, the number of collective bargaining agreements at company level increased over the period, although the relative share of workers covered by such deals remained more or less the same, while the number of sectoral agreements fell from 199 in 1990 to 185 in 2000 (Schilstra and Jongbloed, 2003). In a curious mirror development to the rise in company-level deals, the remaining sectoral agreements now cover a greater number of workers than before. Collective bargaining at both sectoral and company level remains important in Dutch industrial relations, and to reiterate, still covers about 85 per cent of all employees. What is certainly true about the trend towards decentralization in the 1980s and 1990s is that it implied a more detached role of the national government, although this came to an end in the late 1990s.[5]

The second trend has been a growing interest among Dutch managers in human resource management, or HRM (see Paauwe, 1995; Boselie, Paauwe and Jansen, 2001).[6] Both professional journals for personnel managers and formal training programmes for personnel managers in the 1990s demonstrated an increased interest in a more strategic role of personnel management and a better alignment between corporate/business strategy and HRM. This suggests an increase in internal regulation, albeit that practice itself is always lagging behind with respect to the content and intentions written down in the professional press and disseminated at training programmes for professionals.

In sum, both trends share a common implication for the period during which the case studies were carried out; internal regulation is gradually replacing external regulation in the Netherlands.

7.4 Research questions and methodology

We chose to examine these assumptions by studying the decision-making of the 'dominant coalitions' in 13 firms spread across two contrasting sectors, the

HRM and Performance

Dutch metal industry and the Dutch IT industry. These offer an ideal contrast, as they are based on the very different characteristics that each displays on the PMT and SCL dimensions and on the degree of institutionalization of the employment relationship (very strong and long-established in the metal industry, considerably weaker in the IT industry). In other words, the extent of constraining factors acting upon firms' HRM policy-making discretion (i.e. their 'degree of leeway') differs markedly between the two sectors.

We conducted our research at the company level, rather than the sectoral level, because it is at this level that the two key trends in Dutch industrial relations described above meet. Specifically, we set out to examine how the actors involved have been able (or not) to introduce flexible employment practices. Following Atkinson (1987), we assess three forms of flexibility: numerical, functional, and financial (see Figure 7.2). They can take varying forms and can be agreed internally or in conjunction with external actors. Taking each in turn, *numerical flexibility* refers to the ability of organizations to adjust the numbers of workers and/or the level of hours worked, in line with the organization's workload. *Functional flexibility* refers to the ability of organizations to reorganize jobs along a broad or narrow range of tasks or to have them co-ordinated in multi-skilled project groups. Finally, *financial flexibility* refers to the ability of organizations to design their wage systems according to circumstantial requirements.

This is an ideal subject to investigate for two reasons. First, research has indicated that recent trends in Dutch industrial relations have made 'flexible' work practices a prescient and controversial issue for research (Smit *et al.*, 1995; Schilstra *et al.*, 1996; Remery *et al.*, 2002; Horbeek, 2003). Second, the extensive institutionalization of the Dutch system of industrial relations might be

	Internal	External
Numerical	Overtime Flexible working hours Shift patterns	Temporary employees 'Labour pools' Short-term contracts
Functional	Job enlargement/rotation Job enrichment Multi-skilling	Outsourcing Specialized employment agencies Sub-contracting
Financial	Individualized or team-based PRP (agreed at company level)	Individualized or team-based PRP (agreed at sector level)

Fig 7.2. Forms of flexibility

Source: based on de Haan *et al.* (1994).

expected to present considerable obstacles to more flexible forms of employment.

Our interest in each firm's decision-making is essentially five-fold:

1. Which bodies or organizations comprise the 'dominant coalition' in different sectors?
2. What is the 'degree of leeway' for human resource management policy amid the competing interests of the main stakeholders inside and outside the firm and within the constraints imposed by any sectoral institutional arrangements?
3. Which aspects of the actors' environment exercise constraints on their options for selecting HRM policy (i.e. whether on the PMT dimension or the SCL, or a combination of both)?
4. What have been the choices taken in each firm?
5. What have been the outcomes for the actors involved?

The 13 firms were selected on two main criteria: number of employees, and breadth of employees' tasks. We selected the first dimension because, following Dunlop (1958), larger workforces typically require formal co-ordination and management processes and hence there is a corresponding need for greater degree of regulation. We set a minimum headcount of 100, so that all of the firms would be covered by Dutch works council legislation. The second criterion was selected because broader task structures (i.e. different task responsibilities, non-fixed performance routines) tend to be much harder to regulate. The characteristics of the 13 companies—seven from the metal industry and six from the IT/computer industry—are summarized in Figures 7.3 and 7.4.[7]

Our primary data came from five interviews in each company, typically including the head of personnel/HRM, a senior member of the works council, a senior trade union official (where present), and a representative from the relevant employers' association. We solicited information on the conduct of six relationships overall (see Figure 7.1): those between the firm's managers and any trade unions present; between managers and the firm's works council; between the works council and the trade unions; between managers and their

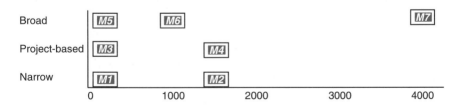

Fig 7.3. Seven metal industry companies by number of employees and task breadth

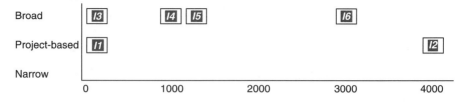

Fig 7.4. Six IT industry companies by number of employees and task breadth

employers' association; between the trade unions and the employers' association; and finally between the works council and the employers' association. We asked questions on parties' goals and strategies and then more detailed questions on how they sought to establish more flexible working practices. Finally, we gathered data on the outcomes secured.

7.5 The metal industry

The metal industry in the Netherlands comprises six industrial sub-sectors: the production of machines; the production of vehicles, planes, and ships; electro-technical activities (e.g. Philips, the wiring of ships); the production of metal objects (e.g. furniture); the instruments and optical industry; and various other metal concerns.

The actors in the 'dominant coalition'

The key characteristics of the seven companies studied from the metal industry, and the nature of their relations with other members in their 'dominant coalition', are set out in Table 7.1. Each is set in position on the two dimensions (headcount size and task complexity) in Figure 7.3 above.

The employers' organization, FME/CWM, represents around 130 economic–technical associations, which in turn comprise approximately 3,500 individual firms. All seven of our sample are members. It is one of the largest sectoral employers' associations in the Netherlands. Its primary strategic goals in collective bargaining are to maintain low gross wage costs, and to 'protect' its members' entrepreneurial freedom. Accordingly, the FME/CWM is not inclined to condone clauses in the sector-wide agreement that might initiate company-specific arrangements, as these could lead to duplicate negotiations on a single topic. It also might provide union representatives the right to company-level negotiations inside firms where management opposes them. Should individual firms themselves decide unilaterally to grant additional

TABLE 7.1 Profiles: seven metal industry firms

Firm	Company details	Agreement coverage	Union density in (central) council	Council–management meetings	Union–council meetings	Union–management meetings
M1: Measure Maker	Measuring tools manufacturer 160 employees Union density: 30%	Almost everyone	100% (6/6)	6 per year	6 per year; information not always passed on	2 per year
M2: Presscar	Manufacturer 1,400 employees (600 in Automotive Division) Union density: 30%	Almost everyone	80% (9/11)	6–8 per year	4 per year; council passes all information	2 per year
M3: Fasttire	Production machines; PLC 235 employees Union density: 50%	Almost everyone	100% (9/9)	6 per year	6 per year; information not always passed on	3–4 per year
M4: High Voltage	Electro-technical installations; PLC 1,400 employees Union density: 30%–40%	Almost everyone	55% (8/15)	6–8 per year	12 per year; council passes all information	2–3 year

(Continued)

TABLE 7.1 (*Contd*)

Firm	Company details	Agreement coverage	Union density in (central) council	Council–management meetings	Union–council meetings	Union–management meetings
M5: C&W	Cable manufacturer 350 employees Union density: 60%	Almost everyone	100% (9/9)	6 per year	4 per year; information not always passed on	2 per year
M6: Windress	International; PLC 830 employees Union density: 20%–40%	Almost everyone	35% (4/11)	6 per year	Weak link	2–3 per year
M7: DuCa	Mass car production Private firm 4,000 employees Union density: 30%–40%	Almost everyone	70% (16/23)	11 per year	15 per year; council passes all information	6 per year

terms of labour or to extend co-determination rights to unions, the FME/CWM will not extend any subsequent practices sector-wide. The FME/CWM has the image of a hard bargainer, although the association prefers to claim that it merely takes a clear, industrial stance.

Four unions (one affiliated to the FNV, one to the CNV, plus Unie and the VHP-M) negotiate on behalf of metal industry employees. Total union density in the sector overall is around 30 per cent, but this is by no means evenly distributed. Some firms are not unionized at all, while others approach 80–100 per cent density, with higher rates of unionization being observable in the larger companies. The metal industry unions' sectoral goals are derived from general union-wide policy on members' terms and conditions of labour. General policy aims are co-determined by negotiators and are then approved by the union members. They can be summarized as strengthening unions' position in sectoral-level and company-level networks in order to influence substantial decisions and support for programmes to improve 'employability'; social security; pension schemes; skill training; and of course acceptable, moderate wage increases.

Many metal industry firms with more than one workplace run works councils for each, as well as a central works council for the firm as a whole. All seven firms in our sample have at least one works council, many of which have been in existence since before the 1979 legislation; four operate additional workplace councils. The average union density on the works councils is greater than the national average (65 per cent) in all but two cases.

The 'degree of leeway'

The metal industry has long-standing institutional arrangements for the regulation of the sector's employment relations, with a reputation and image that exemplifies traditional collective bargaining. It has a two-tier system of negotiations. At the sectoral level, the unions and the employers' association conclude a bargaining agreement for the primary terms of labour for the whole sector (e.g. salary levels, general working hours, pension, and retirement provisions). These terms formally cover every employee in the metal industry: approximately 189,000 in about 1,250 companies (1996 figures). While the agreement's coverage is taken to be identical to the industry itself, this is somewhat misleading, since an unknown number of firms adhere to the agreement on a voluntary basis and senior-level employees in the sector are covered by a separate agreement.

The sectoral agreement permits companies to augment these minimum standards as well as to produce their own policies on all other topics. In this case any such company-level deviations from the sectoral arrangements very often need to be approved by local union representatives and/or the company's works council. Around 500 companies (employing around 80 per cent of the total sector) have these additional company-level agreements. They tend to be larger firms and firms located in the more affluent western regions of the country. The sectoral agreement specifies company-level works councils' areas of influence, including flexible working time such as rosters, shift patterns, and holidays, the use of temporary employees, and several procedural matters.

In short, the extended collective bargaining arrangements in the metal industry leave companies little choice in shaping their regulatory network. The SCL dimension is in this sector quite powerful and exercises a lot of influence on the shaping of the employment relationship.

7.6 The IT sector

The IT sector consists of companies that produce, sell, and/or repair information technology equipment ('hardware') and/or programmes, including consultancy, software development, and services.[8] Actual production is quite limited, but around 60 per cent of all European distribution centres of large American and Japanese companies are located in the Netherlands (for a review, see Bouwman *et al.*, 1994). The sector overall shows little homogeneity, because it is relatively young; moreover, most firms operate in different markets and sub-sectors, a significant proportion of the firms are international, and most firms try their utmost to distinguish themselves in a highly competitive labour market.

The actors in the 'dominant coalition'

The key characteristics of the six companies studied from the IT industry, and the nature of their relations with other members in their 'dominant coalition', are set out in Table 7.2. Each is set in position on the two dimensions (headcount size and task complexity) in Figure 7.4 above.

For simplicity's sake, the main employers' association for the sector is the Vifka-IT, part of the larger federation of IT-related employers' associations. Vifka-IT has around 150 member firms, three-quarters of whom employ less than 100 people. Only one of the six IT firms studied here is a member. As a small organization, Vifka-IT relies to a considerable extent on the expertise of HR professionals working for its larger member companies, including the HR manager from 'Purplish' (see case study below). Its main goal is to resist the

TABLE 7.2 Profiles: six IT industry firms

Firm	Company details	Agreement coverage	Union density in (central) council	Council–management meetings	Union–council meetings	Union–management meetings
I1: ISP	Software producer; PLC 450 employees Union density: < 5%	0	15% (1/7)	6–8 per year	None; informal contact in platform	None
I2: Teletron	Consultancy; PLC 5,300 employees Union density: 10%	80% (company level)	55% (5/9)	4–8 per year	None; informal contact in platform	None
I3: Docuprocess	Software; PLC 500 employees Union density: < 5% (varies)	0	85% (6/7)	10 per year	None	1 per year
I4: Sure	Software supplier 1,100 employees Union density: < 5%	0	25% (3/13)	6 per year	None; informal contact in platform	None
I5: Zipper	PLC 1,300 employees Union density: 15%–20%	c.95% (company level)	80%	6–8 per year	4 per year	1 per year
I6: Purplish	US-owned; PLC 3,000 employees Union density: 10%	20% (sectoral level)	5% (3/65)	11 per year	Union is occasional adviser to works council & 'hardware platform'	None

imposition of any collective regulation upon those of its members who prefer to set their own internal arrangements, 'protecting'—as they would see it—their members' prerogative to set their own company-specific wage policies. The second objective is to resist standardized reductions in working hours. Vifka-IT does facilitate collective bargaining agreements for those members in favour of having one, and ensures that any collective agreements with trade unions do not impede the widespread practice of works council negotiations at the company level.

Four trade unions (one affiliated to the FNV, one to the CNV, plus Unie and the VHP-I) are involved in bargaining for the IT sector. The unions' goals are generally the same as those for the metal industry unions, with the added objective of increasing collective bargaining coverage and co-ordinating campaigns across different firms. However, they are in a much weaker position than their metal industry counterparts. They score low on their most important resource: membership. No more than 10 per cent of the sector are union members; it is probably closer to 5 per cent. (There are no reliable figures for such a dynamic, constantly changing, sector prone to changes in ownership and high labour turnover.) Union recruitment is difficult in the sector. IT firms are generally hostile toward trade unions almost to the point of loathing. They prize decentralization and autonomy from 'external' parties and perceive trade unions to be inflexible. In addition, IT employees are not the type to join a trade union, still less to strike. Even if they were so inclined, the sector's long working hours constitutes a significant barrier to unionization and activism. The four unions have hardly helped their cause with campaigns from radical activists that have turned many IT workers off and the counter-productive split into two factions around the time of the sector's 1997 agreement (Unie and VHP-I versus the FNV and CNV unions).

The works council is the primary employee representative body. The sector agreement does not prohibit works councils from negotiating primary terms of labour instead of trade unions, but in practice the role of most works councils is to act as a consultative body. Few act as formal bargaining partners with their employer. Some IT firms with multiple sites elect to have works councils for each division or workplace, with an 'umbrella' central works council for the firm as a whole; this is the case for two in our sample. The others have just the one works council. Union density among IT works council representatives is modest at best. A number of reasons have been put forward for this. First, IT managers are rarely proponents of co-determination and for the most part tend to resist its imposition and dislike the presence of unions. Second, it is often the behaviour and decisions of the firm's clients, and not its management, that determines the employee's agenda. But perhaps most importantly, works council participation places considerable strain on employees' time and resources and requires a demanding skill-set to fulfil the role effectively. Most IT employees are simply too short of time, despite legal exemptions from work duties. The IT unions are unable to direct works councils' attitudes as they do in the metal industry. There is not much contact between works councils and local trade unions, and, particularly in software firms, where contact does take place the unions are typically confined to an advisory capacity.

Finally, there is a fourth contributing 'actor' in this sector. The two sets of works councils—one in each sub-sector—established two 'platforms' of works councils one for hardware and one for software and services so that employee works council representatives from different firms could meet each other and benefit from each other's skills, knowledge, and information. Each platform sends one member to the other platforms' meetings—there are normally three per year—and each receives the others' minutes. All six IT works councils are members of their relevant platform. The hardware platform is rather more proactive, perhaps as a consequence of the involvement of several trade unionists, whose aim is to secure a sectoral collective bargaining agreement that would also enhance the procedural position of works councils. Collaboration between the unions and the two platforms of works councils has facilitated a number of company-wide bargaining agreements. At the same time, collective bargaining has been enhanced in this sector as a result of the outsourcing of IT departments from traditional large unionized companies (examples are the Dutch Railways, Philips and RCC) to specialized IT companies.

The 'degree of leeway'

The four unions and the employers' association conclude the sector-wide agreement for Dutch IT firms. In practice this applies only to the hardware companies, since the Vifka-IT does not represent sufficient software and services companies. Additionally, the agreement is limited to employees with wages below a certain level (less than €42,650). Thus, the agreement actually covers around 40,000 employees, a modest proportion (18 per cent) of the estimated 220,000 full-time employees in the sector. Non-Vifka-IT members may adhere to its terms on a voluntary basis.

In practice, neither the sector-wide agreement nor the company-level bargaining arrangements exercises significant restraints on management teams. Thus, the low degree of institutionalization (SCL dimension) in the sector accounts for the considerable leeway and freedom that management teams in IT firms enjoy to determine their own HRM policies.

7.7 The sectors contrasted

We are now in a position to draw simple comparisons between the respective 'dominant coalitions' in each sector. The extended collective bargaining agreement in the metal industry leaves companies little choice in shaping their regulatory framework and with whom they must deal. Its actors engage in intensive, multiple relationships both inside and outside companies. Representing employees' interests on the primary terms of labour is clearly the unions' remit at both the sectoral and company level.

By contrast, the looser institutional structures in the IT industry afford managers much greater leeway. For trade unions to secure a comparably dominant position to that enjoyed in the metal industry requires at the least a collective bargaining agreement, and even that is no guarantee. Instead, both sectoral and company-level agreements for IT firms accord the works council an influential position, and this forum most often constitutes the primary employees' representative and the sole formal relationship between company management and its employees.

Relations between trade unions and works council members also differ between the two industries. In the metal industry the unions' influence over council members is predominant; in the IT sector, if anything, the opposite is the case.

In summary, HRM strategy inside the seven metal companies is determined mainly in the arena between the business strategy and the trade unions' goals and is conducted at both the sectoral and company level. HRM strategy inside the six IT companies is determined mainly in the arena between business strategies and the works council's goals and is conducted primarily at the company level. In the next section we describe the introduction of measures in order to enhance flexibility and the way in which the different flexibility arrangements are regulated in the two sectors.

7.8 Flexibility in the employment relationship: choices made and outcomes

Tables 7.3 and 7.4 summarize the extent of the three different forms of flexibility in the metal and IT industries, respectively.

All companies appear to make a similar trade-off between internal and external numerical flexibility. Metal companies tend to make widespread use of external forms, often hiring large percentages of temporary employees to deal with peak loads (10–30 per cent). At the same time they also use

TABLE 7.3 Flexibility in the metal industry

Firm	Numerical flexibility	Functional flexibility	Financial flexibility
M1: Measure Maker	Outsources repair work Rare use of temporary or part-time employees	—	Profit-sharing scheme
M2: Presscar	Few temporary employees Overtime Rare use of outsourcing	Poor functional flexibility in production	Profit-sharing scheme
M3: Fasttire	Temporary employees Outsourced parts of production	Broad skills base Little cross-functional work	Profit-sharing scheme
M4: High Voltage	Temporary employees Labour pool	Project teams Multi-skilling	Profit-sharing scheme
M5: C&W	Extensive use of temporary employees	Multi-skilling (2 of 3 sites) Autonomous work groups	—
M6: Windress	Agency workers	Task groups	Profit-sharing scheme (trial resisted by works council)
M7: DuCa	Flexitime (weekly hours) No outsourcing	Task groups Multi-skilling	Small PRP element

internal forms, especially overtime and a variety of rosters. Interestingly, the more 'Tayloristic' metal companies, with little evidence of practices such as task groups and self-directed teams, are less dependent on both numerical and functional flexibility. This could be a consequence of a more predictable work flow. The situation is very different in the IT sector, where there is evidence that the larger companies make a trade-off between internal and external flexibility. The difference between the sectors may result from different average educational levels; the sectors recruit from separate labour markets. IT companies also prefer issuing short-term contracts to employing temporary staff. (Apparently IT companies use temporary contracts as an elaborate selection procedure.) Metal companies displaying high numerical flexibility also display reasonably high internal functional flexibility. Conversely, those with low levels of internal functional flexibility need little numerical flexibility. It seems that the metal companies either require short-term flexibility (apparently either numerical or internal functional) or can predict market developments ahead of time (few flexibility requirements).

TABLE 7.4 Flexibility in the IT industry

Firm	Numerical flexibility	Functional flexibility	Financial flexibility
I1: ISP	Rare use of all forms	Project-based work teams	Highly standardized terms and conditions Individual PRP (4 × per year)—an employee-led process
I2: Teletron	Temporary labour (9% of workforce) Short-term contracts Flexible working hours Overtime	Project-based work teams Multi-functional employees, alongside specialization Multi-skilling training	PRP for management grades Bonuses for 'exceptional performance'
I3: Docuprocess	Very few part-time or temporary employees	Team-based work (plans for devolving more responsibilities to teams, career planning, training)	Client-assessed PRP; some orchestrated convergence of bonus levels Bonuses for 'exceptional performance' PRP
I4: Sure	Rare use of external flexibility arrangements Extensive reliance on overtime (10% –20% of normal working hours)	Team-based production Multi-skilling Little use of cross-functional working	Profit-sharing scheme Differentiated terms and conditions (based on individual compliance with company pay policy)
I5: Zipper	Outsources some functions (catering, gardening, security) Use of short-term contracts Temporary hires during peak times Flexible working hours	Extensive technical training Emphasis on employability	Job-ranking Individual PRP (up to 25% of income)
I6: Purplish	Sub-contracts some functions Use of short-term contracts (15% of workforce) Some part-time workers Overtime and flexible work hours	Project-based work teams Efforts to collate a skill-set database	Job-rating Individual merit bonus

The metal firms showed various refinements of internal functional flexibility. An example would be whether 'group' tasks include administrative tasks like production planning, project planning, or personnel planning and whether they include technical support tasks like maintenance and repairs. The distinction into three such categories is more clear-cut in most IT companies. Task breadth varies, from project groups with somewhat specialized employees subcontracted to clients, to multi-skilled employees performing several tasks in multiple projects. The exact number of ancillary tasks performed by these project groups differs in each firm and/or project, but is generally high.

The importance of external functional flexibility is hard to discern, especially in the metal industry. Most companies have a clear position in the chain of production: they buy, and often sell, semi-finished products from business-to-business suppliers. Make-or-buy decisions in the past are often forgotten. Parties are aware of outsourcing during the decision-making process, and recollections fade shortly after the associated production equipment is removed. However, IT companies and their clients continuously make outsourcing decisions, although most claim they outsource only routine tasks, highly specialized tasks, and tasks for which they themselves are not equipped.

Almost all IT companies reward individual or group performance, often negotiated in the company's works council. The company's performance has a stronger influence on these negotiations when unions are not involved, as unions tend to resist this link. Many IT firms employ mechanisms that automatically adjust part of their wage bill to the market developments. This may happen as a result of pay-for-performance and/or a profit sharing scheme, or from the fact that works council and management negotiate on the wage bill. The latter takes place at three companies in this sample. Although no precise data are available, it appears that wages in the metal industry are less performance-related (rarely over 10 per cent flexible) than those in the IT sector (sometimes up to 30 per cent). Wages are linked to the firm's performance at all these firms; half of the companies reward individual performance, and even more have a profit-sharing scheme; at two of the firms the collective bargaining agreements have a similar wage structure. In short, most metal companies try to maintain or increase some form of financial flexibility. Many of the IT companies, on the other hand, aim to reduce the variety in terms of labour by standardizing or at least harmonizing them. This variety results from both mergers and takeovers and from employees disagreeing with alteration to their terms of labour.

7.9 Case studies

The following four case studies illustrate these patterns, and the use made of external and internal regulation of these terms and conditions.

Presscar

Presscar is a Dutch public limited liability company, with its headquarters in a devout Protestant region of the country, from which it recruits the vast majority of its employees. Worldwide it employs around 2,000, of which 1,400 are based in the Netherlands, employed across four business units: automobile parts, building components, installation products, and thermoplastic materials. Union density at the main site, for automobile parts, stands at around 30 per cent (see Table 7.5).

The peculiarities of the market for Presscar's core product—pressed sheet metal—mean that most of the firm's clients manufacture this product themselves; in other words, many of its customers are also competitors. The technological demands of the business are formidable, as are the logistical planning required to deliver optimum use of Presscar's machinery. Downtime, or under-utilization, is very costly indeed. Accordingly, Presscar operates a just-in-time (JIT) production system which each business is expected to apply to secure long-term client relationships.

The metal industry agreement covers all Presscar employees except the senior management team. This is then augmented and enhanced with company-level policies, all of which are set out in the firm's personnel guide. Management and the unions enjoy a good working relationship, with regular monthly contact above and beyond the periodical consultations. Presscar also has four works councils: one central council and one apiece for the business units (except the two sites at HQ which share a council). Union density is 80 per cent inside the central works council. By and large, the central council is supportive of Presscar management plans, reasoning that what is good for the firm is good for the workforce—both managers and employees want a viable and competitive company.

Presscar makes little use of numerical flexibility in terms of contractual arrangements; for example, only a handful are on part-time contracts. Moreover, it has its own subsidiaries responsible for the 'usual suspects' for outsourcing, such as catering, security, and internal administration. However, it does make extensive use of overtime, although neither management nor the recognized unions are especially enamoured of the arrangements (the former because of the high costs, the latter because better planning might create new jobs).

TABLE 7.5 Profile: Presscar

Firm	Company details	Agreement coverage	Union density in (central) council	Council–management meetings	Union–council meetings	Union–management meetings
M2: Presscar	Manufacturer 1,400 employees (600 in Automotive division) Union density: 30%	Almost everyone	80% (9/11)	6–8 per year	4 per year; council passes all information	2 per year

HRM and Performance

Functional flexibility is not developed within Presscar, and certainly no cross-functional working. Presscar work tasks are typically short-cycled and there is neither job enlargement nor job enrichment, unless one includes oiling the machines. The workforce has resisted task group initiatives, fearing job losses.

Presscar also makes little use of financial flexibility programmes, eschewing tailor-made pay packages except for senior management. All of its employees are covered by the sectoral agreement, with only one company-level embellishment, a profit-sharing plan for its Dutch employees, which was devised in consultation with the works council in the early 1990s.

Windress

Windress Aluminium Constructions belongs to an international industrial public limited liability company. Windress's activities—window dressing products—constitutes the most significant of the three main markets for the conglomerate, the others being trade in primary and secondary metals and precision machinery. Windress began in the Netherlands in the 1950s. It sells most of its products, especially the quality brands, through a network of franchised distribution licensees to which Windress supplies not only the materials and components for the products, but also the specialized machinery for their assembly (see Table 7.6).

The firm has some 830 employees, of whom around 40 per cent work in production and a comparable percentage in sales and marketing. Unionization density varies in estimates from 20 to 40 per cent throughout the firm and stands at around 75 per cent in the production grades. While the majority of the workforce is passive or neutral in industrial relations matters, there is a small but vocal radicalized group that would prefer to see both the unions and the works council confront the management 'enemy' more directly.

The company and the union representatives have developed a fairly constructive relationship since the restructuring during the 1990s and are usually able to pursue compromises on the firm's more contentious objectives.

The company's central works council is long-established, originally formed during the early 1970s. It has 15 seats, ten of which come from the shop-floor. The main site occupies nine seats; the other two sites three apiece. Each site has its own specific works council as well. Each local council meets with management six times a year officially, although typically a further six joint meetings at the company level also take place each year.

Windress adheres to the terms concluded in the sectoral agreement, which automatically increases wages for all but the senior management team. However, in contrast to Presscar, these are supplemented with company-specific arrangements on almost every topic concerning the terms of labour. All of

TABLE 7.6 Profile: Windress

Firm	Company details	Agreement coverage	Union density in (central) council	Council–management meetings	Union–council meetings	Union–management meetings
M6: Windress	International PLC 830 employees Union density: 20%–40%	Almost everyone	35% (4/11)	6 per year	Weak link	2–3 per year

these are detailed in the firm's comprehensive personnel guide. Any amendments to terms and conditions within Windress require an endorsement from either the trade unions (for primary terms of labour) or the works council (for the secondary and tertiary terms).

During the mid-1990s Windress responded to increasing demands of its customers on quality by reappraising its production methods. In its intended shift towards a 'mean and lean' approach, the firm concluded that both its existing facilities and its workforce were incompatible with efforts to make the process more flexible. In particular, the workforce was felt to lack sufficient skills and education to adapt to more flexible work practices and so would require additional training. Further, changes to production techniques would mean that some of the workforce would be 'under-utilized'. In consultation with its works council and local union representatives, Windress implemented compulsory training courses for all of its production work groups. Today, each employee must be capable of performing at least two main tasks. Moreover, each work group is responsible for its own planning and quality control.

The production workers' flexibility is rewarded with additional pay, and the firm operates a profit-sharing scheme. This was briefly linked to absenteeism, until both the unions and the works council objected.

On numerical flexibility, the firm uses a small number of agency labourers (around 25 a time) to smooth out production peaks. This is not a popular strategy among the employees, however. Satisfactory 'temporary' employees are offered a one-year contract.

In sum, the degree of leeway that management has in determining its HRM policies, and policies in other areas, is more or less determined by expanding the boundaries set down in the Works Council Act and the sectoral bargaining agreement. What is noteworthy about Windress is that some company agreements involve *both* the works councils and the local trade unions, including reductions in shift bonuses and the link between absenteeism and the profit-sharing scheme mentioned above. On the latter, when the unions objected, the management team sought to persuade the works councils of the virtues of the scheme. When this too failed—because, management is convinced, the unions were more persuasive behind the scenes—the firm abandoned the idea. In other words, the firm makes use of either party (unions or works council), depending on the issue.

Zipper Automated

Zipper is a Dutch public limited liability company. It has a headcount figure of just over 1,300, roughly half of what it used to employ before the early 1990s recession damaged the business. Although for a long time it operated as an independent company, its status at the time of the research was as a joint venture with two other firms. It is active in four sectors, primarily in its domestic market: automating government organizations; employers' information database systems and salary records; office IT equipment (both hardware and software); and tailor-made software and project secondment services. Its cash-cow is salary administration. All four markets are dynamic and very much client-driven, and of course Zipper is required to maintain up-to-date knowledge and application of the latest technologies. Union density is surprisingly high for the sector at around 15 per cent, perhaps even as high as 20 per cent (see Table 7.7).

Zipper is an unusual case study, in that it was one of the few firms in the IT sector to have a company-level collective bargaining agreement. The four unions involved in the sectoral bargaining agreement meet with Zipper management once a year to conduct negotiations. Indeed, Zipper management actually prefers to arrange primary terms of labour with these external partners. Accordingly, the unions are given extensive access to company information and relations are good.

The terms of the agreement cover all Zipper staff, except the senior managers. It consists of three parts: a general framework agreement for all employees (including basic definitions of terms, negotiations on the wage bill but not on actual salary levels, and parameters surrounding secondary terms of labour), plus two 'specifications'. The 'specifications' pertain to different business units, allowing Zipper greater flexibility in employees' terms and conditions to match the different standards in the different sub-markets within which it operates. (The unions objected to this, but had little option but to go along with it.) While Zipper management seems to appreciate the valuable role that the unions perform in the collective bargaining agreement, it remains ambivalent on the extent to which these external players should enjoy influence over other concerns within the company. So, although the unions' input is welcome on the general direction of Zipper's HRM strategy and policies, management continues to resist the unions' efforts to negotiate on individual wage levels.

Zipper has one central works council, which it has had since the early 1970s, and in addition runs separate works councils for the four business units. Each business unit council sends two delegates to the central works council. Union density across the councils approaches 80 per cent. In this respect, the aims of the works council and those of the four negotiating unions converge considerably. While the company-level collective bargaining agreement delimits the remit of the central works council, in practice the council members and the unions consult regularly. Management–works council relations are generally very good indeed, with managers regularly providing the central works council with information prior to major decisions and enjoining them to share in the

TABLE 7.7 Profile: Zipper Automated

Firm	Company details	Agreement coverage	Union density in (central) council	Council–management meetings	Union–council meetings	Union–management meetings
I5: Zipper	PLC 1,300 employees Union density: 15%–20%	c.95% (company level)	80%	6–8 per year	4 per year	1 per year

decision-making process. The works council seeks to balance the company's interests with those of its employees and tends to get proactively involved in firm decision-making.

Numerical flexibility is modest within Zipper. The vast majority (some 1,100) of Zipper staff work in either the production or the delivery of Zipper's services, with a further 200 in support staff roles. Zipper has very few employees on part-time contracts. But, in common with the rest of the IT industry, it does make use of short-term contracts and temporary contracts to fulfil certain projects; around 100 employees fall into these two categories. A third form of numerical flexibility concerns the facilitation of irregular working hours. Finally, it has outsourced many of its non-core activities, such as catering and security.

Given such dynamic and competitive markets, and such demanding clients, the functional flexibility of employees is of great importance. The company aims to broaden their education and technical knowledge, but is also acutely aware that their intimate knowledge of Zipper's customers, each with its own idiosyncrasies and specific requirements, is an additional source of competitive advantage. Maintaining this close working relationship with clients delimits the extent to which Zipper can deploy its staff using functional flexibility.

Financial flexibility is in the first instance facilitated by the two 'specifications' in the company-level agreement. In addition, Zipper determines individual wages through a job-ranking system that is widely used within the industry, in which jobs are grouped into task-based 'families' and wage levels are then compared across different firms. This is coupled with a pay-for-performance system of bonuses which may amount to a quarter of employees' total income. An element of the performance appraisal informs employees' career progression. The total sum of money available for performance-related bonuses is subject to Zipper profit levels, and is also subject to negotiations at the company level with the four unions.

Purplish

Purplish is a Dutch public limited liability company owned by a large American holding. Its ten separate fully owned subsidiaries provide both hardware and software services, customized to clients' detailed requirements. The Dutch operation has five major departments: international, information systems, services, specialized support staff, and marketing. In total, it employs around 4,000 employees, but of these 800 work for various subsidiaries with separate terms and conditions for labour. Thus, Purplish itself has a little over 3,000 employees. As at Zipper, union density is surprisingly high for the sector, standing at around 10 per cent and dominated by the VHP union (see Table 7.8).

TABLE 7.8 Profile: Purplish

Firm	Company details	Agreement coverage	Union density in (central) council	Council–management meetings	Union–council meetings	Union–management meetings
I6: Purplish	PLC. US-owned 3,000 employees Union density: 10%	20% (sectoral level)	5% (3/65)	11 per year	Union is occasional adviser to works council & 'hardware platform'	None

Once the American HQ has communicated its general HRM strategy to its subsidiaries, Purplish in the Netherlands translates this into a viable set of policies compliant with local law and then disseminates this to its business units, which enjoy considerable discretion on matters of implementation. At the time of the research Purplish was in the process of reconfiguring its operations into a matrix structure based on project management for its clients; thus, the different subsidiaries will soon be categorized by region, then by country, and then by sub-sector. Each employee is responsible to her or his own business unit, but has an employment contract with the local subsidiary (country-based). Accordingly, it is difficult to generalize about Purplish terms and conditions and ways of operating, since by definition these may be subject to the stipulations of the client. That said, the firm has sought to standardize its skill-sets as far as possible and to establish a database of the abilities of each member of staff.

The unique aspect of Purplish's HRM strategy is that the sector-wide agreement covers a substantial proportion of its workforce (600 employees: around 18 per cent of the full-time staff)—the only IT firm in our sample to comply with the sectoral agreement.[9] Despite this, and interestingly, the management team has hardly any formal dealings with the recognized trade unions. In other words, the decision from Purplish to sign up to the sectoral agreement has very little to do with pressure exerted by its unionized workforce. The unions' only input is in an informal advisory capacity to the company's works councils.

Purplish has five works councils, one for each department, plus a central works council for the whole of the company. In many respects the central works council adopts the traditional remit of external recognized trade unions. It meets with senior management once a month, as do the five departmental works councils with their respective management teams. There is little scope for the central works council to formulate long-term strategies on behalf of the Purplish workforce, given the dynamic nature of the market and operations and the constraints imposed by the firm's headquarters. The works council and management teams tend to approach issues as distinct challenges rather than bundling them together as a piece.

The one particularly noteworthy, and also unique, aspect of Purplish is that it negotiates with a special committee of its central works council over the internal allocation of various terms of labour. Any company-specific arrangements are subject to the firm's overall business performance, but are then rolled out to cover all staff. This is remarkable for the sector. However, it should be pointed out that these joint negotiations are hardly the first-choice strategy for management, which has tried to limit the council's influence after years of extending its rights in order to keep the unions out.

Purplish makes extensive use of different forms of numerical flexibility. Around 500 employees are on short-term contracts, mainly of between two and four years' duration; another hundred or so work part-time. In addition, the firm has sub-contracting arrangements with suppliers in order to fulfil those clients' demands that its own project teams are unable to achieve. Overtime and flexible working hours are an accepted part of the job.

Similarly, the nature of the business demands of employees that they be technically adept and highly flexible in responding to the specifications of clients' needs. Purplish employees work in project teams that can vary in membership, forming and disbanding as projects demand.

Each employee receives a merit bonus based on the outcomes of the annual performance appraisal/job-ranking system.

7.10 Conclusions

We suggested in the introduction that, given the trend in the 1980s and 1990s in the Netherlands toward decentralized industrial relations, combined with growing managerial interest in HRM, we might expect to observe in our case studies an increase in internal regulation of the employment relationship and a corresponding reduction in external regulation. This study rather suggests an alternative picture.

The research found, firstly, that few companies faced serious constraints, either internally or externally, on their plans for introducing more flexible arrangements in their employment relationships. The few examples of works council or trade union opposition to management programmes seemed not to have heralded a collapse in relations, while for the most part both works councils and/or trade unions have proactively engaged with management proposals on flexible work practices and systems. Contrary to Dunlop's (1958) claim, market changes did not necessarily lead to changes in procedural or substantial rules. In the institutionalized Dutch system of statutory information and consultation arrangements, all actors enjoy insight into the company's market position, and so decreasing performance rarely influences the structure or atmosphere of relations. When market developments did force management to cut the terms of labour (substantial regulation), this rarely led to a bad atmosphere since the information was already common currency and the problem-solving process was undertaken jointly. In the few cases where salary cuts did serious damage to relations, the unpopular substantive changes exacerbated an already fraught atmosphere.

The second finding is more significant. The research found considerable evidence that both internal and external regulation have their advantages, from a management point of view. Some management teams have forgone the presumed orthodoxy for 'economically rational' HRM policy—internal regulation wherever possible—and have deliberately chosen to involve other actors in the process of determining its HRM policies. The most dramatic examples of external regulation are the bargaining agreements forged in the IT sector, especially Purplish (which voluntarily subscribes to the sector-wide agreement) and Zipper (where labour negotiations have effectively been 'sub-contracted' out to the trade unions). While the analysis certainly does not prove that these firms *favour* external collective regulation over internal regulation, many have nevertheless taken advantage of it—albeit in a somewhat calculated manner. In addition, the IT companies without extensive collective agreement coverage all involved their works councils in the determination of salaries, bonuses, etc., rather than have management decide and act unilaterally. Similarly, several of the metal industry companies, enmeshed in the sector's external regulatory networks, indicated a clear preference for making use of *supplementary* internal regulation through their works council(s). Perhaps the most striking example is that of Windress.

Why might this be the case? The contextually based human resource theory offers an insight. An advantage to managers in engaging in supplementary regulation is that other actors' involvement provides managers with access to valuable power bases that they lack. Put simply, it gives management access to *legitimacy* (as indicated by the SCL dimension). For example, many IT management teams reason that trade union involvement in company decision-making accords the final outcome greater authority and credibility than might be secured through unilateral imposition. Purplish explained that their decision to adhere to the sectoral agreement rested on its strength in helping to override works council and/or individual objections to changes in terms and conditions. Similarly, Zipper management offered two main reasons for preferring to bargain with trade unions rather than their own works council: the value of dealing with professional negotiators, and the impartiality of union negotiators unaffected by the terms and conditions under discussion. Yet what is also interesting is that in the absence of unions many employers still seem to prefer additional works council involvement in the regulation of the employment relationship, notwithstanding the potential legal uncertainties. (The Works Council Act and related legislation provides only a weak legal foundation for these bodies' input into negotiations on the primary terms of labour.) Two examples are Docupress and ISP. Note that the IT firms with company-wide bargaining agreements do not have substantial numbers of unionized workers who might be expected to have pressurized their employer into adopting formal collective bargaining arrangements. This has been a management decision.

Our empirical research also offers insights into factors determining the composition of the dominant coalition which shed light on these surprising findings. Trade union involvement was found to be almost completely contingent upon the presence or absence of a collective bargaining agreement. If the company is covered by such arrangements, local union representatives are the dominant actors on behalf of the employees. In the absence of a collective agreement trade union input, management contact with trade unions is minimal, except for irregular occasions such as talks over the 'social plans' required for mergers, restructurings, and/or large-scale redundancies. Instead, firms seeking legitimacy for their decisions turn to their works councils, and many are happy to negotiate primary terms of labour with their employees in this forum. However, as we have seen, some managers do turn to trade unions, regardless of union density levels. Thus, it appears that some companies do see merits in external regulation, negotiating with weakly represented trade unions instead of with their own works councils. Regardless of the 'partner' to whom management appeals for this legitimacy, doing so is clearly felt to benefit the firm because this can override significant objections from the firm's own works council and/or individuals, thereby preventing an inside-oriented 'politicizing' of their (HR) management policies and at the same time reducing administration costs. Settling an agreement with trade unions also provides managers with a stronger legal status to the agreement (thus increasing the deal's legitimacy). This suggests that the differing legal status of the actors is perhaps the most compelling power base sought by management in evaluating the respective merits of internal versus external regulation. The superiority in this regard of agreements with recognized trade unions may provide one explanation for some firms' preference for dealing with them rather than the internal works council. In the case of firms with several subsidiaries under a holding, management can adjust the terms of labour for all employees by a holding-wide collective bargaining agreement with a trade union; to achieve the same coverage in collaboration with the firm's works councils would require the consent of each and every council. Furthermore, the works councils' consent provides less of a judicial safeguard against individual employees who reject alterations of their terms of labour. Hence, the power bases are derived from legal prerogatives.

This research suggests that 'layered' collective bargaining agreements—with general regulations at sectoral (or company) level complemented by substantial leeway for tailored specifications at company (or business unit) level—seem to, or can, offer a 'happy marriage' of the employer's and employees' desires. This type of agreement explicitly allows for company and/or business unit specifications but is binding to individual employees and works councils. The layered agreement combines high regulatory involvement of both employee representatives (unions and works councils). However, it also implies a great deal of additional work for both trade union officials and works council members (Schilstra and Jongbloed, 2003).

Since the nineties, we can discern employers and trade unions at the sectoral level favouring so-called *à la carte* collective bargaining agreements. These contain an options package of terms and conditions from which the employees can compose, at least to a certain degree, their own set of labour conditions and can even change their terms once or a few times a year. Choice options include leisure time, pension schemes, child care, computer facilities, etc. We see that with respect to these arrangements the bargaining partners can take into greater account the specific situation of separate enterprises and workplaces, as well as accommodate the idiosyncratic preferences of individual employees. These *à la carte* agreements thus may create more leeway for HRM practices.

In conclusion, our findings endorse Powell's claim that extensive interactions among different parties may 'increase transaction costs, but in return they provide concrete benefits or intangible assets that are far more valuable. The reduction of uncertainty, fast access to information, reliability, and responsiveness are among the paramount concerns that motivate the participants in exchange networks' (1990: 323). While reaching consent among the actors may be time-consuming, this drawback is offset by the relatively smooth implementation of any adjusted regulations derived in large part from the perceived legitimacy of the decision-making secured with employee representatives' involvement. Our research challenges the assumptions that external regulation is necessarily less responsive. It suggests instead that external regulation can be just as responsive to the individual company's objectives as internal collective regulation.

Notes

1. Individual internal regulation, in which the employer and an individual employee regulate the employment relationship, is excluded from this study. Examples of this regulation are the organization's specification of the employee's tasks and functions or the individual's employment contract.
2. Note that industrial or craft unions negotiating at company level are a form of external regulation, as they generally negotiate with more than one employer.
3. For more detailed overviews see Smit *et al.* (1995), Visser and Hemerijck (1997) and Visser (1998).
4. In 1998, the 1979 Works Councils Act was revised, including a reduction in the threshold level of staff required for initiating a works council to 50. However, in this chapter we use case studies that precede the 1998 amendments, and hence here we describe the legal and industrial relations situation prior to 1998.

HRM and Performance

5. The late 1990s witnessed a fresh programme of legislation related to labour conditions on, e.g., flexibility and security, working times, and facilities for combining work with child care.
6. See also Chapter 4 of this book for an overview of Dutch research in this area in the 1990s.
7. One bias among our metal industry sample is that the smallest participating firm is more than four times larger then the smallest companies in the IT sector. Also, the six participating IT companies are somewhat atypical for their industry, since two have a collective bargaining agreement with a union and all six have at least one works council. It might be, then, that these companies devote more time to labour relations than the average IT company.
8. Note that this does not include telecommunications companies.
9. Indeed, the company used to apply its terms automatically to all staff until the mid-1980s, when the agreement enshrined a reduction in working hours that Purplish judged incompatible with its operating procedures. It bought off the clause among its own staff with a lump sum.

8   Continuing Divergence of HRM Practices: US and European-Based Company-Level HRM Practices

Ferrie Pot and Jaap Paauwe

8.1 Introduction

This book argues against a universal prescription for human resource management. Instead, human resource managers should be sensitive to the institutional environment in which their organization is embedded. The institutional environment is made up of many dimensions. The origins of the institutions that affect the performance of HRM practices are various. We can distinguish institutional influences that are specific to an industry, region, corporation, locality, plant, etc. One of the major sources of institutional influence on the performance of human resource management practices is the nation state. The specific set of national institutions is often referred to as 'national culture'. In the organizational literature various contributions assess the cultural peculiarities of employment relationships in a particular nation state (see Box 8.1).

Although adjacent disciplines do recognize diversity across nations, the literature on HRM is on the whole still quite universal in nature. The institutional impact of the nation state on corporate HRM practices is a matter of debate. It has been argued that national variations disappear as the economic realm becomes more and more globally integrated. Culturally based differences will vanish as obsolete national economic practices are sanctioned by the iron hand of the global market. 'Globalization' is the buzz-word (Waters, 1995). Child (2000) is less outspoken in his overview of the state of the art in international business research. Based on his overview, he distinguishes research that pays considerable attention to national contexts (the so-called 'high context' perspectives) from research that emphasizes universal rationales and is insensitive to specific national contexts (the so-called 'low context' perspectives). Child makes a plea for research in transnational organizations that

---

Box 8.1

Various disciplines in the social sciences have contributed to the identification of nation-specific features of employment relationships. In a seminal work in the study of industrial relations, Dunlop (1958) introduced the concept of a 'national industrial relations system'. Drawing on this framework, Bean (1985) and Poole (1986) collected evidence on the broad variety of national systems of industrial relations. In the field of management and organization studies, Whitley (1999) developed the concept of 'national work system' to capture the manner in which employment relations are socially regulated. In the same discipline, Begin (1997) developed the concept of a 'human resource system' to model the systematic differences of corporate employment practices across six major developed nations. Using a Marxist perspective, Edwards (1994) employed the concept of a 'national regime of labour regulation' to grasp the distinct approach to labour management that unifies employers within a single country. In the domain of the sociology of work, a group of French researchers demonstrated a 'societal effect' on the organization of work (Maurice et al., 1986; Maurice and Sorge, 2000). Finally, from a collaborative research effort of an economist and a political scientist, the concept of a 'social system of production' was born (Hollingsworth and Boyer, 1997).

---

integrates both perspectives. Geppart et al. (2003: 3) reaffirm and emphasize this by stating that

globalization, on the one hand strengthens the arguments of the low-context perspectives as it leads to an increasing worldwide convergence and standardization of market conditions, technologies, HRM practices and decision-making processes in corporations. On the other hand, globalization also makes the differences in national cultures and institutions even more visible as it brings these, often diverse, contexts closer together.

So the still highly relevant research issue is whether, within an overall trend towards globalization, national cultures and institutions will continue to shape organizational form and behaviour (Child, 2000: 54–5).

Following Child's challenge, in this chapter we analyse the extent to which a nation state exerts an influence on the design of human resource management practices. In doing this we will refer to HRM change processes in the United States and the Netherlands that were initiated in chemical plants during the 1990s.

We performed an in-depth comparative study of multinational companies (MNCs) in the chemical industry that are based, and have head offices, in the USA or Holland. From our comparisons, we outline how these companies introduce change into their work systems and HRM practices. Because these companies operate in global markets, they are confronted with the need to conform to global best-practice HRM principles. In spite of the fact that companies introduce changes that are in line with such a global best-practice model, we see different patterns in how these changes are implemented and in the way the various parties/stakeholders are involved. These divergent patterns are related to the different cultural and institutional settings of the various home bases of the MNCs. From a managerial perspective, it is important (especially for managers operating in international settings) to be aware that change will proceed in different ways even when, more or less, the same organizational measures are implemented.

Preceding the description and analysis of our case studies, we present a brief summary of the convergence–divergence debate and the main stages in this debate over the last several decades (Section 8.2). In Section 8.3 we focus on the possibilities for cross-national learning for the two countries—the United States and the Netherlands—in which our chemical plants are based. Section 8.4 deals with the case studies in more detail. In Section 8.5 we analyse the actual outcomes of the case studies from the perspective of the differences in change procedure, which has its roots in differences in business culture in the two countries (Section 8.6). In Section 8.7 we present the main conclusions.

8.2 The convergence-divergence debate

Proponents of convergence and divergence theories argue about the persistence of cultural diversity in economic organizations. The former group views diversity as a temporary state of affairs and draws attention to the observation that societies have a tendency to grow more alike. The latter maintains that the existence of cultural variety is an enduring aspect of socio-economic reality. Convergence and divergence theories have been formulated in literature in a wide variety of ways ever since the Second World War (Kerr, 1983; Boyer, 1996; Strange, 1997; Child, 2000; Morgan, Kristensen and Whitley, 2001).

With respect to employment relationships, the convergence–divergence debate passed through two distinct stages during its development (Smith and Meiksins, 1995). The first stage refers to the period when the case for convergence was put forward by Kerr et al. (1960). He proposed a 'logic of industrialization' that entailed the adoption of the same social, political, and economic structures by capitalist and communist societies alike. The unifying effect of technology was thought to underlie the 'logic of industrialization'. The more closely social arrangements were tied to technology, the more uniform they were held to be across various societies. Theorists of the so-called 'contingency school' explored this perspective in organizational theory. They argued that a firm's structure is largely free from cultural influence and that its structure is determined by external contingencies such as size and technology (Pugh, 1981).

This culture-free thesis provoked counter-reaction from researchers who supported the view that cultural differences are always mirrored in economic organizations. Various studies emerged that found evidence of diversity among organizations across nations that could not be explained by the influences of technology alone (Dore, 1973; Gallie, 1978; Maurice, Sorge and Warner, 1980; Sorge and Warner, 1986). Most importantly, these studies demonstrated that, in contrast to what is assumed in the convergence thesis, organizations cannot be divided up into distinct technological and cultural spheres (Sorge, 1983). For human actors are not guided by either economic or social motives; instead, their economic preferences are socially constructed by their particular national environment, so producing different ways in which they relate to each other and to their firms.

Although the evidence seemed to support the cultural viewpoint, the convergence thesis was reformulated and entered a second stage in the 1990s. Instead of seeing the organization of employment relationships as being determined by technology, new versions of the convergence theory argued that economic globalization is the determining influence. They claimed that the ongoing globalization of the economic world has freed former 'national economies' from the influence of national institutions. In semi-professional business literature, the new prophets of globalization speak of newly emerging 'forces' that are breaking down national borders and creating global markets that cannot be curbed by national intervention (Ohmae, 1990). This progressive erosion of the sovereignty of nation states has cast increasing doubt on whether nation-specific institutions will act as barriers against global convergence. However, as there is no clear definition of a universal standard of competitiveness, the path that convergence will take is under debate.

Three options can be considered. The *neo-liberal perspective* takes the position that, in order to survive and to sustain affluence in the new world order, national governments must tailor their economic policies to enforce the optimal functioning of markets (Friedman, 1982). In this respect, the United States leads the way (*Economist*, 1996). At an organizational level, this trend was reflected in the advice given to employers to introduce more market mechanisms into the employment relationship: people should be seen as 'resources' that should be managed according to economic principles. Dore (1986) proposed a contrasting convergence theory which originated in the Japanese model of economic organization. According to his proposition, market mechanisms should be augmented by the fostering of *long-term relationships between firms and employees* based on trust and a sense of solidarity, as this will encourage the development of knowledge and skills. A third convergence theory advocates the reconfiguration of existing models of economic organization by *cross-fertilization*. This means that competitive pressures will push 'nations' to correct the flaws in their systems by adopting global 'best practices' (Groenewegen, 1997).

However, institutionalist writers challenge these new versions of convergence theory. Although the changed state of the global economy is acknowledged, Hollingsworth and Streeck (1994) identify eight reasons why it is unlikely that convergence will occur. The most important is the argument that the evolution of an institutional configuration is path-dependent. A nation's developmental trajectories are determined by its specific historical development and are therefore inevitably limited (Hollingsworth, 1997). Moreover, it has been argued that efficiency is a multidimensional concept. There are alternative standards of good economic performance that cannot be optimized by a single institutional configuration. Each model of capitalism possesses its own relative strengths and weaknesses (Streeck, 1992; Whitley, 1999). In the same vein, the evidence for convergence at the organizational level is far from conclusive. Although the American model of human resource management has found worldwide appeal, various studies observe continuing diversity in corporate human resource management practices (Sparrow *et al.*, 1994; Brewster *et al.*, 1994; Dowling *et al.*, 1999). Some have argued that, because the human resource management model originated in America, it is less suitable for the distinct cultural contexts of European countries (Brewster, 1995).

8.3 Claiming convergence: cross-national learning between the Anglo-Saxon and the Rhineland models

The United States and the Netherlands are two leading countries in terms of economic performance. Nevertheless, these two countries have traditionally organized their economic activity by means of different economic models. Economic organization in the United States is an example of the so-called Anglo-Saxon model, whereas the Netherlands is commonly grouped among the nations that organize economic activity on the basis of the so-called Rhineland principles that are widespread in continental western Europe (Albert, 1990). Using Beer's classic HRM model and its fourfold categorization of the field of employment relations (Beer *et al.*, 1984), we can compare the features of both models (see Table 8.1).

Globalization is believed to be a powerful force that will eradicate diversity in employment relations among nations that compete in global markets. How has globalization affected employment relationships in the United States and the Netherlands? A broad overview of the development of the employment

TABLE 8.1 American versus Dutch organization of the employment relationship

	United States	The Netherlands
Work organization	Taylorist	Socio-technique
Human resource flow	External labour	Internal labour market
Reward system	Individualized, tangible	Collective, intangible
Employee participation	Low (management prerogative)	High (co-determination)

relationship in both nations indicates that the traditional models have been subject to substantial change. Both US and Dutch firms have felt the pressure to adjust to new market demands. Some general patterns can be discerned in the way firms have responded in the United States and the Netherlands to the new challenges posed by globalization. Since the 1980s, the need to introduce group work and to enhance the level of employee participation has been consistently emphasized in US management literature. Strong corporate cultures, total quality management, decentralization, team work, and reducing anxiety in the workplace to increase employee commitment have all been put forward as measures by which US firms can remain competitive in the global business environment (Peters and Waterman, 1982; Deming, 1986; Pfeffer, 1994).

US enterprises have experimented with new forms of work organization that de-emphasize hierarchy and emphasize collaboration and teamwork (Appelbaum and Batt, 1994; MacDuffie, 1995; Appelbaum et al., 2000). Lawler et al. (1992) found that 86 per cent of US firms used some form of employee involvement programme and in 66 per cent of firms quality circles were being used. Osterman (1994) estimates that in 37 per cent of US work places more than half of the workers are involved in at least two of the following new labour management initiatives: self-directed teams, job rotation, quality circles, and total quality management. In contrast, since the 1980s the tendency in the Netherlands has been to loosen the ties between employers and employees. The Dutch answer to intensified international competition has been growing flexibility of employment conditions (Bolweg and Kluytmans, 1989; SER, 1991; Albeda and Dercksen, 1994; CBS, 1996; Visser and Hemerijck, 1997). This shift to more flexibility is reflected in the increased number of flexible labour contracts (Haan, de Vos and de Jong, 1994; Remery, van Doorne-Huiskens and Schippers, 2002), the emphasis on the employability of the employee (Gaspersz and Ott, 1996), and the closer match between employment conditions and individual preferences or employee performance (Goslinga and Klandermans, 1996).

What do these developments contribute to the convergence–divergence debate? As we have just shown, the convergence arguments can be grouped into three main approaches. The first and second convergence of these can summarily be dismissed. According to the first convergence thesis, convergence will occur in keeping with the Anglo-Saxon model. Although some 'Americanization' of employment relations has been observed in the Netherlands, the case for global convergence in line with the US model neglects developments within the United States itself. Organizational concepts that fit more in the Rhineland model, such as team production and employee involvement, also have widespread appeal in the US business environment. According to the second convergence thesis, convergence will occur along the lines of the Rhineland model. This thesis too must be rejected, because some of the elements that fit the Anglo-Saxon model, such as flexibility, pay for performance, and relaxation of dismissal protection, have also been increasingly stressed in the Dutch business environment. It can be seen that global convergence along the lines of either the Rhineland model or the Anglo-Saxon model is refuted. Those committed to a convergence model will have to put their chips on the third convergence thesis described above, which advocates the reconfiguration of existing models of economic organization in order to create a new best-practice model through a process of cross-cultural fertilization.

A comparison between, on the one hand, the US and Dutch models of employment relations and, on the other hand, a global best-practice model makes this claim clear. 'Best practice' refers to the suggestions that dominate management literature and are dispersed by management teaching and consultantancy agencies. Table 8.2 presents the best practices in employment relations according to the four-fold categorization described earlier. The Taylor method for designing work systems needs to be replaced by a more flexible form of teamwork such as that proposed by the proponents of socio-technical work design. With regard to human resource flow, management should abandon the rigid, collective regulations that are characteristic of internal labour markets: external labour market mechanisms provide more flexibility. In addition, rewards systems should target individual performance instead of being collective. Finally, employee participation is considered an indispensable element in achieving improvements in the productive process.

From Table 8.2 it could be concluded that the dominant practices of the Dutch companies in the realm of work organization and employee participation are considered to be in alignment with global best practice, and that Dutch employment practices diverge from global best practice, in terms of flow and reward management. In contrast, in US companies the dominant employment practices are in line with global best practices in terms of how human resource

TABLE 8.2 Convergence to a best practice model

	Best practice	Cross-fertilization
Work organization	Socio-technical work design is superior in making use of new micro-electronic technologies	USA needs to adjust
Human resource flow	Reliance on external labour market mechanisms makes the firm more flexible to adjust to volatile market demands	NL needs to adjust
Reward system	Focus on individual rewards is necessary as the modern employee is guided by an individualized value pattern	NL needs to adjust
Employee participation	High; to be innovative firms should be able to harness workers' intelligence and knowledge of production system	USA needs to adjust

flows and rewards are managed. However, the prevailing fragmentation of job content and antagonistic supervisor–subordinate relationships in traditional US work organization can be considered to fall short of the best-practice model.

In sum, the third convergence thesis, which claims that various national models converge to a universal best-practice model, appears to be most appropriate. The developments seen in the Netherlands and the United States can be explained as ongoing attempts to improve on weaknesses in their traditional models of organizing employment relationships. Nation specific features within employment organization systems are doomed to disappear as Dutch and US managers adhere more and more to a common best-practice model. However, such conclusions are premature. To argue conclusively that there is convergence requires evidence on actual outcomes rather than mere strategic intentions. Are strategic initiatives converted into actual outcomes? Are attempts by US firms to transform the US workplace through the introduction of team-based forms of work organization proving successful? Are employment relationships in the Netherlands really becoming more flexible?

The next section addresses these questions by reference to empirical evidence at the level of the firm.

8.4 Claiming divergence: evidence from case studies

Pot (1998; 2000) provides a detailed description of developments in employment relationships in the United States and the Netherlands. His empirical data are derived from case studies of four multinational firms in the chemical industry. The case studies concentrate on the major change processes in the realm of employment relations over 1985–97 that were initiated at the various hierarchical levels of the companies, e.g. the corporate, business unit, geographical and plant levels. The cases were selected in such a way that differences in the change processes among the companies can be meaningfully interpreted in terms of cultural differences between the Netherlands and the United States. Two of the companies have headquarters in the Netherlands (Akzo Nobel and DSM) while the other two have headquarters in the United States (Dow Chemical and General Electric). This aspect of the research design helps to identify the kind of impact that the national cultural background of the company's home base has had on the way the company's labour management practices have been adapted. Moreover, we were able to reveal the impact of the national cultural context on change processes at the plant level, by comparing developments at a production plant in the Netherlands with a 'matched' production plant located in the United States. This procedure was performed for each of the four companies separately. The design of our research allows for two types of comparison (see Figure 8.1).

The comparative analysis yielded a broad pool of information. For our current purposes only a portion of the results are relevant. The analysis will focus on the implementation of empowered teams in the US plants of General

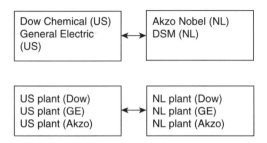

Fig 8.1. Two types of comparison

Electric and Dow Chemical and on the introduction of measures to enhance flexibility in employment relations in the Dutch firms Akzo Nobel and DSM.

Transformation of the US workplace

Let us first consider the claim that the US workplace is transformed by the introduction of team-based forms of work organization. In theory, the concept of empowered teams can rectify the shortcomings in the traditional US model of employment relations, such as fragmentation of job content and the antagonistic nature of the supervisor–subordinate relationships (Appelbaum and Batt, 1994). The introduction of empowered teams should lead to broadly skilled workers who are able to take up various tasks in the production process. Extensive job rotation should eliminate the situation where there are workers who can perform only a limited number of production tasks. Moreover, giving the worker more decision-making authority should defuse antagonistic supervisor–subordinate relationships.

We next evaluate the actual operation of the team-based work forms at the US plants of General Electric and Dow Chemical. It seems that the characteristic features of the work-related culture in the United States are reproduced in the newly instigated forms of work organization.

Consider first the attempt to introduce 'high involvement work teams' at General Electric. The 'high involvement' work organization was pre-designed by management. The organizational changes were to be implemented over a period of 18 months according to an extensive training manual. This new model aimed to increase employees' range of skills relating to the production process, and to increase the decision-making authority of the operators. However, both objectives seem to have been frustrated by the manner in which the organizational changes were introduced. Insufficient employee involvement in the design of the new organization and an unrealistically tight time schedule in which to implement organizational change inhibited the smooth transition from a traditional work organization to a self-directed workforce. Instead, the workforce stuck to old rules and habits; the antagonistic relationship between supervisors and operators remained; production supervisors still made the decisions. As an operator comments,

'There are still supervisors. The production lead runs the show. They don't leave their men alone. We still don't have control over the line. On meetings they say we should decide ourselves to shut a line, but the production lead still tells us that the line should be running to get the tons right. Although management tells us they want us to be self-directed, they have left us with that guy who tells us what to do. Management overlooks it, they just let go. You can't teach an old dog new tricks.' (Pot, 1998: footnote 41)

Furthermore, the operators' range of skills has not increased. In contrast, a return to higher specialization was observed. Former team responsibilities, such as 'pigment weighing' and 'colour operations', were reassigned to individual operators. Moreover, the frequency of job rotation for operators was set to 18 months. Given the low frequency of job rotation, the workforce cannot truly be considered to be made up of multi-skilled operators. As they openly admitted themselves, production management prefers specialization, because it ensures individual accountability and a higher production quality. A production supervisor commented:

'I like specialists in my shift. I only need a few operators for rotation. Let's face it, experts get the product out. They can fix something, they are good for the yield and they have less red tags. As a rule, you can say that shifts with experts run the lines better.' (Pot, 1998: footnote 43).

Accordingly, the 'high involvement teams' that operate at the General Electric plant in Selkirk are best characterized as baseball teams, as has been suggested by the local human resource manager:

'We will still have teams in the future, but it depends on how you see a team. Look at baseball. They never change a winning team. If the pitcher knows how to throw and the catcher catches the balls, you should not remove them from their posts.'

Consider next an attempt at the American plant of Dow Chemicals to implement 'empowered teams' on the shop-floor. Guided by 'Strategic Blueprint', the Dow's global change management model, the introduction of empowered teams promised to endow operators with broader skill levels and more decision-making authority. However, the theoretical merits of team-based forms of work organization do not seem to have been realized. The traditional features of the US workplace have reappeared in the new 'team-based' work organization. First of all, managerial prerogatives were upheld. Second, although Dow's global change management model prescribed employee participation through the instalment of so-called 'design teams', operators were not convinced that they actually gained true influence. Their doubts were supported by the fact that important changes, such as the move from a five to a four-shift schedule, were decided by management. Moreover, operators felt manipulated by management to steer a certain course. As one operator recalled,

'I think, we were guided on how to design. Our ISB-leader (ISB: Implementing the Strategic Blueprint) came back from Canada with a bunch of paper that we were supposed to use as a starting point.' (Pot, 1998: footnote 76).

Furthermore, the instalment of a plant decision-making body, the so-called 'Operate Plant Team', did not affect managerial prerogatives. Although shift operators were represented in the team, its potency was disputed. To begin with, its democratic intent was frustrated by majority rule since shift operators could never constitute a majority:

'Decisions in the OPT are already pre-decided by the day technicians and leave little influence to the schedules... It doesn't matter what we say, they will do what they want... If you don't nod your head, you'll get banned.' (Pot, 1998: footnote 85 and 86).

Moreover, the aims of consensual decision-making were not fully understood by the operators:

'The OPT doesn't make clear decisions, but tries to please everybody. They ask everybody whether they can live with it, or support it. I don't think it's important whether I can live with it. The key is whether a decision is good for Dow because that's where the money comes from.' (Pot, 1998: footnote 87).

Next, although in the new organizational scheme all supervisory positions were removed from the hierarchy, new antagonistic relationships emerged. The breaking down of the original chain of command did not stimulate a co-operative attitude. Instead, the senior operators, the day technicians, and the production engineers became involved in a new struggle for decision-making authority. According to the operators, the new organization is characterized by disorganization:

'Now there are too many chiefs and too few Indians. Everybody is on the same layer and everybody wants to be the boss... it is disorganized which causes confusion and frustration, because one person says this and the other tells us something else... there is no chain of command. Sometimes there must be a leader who shows the direction.'

Finally, the development of a multi-skilled workforce remains a theoretical goal rather than a practical outcome. Although some operators are cross-trained, their actual job content was not broadened. Accordingly, the operators perceived cross-training as a waste of time and effort (Pot, 1998: footnote 80).

The above findings cast doubts on claims that the traditional US work-related culture has been transformed following the introduction of new, team-based forms of work organization. The evidence shows that the characteristic features of traditional US work culture, such as the antagonistic supervisor–worker relationship, the prevalence of management prerogatives, the limited decision-making authority of workers, and the narrow definition of individual job contents, have been reproduced in the new forms of work organization.

The transformation of Dutch employment relationships

Let us next consider the claim that the recent emphasis in the Netherlands on labour flexibility is an improvement on the weak features in the traditional

Dutch employment organization, namely the rigid internal labour market arrangements and the collective reward system which lacks individual incentives. Developments at Akzo Nobel and DSM provide us with some crucial insights.

The issue of flexibility has been subject to extensive discussion between Akzo Nobel Netherlands, the national trade unions, and the works council. Since the change process allowed for the interaction between the various stakeholders, the outcomes demonstrate a balance of interests. Initiatives that were introduced to enhance the flexibility of employment relationships have not been pursued solely at the cost of employees. The trade-off between a reduction in working hours and flexible working hours is illustrative. The management of Akzo Nobel Netherlands aimed at more flexible working hours so that the productive capacity would be better aligned with the demands of the market (longer working hours when business demand is high). Unions, in their aim to preserve employment and improve employment conditions, made the reduction of working hours their prime objective. Negotiation and consultation resulted in an agreement that combined both objectives. On the one hand, managers were allowed, within certain limits, to adjust working times of Akzo Nobel workers. On the other hand, the average working week was reduced from 38 to 36 hours.

A similar example of a compromise between managerial intentions and labour demands concerns the introduction of performance-based rewards at DSM. Management aimed to increase managerial discretion in setting rewards for individual employees. Rewards of relatively well-performing employees should be higher than for low performers. Unions, given their objective of defending employment conditions for the collective of workers, were unwilling to accept such an encroachment on the traditionally collective manner of setting rewards. In the end, after a series of negotiations and consultation, the unions agreed to link performance ranking with payment on the condition that the level of base salary was not affected. Another example taken from DSM concerns the use of labour 'pools'. Employees that became redundant were not laid off but were grouped together in so-called labour pools. Members of the labour pool are presumed to be flexibly employable across the various production plants of DSM. As such, employees have held on to their employment conditions as employees of DSM, and the company has gained a flexible depot of labour capacity.

At the level of national government, a similar example of compromise between managerial demands for more flexibility and worker need for employment security can be observed. The growing use of temporary labour has initiated debate at national level about their employment conditions. The Dutch institutional structure allows for consultation between collective representations of employers and employees by independent bodies such as the

Foundation of Labour and the Social-Economic Council. On the side of the employers, the need for such flexibility was stressed. The trade unions emphasized the inadequate employee benefits for this group of temporary workers. In 1996 a compromise was reached by which it became simpler for firms to hire temporary labour, and at the same time the rights of such temporary workers were guaranteed by the agencies that acted as intermediaries (Ministerie van Sociale Zaken en Werkgelegenheid, 1995; Stichting van de Arbeid, 1996; van der Meer et al., 2003: 66). The resulting law, the so-called 'Flex-Act', has been operational since 1999 (Koene and Paauwe, 2002).

A final illustration of the growing flexibility in employment relationships concerns the notion of 'employability'. Some commentators, when speaking about 'employability', imagine a perfectly flexible labour market that is populated by workers who sell their skills temporarily to an employer. To ensure job security, workers need to ensure the 'employability' of their own skills. Such a perspective of the labour market contrasts with the traditional work-related culture of the Netherlands, which emphasizes internal labour market arrangements. As such, the notion of 'employability' has given rise to extensive debate in both academic and popular business literature in the Netherlands. The cases of Akzo Nobel and DSM demonstrate that the actual implementation of the notion of employability does not challenge traditional Dutch views on employment relationships. The agreements that Akzo Nobel and DSM made with the trade unions on the notion of employability implicitly assume long-term employment relationships. Strengthening the internal labour market is the dominant idea in the agreement between DSM and the trade unions on employability. Similarly, at Akzo Nobel employability refers to the joint responsibility of employer and employee to maintain the skills of the employee at a productive level by means of continuous training. In sum, 'employability' is used in a manner that reinforces the traditional reliance of Dutch companies on internal labour market mechanisms. The notion of employability is in line with qualitative or internal flexibility rather than with quantitative or external flexibility.

8.5 Explanatory mechanisms: the procedure of change

On the basis of broad strategic intentions announced by management, we could expect convergence between employment relationships in the United States and the Netherlands to become apparent. Our analyses of the introduction of empowered teams in the US business context and of flexibility in the Dutch context question this claim. How can we explain the divergence between strategic intentions and actual outcomes? The comparative analysis suggests that the design of the change procedure is the major explanatory mechanism. The deviation between the strategic management goals and their realization can be understood by reference to the procedure by which the changes are realized. The change procedure constitutes the link between the formulation of change objectives and the way things turn out in reality.

The comparative analysis suggests significant differences between the design of the change procedure in the United States and the Netherlands. These differences can be summarized by use of the concepts of 'planned' and 'emergent' change (Wilson, 1992). The concepts can be distinguished on the basis of three interrelated elements:

- The formulation of the content of change
- The time span of the change process
- The extent of interaction between management and non-managerial employees.

In a 'planned' change process, the objectives are defined beforehand by higher management. This leaves no room for participation by employees at lower hierarchical levels or by other stakeholders. The change objectives are communicated top-down, and the primary task of lower hierarchical levels is to implement such changes within a set time. In contrast, in an 'emergent' change process the organizational change develops during the course of a long-term change trajectory. While management does set some of the desired outcomes, the actual content of change evolves during a process of interaction between the various stakeholders. Using evidence from the case studies of Pot (1998), we will demonstrate that the change process in the United States can be characterized as 'planned', whereas in the Netherlands it is dominantly 'emergent'. We look first at design at higher management levels, then at design at plant level.

Procedural differences at higher management levels

The dominant actors shaping the organization of employment relationships at the two US companies, General Electric and Dow Chemical, are the managers at corporate level and external management consultants. At both General Electric and Dow Chemical, managements at the corporate level have designed a labour management strategy and associated labour management tools that apply to all local establishments, irrespective of national boundaries. The dominant position of the corporate-level managers means that the position of the other (lower) hierarchical layers is limited with regard to labour management initiatives. The role of business unit management and geographical management is restricted to the proper implementation of the global programmes.

In contrast, the two Dutch companies have followed a different procedure to effect changes in the organization of the employment relationship. Both at Akzo Nobel and at DSM, the role of corporate management is limited with regard to labour management strategy. Ample autonomy is left to lower management layers. Accordingly, both the business unit layer and the geographical layer play an important role in creating new labour management strategies. Especially important is the presence of a distinct hierarchical layer for employment issues that concern the Dutch employees. While in US companies no distinct labour management division separates the corporate level from the local sites, the Dutch companies have installed a distinct Dutch labour management department. At this level, a set of labour management strategies is defined that applies to all workers in the Netherlands. The relevant set of actors at this level is not confined to the management of the geographical unit. Instead, Dutch management develops its labour management strategy in close collaboration with the national trade unions and the national works council. Through regular consultation and joint study groups, management and unions develop new labour management strategies that are acceptable to both. The collective bargaining agreement formalizes their interaction. So both parties demonstrate in their behaviour that they take the institutional setting for granted.

It should be noted that the interaction between management and representatives of the trade unions does not take the form of isolated negotiations. The case studies of Akzo Nobel and DSM demonstrate that potential problem areas are identified at an early stage. Such problem identification is followed by the instalment of research teams in which both management and unions participate. It can take years of study and consultation before consensus is reached on concrete actions that are formalized in collective bargaining agreements. Since such a change procedure allows for the interaction between the various stakeholders, it is not surprising that the outcome represents a balance of interests. The manner in which Dutch firms have dealt with the issue of flexibility is an illustration of such a balance and is representative of the way in which consultation takes place in the wider institutional context.

Procedural differences at plant level

Among the US plants, it can be observed that the change process is defined in project terms with clearly defined objectives and time schedules. In contrast, among the Dutch plants the change process was found to be defined in process terms, without an explicit formulation of the final objectives.

An example of this is the contrast between the plants of General Electric in Selkirk (USA) and in Bergen op Zoom (NL). Both plants initiated a move towards 'empowered teams'. Since the changes were not carried out according to a corporate blueprint, management at both sites could shape the transformation according to their own insights. In the Netherlands, the resulting transition can best be characterized as a gradual change process ('like a flower that grows': Pot, 1998, footnote 16), which was not confined to a set time period ('it is a continuous process in which, in the end, everybody is doing other things than they did before': Pot, 1998, footnote 35), and for which no clear objectives were prescribed ('if we eventually get to self direction, that's fine, but that's not the objective: the objective is to deliver on business targets': Pot, 1998, footnote 12). In contrast, in the United States the shift towards high involvement teams was implemented more drastically with a set start-off time ('They gave us a date, then it's gonna happen, then you'll be self-directed whether you are or are not ready for it': Pot, 1998, footnote 40). The objectives were clearly set from the outset and had to be achieved within a period of 18 months.

Related to the distinction between process and project is the factor of time in the change process. In the Dutch plants, the time span of the change process is consistently longer than that observed in US plants. Consider the change process at the plants of Dow Chemical in Oyster Creek (US) and Terneuzen (NL). Both plants faced a similar 'change management model'. At the US plant the whole change process was effectuated within six months. At the Dutch plant the implementation of the change process according to the change management model failed; a new change process was initiated with long-term objectives. Another example of differences in the time factor was seen in Akzo Nobel. Plant management in the Netherlands initiated a change process that was expected to lead to self-direction over a period of ten years ('We will gradually introduce the new work organization to the operators. First, we need to create acceptance . . . it is a long-term process. It is important to think before you jump. Everybody should be on the same line': Pot, 1998, pp. 128–9). In contrast, the management of the Akzo site in Pasadena completed an organizational change within a couple of months.

A final procedural difference that distinguishes Dutch from US change processes concerns the quality of interaction between management and operators. In the Dutch plants, changes are effected by means of interaction between operators and management. In contrast, in the United States the control of change processes resides solely with management. Developments at DSM illustrate this point. The organizational change at the US DSM plant was completely directed by site management ('they announced the new organizational structure and, thereafter, I was asked to become manager of the polymerisation section': Pot, 1998, footnote 176). At the Dutch DSM plant, organizational change involved interaction between management and operators. After management had convinced the shift supervisors of the need for change, the supervisors themselves designed a new organizational structure; they proposed a model that was then accepted by higher managerial layers. Similar observations on the extent of management–worker interaction during the change processes have been made at the other cases. At both the Dutch and the US plants of General Electric, management reconsidered the role of the shift supervisor. In the Netherlands the shift supervisors themselves (at least in their perception) proposed making their own positions superfluous in the long run ('Management made it clear that change was necessary... we came up with the idea that we, as shift coaches, should make ourselves superfluous': Pot, 1998, footnote 25). Higher management focused on convincing the shift supervisors of the need for change. In contrast, at the US plant no worker input was observed in the change process towards 'high involvement working teams' ('This change has been thrown at us. If the teams would have decided themselves, they would have kept the e-tech and appointed one of the e-techs as co-ordinator': Pot, 1998, footnote 48).

The case of Dow Chemical is also illustrative. A main reason for the failure of the 'first round' of the change process at the Dutch plant was the lack of employee participation. Workers, who felt ignored during the design of the change, were not committed to the objectives of the change. The acknowledgement of workers' involvement during the 'second round' of the change process resulted in a change programme that received broad support. In contrast, at the US plant of Dow, the workers perceived the change process as being imposed by management. Major decisions were made directly by management, while other decisions were perceived as being pre-decided or as being manipulated by management.

In sum, some major differences distinguish the typical design of the change procedure in the United States from that in the Dutch business environment. Table 8.3 summarizes the differences. The planned change procedure employed by US firms should be considered a major factor in the explanation of their failure to move away from the traditional organization of the employment relationship. Similarly, the emergent change procedure that is dominant in the Netherlands prevents the introduction of flexibility in the employment relationship as originally intended by Dutch management.

8.6 Cultural influence on change procedure

The distinct procedures by which organizational changes are implemented in the US and Dutch plants were characterized as, respectively, 'planned' and 'emergent'. Our conclusions are based on case studies of four multi-

TABLE 8.3 Planned versus emergent change procedure

	Planned change (United States)	Emergent change (Netherlands)
Formulation of content of change	The content of change is defined by management in consultation with management consultants. Accordingly, content of change is closely linked to new developments in management thinking.	Content of the change is not defined beforehand. Consensus exists on the need for change, but the content of the change emerges during the process of interaction between management and stakeholders.
Room for employee	Little: employees have room for manoeuvre only within the framework set by management	Ample room for employee influence
Time span of change process	Defined beforehand and usually short-term; implementation of change should be accomplished within a defined time span.	Not defined beforehand, but usually long term. Since the change emerges out of a process, there is no definite beginning and ending

national companies. This section deals with the question of generalization. Are the characterizations of the change procedure in the two countries based on incidental results, or do they represent more persistent features of the work-related cultures of the United States and the Netherlands?

The main feature that distinguishes a 'planned' from an 'emergent' change process concerns the nature of interaction between management and subordinate members of the firm. We agree with Wilson (1992: 12) that 'planned change relies on a model of organization in which there is uncritical acceptance of the managerial role. This appears to be particularly true of North America'. In contrast, emergent change will occur in organizations where the distance between the diverse hierarchical levels is smaller. Below, it will be argued that the prevalence of managerial prerogatives is a dominant feature of the US work-related culture. In contrast, the lack of authoritarian power of the manager is characteristic of the Dutch work-related culture. So differences in the SCL dimension (see the theoretical framework in Chapter 5) offer clues for explaining the difference in change procedure.

Let us first consider the management–worker relationship at higher management levels in the United States. This relation is inextricably bound up with the national system of industrial relations, and the interplay between management representatives, labour representatives, and the state (Dunlop, 1958). The US system of industrial relations is characterized by the weak role of the state and a decentralized system of collective bargaining. In the United States, the role of the state is restricted to ensuring that the bargaining process between management and unions is not obstructed by the abuse of power by either of them. The bargaining process is initiated only after a so-called 'representation ballot' has demonstrated the support for unions by the majority of the workers. Such ballots take place at the level of the 'establishment', such as the production plant, and it is this feature that gives the US system of industrial relations its decentralized nature. Moreover, the system of representation elections has divided US industry into unionized and a non-unionized sectors (Kochan *et al.*, 1986). Since managers in a non-unionized environment have more discretion and control, as they are not hindered by union interference, US management tends to use its power to keep its workforce union-free. This feature contributes to the adversarial relationship between employers and unions (Jacoby, 1991; Lawrence, 1996).

Furthermore, owing to limited government regulation, the US system of industrial relations is greatly influenced by attitudes and judgments of the jurisdiction. Most employees' and employers' rights and obligations are not written down as laws, but are legitimized by the jurisprudence of the US courts. Atleson (1983) concludes, after an analysis of US court decisions, that US courts are motivated by the hidden assumption that 'the enterprise should be under control of management'. The distinction between mandatory and permissive bargaining subjects is also based on court decisions. The distinction holds that unions can play a role only in setting wages and working conditions; management is given the right to manage and retains the initiative with respect to strategic and entrepreneurial decisions ('management prerogatives'). Jaggi (1992) concludes that programmes designed to enhance the participation of workers do not affect the so-called management prerogatives. Instead, programmes to enhance co-operation between management and employees concentrate on the survival of the company. The initiative for employee participation programmes is with management, which supports their introduction as a method to improve effective communication. Programmes such as work committees, employee suggestion schemes, and quality circles are accepted only within the framework of productivity, profitability, and management prerogatives.

In contrast to the US system of industrial relations, state involvement characterizes the Dutch system of industrial relations. The Dutch government has issued numerous laws regulating employment relationships in many areas, including aspects such as dismissal protection, collective bargaining, co-determination, and working hours and conditions. The objective of these legal provisions is to ensure just and fair outcomes and to eliminate conflict between employers and employees.

A further feature of Dutch industrial relations is its centralized nature. At national level the relationship between employers and employees is governed by organizations such as the Foundation of Labour and the Social Economic Council. At the industry level the interaction between employers and employees is formalized by the negotiation of the collective labour agreement. The influence of individual employers and local union officials in this system of industrial relations is limited. At the plant level, the Works Council Act regulates the relationship between management and workers. This Act aims to democratize corporations by giving employees certain rights on managerial issues. Finally, one should note that the attitude of the industrial players is characterized by an emphasis on 'consultation' and 'striving for consensus'. This attitude is in contrast with the principle of bargaining that underpins the interaction in the US industrial relations system (see Table 8.4)

Next, let us consider the management–worker relationship in the workplace. US workplace relations are characterized by distance between the supervisor and his immediate subordinates in terms of power. Extensive discretionary powers for supervisors with regard to performance appraisal, level of pay, and discipline seems to have created a climate of fear in the work place (Starkey and McKinlay, 1993). The following description of unwritten rules appears to be typical of American work floor relations:

'Don't disagree with the boss; Don't rock the boat; Look busy even if you're not; Don't smile, let alone laugh too much; Be obsessive about getting your numbers right, estimates won't help; CYA (cover your ass); If a colleague gets into trouble with the

TABLE 8.4 Distinction between consultation and bargaining

	Consultation (NL)	Bargaining (USA)
Starting point	A problem	A conflict of interest
Objective	Consensus	Contract
Attitude	Co-operative	Competitive
Means	Discussion	Pressure/power

Source: based on Reynaerts, cited in Nijs (1996: 27)

boss—don't help, be grateful it's not you; Observe the dress code.' (Starkey and McKinlay, 1993: 43).

In contrast, d'Iribarne (1989), in a detailed idiographic description of a Dutch, a US and a French plant, characterizes the absence of authoritarian power in work relations as typical of the Dutch workplace. To co-ordinate work organization, a Dutch supervisor cannot make use of his hierarchical position by giving orders or applying sanctions. The only means at his disposal is the power of persuasion, by putting forward convincing arguments within a discussion. During this process it is necessary for him to make use of the recommendations of his subordinates in order to reach consensus. The following observation captures the position of the Dutch supervisor:

'It pays to speak, to discuss, to explain and to convince. The Dutch appear to be as open to good reason as they are allergic to pressure . . . It is necessary to speak a lot. To motivate is easy if one takes the effort to explain. When I give an order, I always have to explain and speak. If I don't, I run the risk that the order will not be carried out. Explaining should be considered as the most efficient way to manage in the Netherlands, in the same way as one speaks about sanctioning in the United States.' (d'Iribarne, 1989: 213)

McFarlin et al. (1992) demonstrate the different attitudes towards employee participation as between US and Dutch managers. First, they observe that US management prefers to implement employee participation by means of formal programmes, such as self-directed work teams. Furthermore, employee participation is considered by US management as a tool to enhance performance ('improving the bottom line'), rather than as a means to improve relationships and the quality of working life. Also, US managers are less convinced that their subordinates desire participation.

In contrast, Dutch managers appear to be sceptical about certain US initiatives. They view participation as a societal obligation to workers. Dutch managers do not understand the need for a separate programme to improve participation, because the works council already provides ample opportunity for this to occur. Furthermore, Dutch managers reject the US 'obsession' with formal efforts to improve productivity via employee participation programmes. They feel that the programmatic, formalized nature of US efforts to improve participation is inconsistent with their own style of dealing with the needs of their subordinates. Societal expectations in the Netherlands force managers to operate on an informal basis. To get anything done, one needs to ask for subordinate input on a regular basis and to rely on persuasion rather than hierarchical power.

In sum, this section has aimed to demonstrate that the 'planned' change procedure is closely linked to the dominant US management–worker relationship in which management prerogatives prevail. In contrast, the 'emergent' change procedure that is characteristic in the Netherlands fits well with the relative lack of managerial authority in that country. The above analysis is restricted to the system of industrial relations. For reasons of space, the management–worker relationship is not linked to other institutional configurations in US and Dutch society. Other institutions that reinforce the difference in the management–worker relationship between the United States and the Netherlands are the education system, the system of corporate governance, the welfare system, and the dominant pattern of values and norms (Pot, 1998; 2000).

8.7 Conclusions

There are features in the nature and evolution of employment relationships that do apply globally, and we do not deny this above. Global trends should be acknowledged as triggers of change in employment relationships. Firms, irrespective of national borders, are compelled to adjust the employment relationships to fit in with current global realities. Yet, we have shown that the triggers of change must be seen independently of their outcomes. The actual response of firms to global challenges depends on the institutional context in which they are situated, of which the relevance is emphasized in the contextually based human resource theory (SCL dimension).

To understand the origin of national specific responses to global challenges in employment relationships, we have emphasized the procedures involved in realizing change processes. The design of the change procedure influences, to a large extent, the actual outcome. This conclusion is based on comparative case studies of US and Dutch firms. It is argued that the difference between the 'planned' change procedure employed in the United States and the 'emergent' change procedure employed in the Netherlands underlies the specifically national developments in the organization of employment relationships in these countries. On the basis of our findings, we challenge the widespread belief that global trends will lead to the homogenization of employment relationships, and claim that a divergence in employment relations will continue to exist.

Can such a strong claim as the thesis of continuing divergence be justified on the basis of only four case studies? To this end, we need to consider the generality of the empirical results. Surely, case studies can constitute a basis for generalization. However, in this respect one should distinguish between analytical generalization and statistical generalization (Mitchell, 1983). Case studies do not constitute a basis for statistical generalization, which is grounded on the logic that a selected sample represents a larger pool of subjects. Accordingly, case studies cannot confirm statistical regularities. The rationale for case studies, however, resides in their ability to identify mechanisms causing certain events to happen. The effect of the identified mechanisms can be generalized to other contexts.

This is exactly what we claim in this chapter. Why has the introduction of empowered teams not led to a transformation of the Taylorist workplace organization in the US business context? Surely, this was the strategic objective of the management that initiated the change. Why is the introduction of measures to increase the flexibility of the Dutch employment relationship accompanied by the introduction of measures that are in the interest of the workers? Surely, management would be expected to introduce flexibility in a more rigorous manner.

The answers to these questions have been given. As a result of the procedure by which the changes are realized, the outcomes deviate from the strategic intentions. Accordingly, the case studies identified the nature of the change procedure as a crucial mechanism for explaining the development of the employment relationship. Convergence of the employment relation, then, can be said to occur if it is preceded by a convergence of the design of the change procedure. Indeed, a harmonization of the change procedures would remove the relevance of the explanatory mechanism proposed by this contribution. However, we have seen that the specific design of the change procedure does not stand by itself, but is inextricably bound up with the national institutional configuration. So far, the impact of globalization has not been powerful enough to arrive at a complete institutional convergence of nations.

In the next and final chapter we will zoom in on the HRM function itself and use our vision of HRM and performance to emphasize the different HRM roles and explain how we can relate these to the different concepts of performance (strategic, professional, and societal). It is crucial for the HRM function/role that it becomes part of the dominant coalition and is able to influence the way in which HRM policies and practices can contribute to viability and a sustained competitive advantage, and can meet the various dimensions of performance as outlined in the previous chapters. To measure the different dimensions of performance (HR effectiveness), we develop the 4logic HRM scorecard, a tool that will appeal to practitioners involved in the implementation of 'aligned' HRM policies and practices, i.e. those that fit both the market place and the institutional setting in a unique and organization-specific way.

9   Changing HRM Roles: Towards a Real Balanced HRM Scorecard

9.1 Introduction

This chapter considers the relationship between the role-set of HR managers and how it relates to HR effectiveness and performance. I first outline the way in which the HRM roles have evolved from 'clerk of works' to change agent and business partner. The increased focus on devising ways of contributing to added value has also resulted in more attention being given to the whole issue of how to measure the contribution of the HRM function. Based on our multidimensional perspective on performance, this raises not only the issue of how to measure, but also such questions as: Measuring for whose sake? Measuring of what? Who is involved in setting the standards, and who decides when corrective action is necessary?

Deliberation of these issues leads to the formulation of the *4logic HRM scorecard*, which is fully in line with the Contextually Based Human Resource Theory (CBHRT) and its multidimensional perspective on performance, outlined in preceding chapters.

I use the label '4logic' because it includes not only the strategic and the professional logics, but also the societal perspective—the dimensions of relational rationality, fairness, legitimacy, viability, and sustainability—instead of focusing solely on profitability for the shareholders. From these three logics, the HRM function has to deliver a range of services and HRM practices for which different delivery channels can be used. Optimizing delivery is important and should be based on both quality and cost effectiveness criteria, which implies our fourth and final logic, i.e. the delivery logic.

This 4logic HRM scorecard has been tested among a range of companies operating both locally and internationally. Examples and outcomes of the testing will be used to illustrate the applicability of this HRM scorecard.

9.2 Changing roles and expectations for the HR manager

A review of the literature throws up many frameworks for considering the evolution and development in HRM tasks, skills, and roles. Some merely list things that HR managers do, while others are more encompassing, considering the HRM pattern from a more ideal-type perspective (e.g. Tyson and Fell, 1986; Ulrich, 1997). Increasingly, companies are beginning to recognize the importance of people to a business's success. More human resource issues are really people-related business issues, in that they influence the essence of the business, profitability, survival, competitiveness, adaptability, and flexibility. The assignment of integral management to line managers, the tendency towards decentralization, and the creation of smaller units all imply that the role and position of personnel/human resource staff functions need to be reconsidered. So an overview of the changing HRM roles is useful.

Tyson's typology (1987) provides a good starting point. Struck by the increased fragmentation of the personnel function, which he describes as its 'Balkanization', he distinguishes three Weberian ideal types or models:

1. *The clerk of works model* This views personnel management as an administrative support activity with no involvement in business planning. All authority is vested in line managers. The principal activities for these personnel staff will be recruitment, record keeping and welfare.
2. *The contract manager model* This approach is concerned with confronting unions with a system, as part of a comprehensive policy network. Acting on behalf of line managers, the personnel department staffs are experts in trade union agreements, in fixing day-to-day issues with the unions, and in responding in a reactive way to problems.
3. *The architect model* Here personnel executives seek to create and build the organization as a whole. This creative vision of personnel entails contributing to the success of the business through explicit policies, that seek to influence the corporate plan, with an integrated system of controls between personnel and line managers. The personnel function is thus represented within the dominant coalition in the organization.

Schuler (1990) discerns an increasing shift from a specialist staff function to the HR manager as business manager and part of the management team. He claims that the following roles became more prominent in the 1990s: that of business person, shaper of change, consultant to the organization, strategy formulator and implementer, talent manager, asset manager, and cost controller (Schuler, 1990: 58). In a more recent overview Schuler and Jackson (2001) foresee the following roles as the most prominent:

- *Linking role*: relating to the linking of HRM issues and challenges to the business
- *Strategic role*: implying involvement in the strategic direction of the company
- *Monitoring role*: reviewing the actual situation against the strategic plan and deciding on corrective actions
- *Innovator role*: developing innovative approaches and solutions to improve productivity and the quality of work, while at the same time complying with the law in an environment of high uncertainty, energy conservation, and intense international competition
- *Change and knowledge facilitator role*: managing the change processes at both the individual and the organizational level, and very often in relation to strategy implementation
- *Enabler role*: enabling line management to make things happen

So the HRM department provides services to line management in the traditional areas of recruitment, selection, rewarding, counselling, promoting, and firing. This is a method of service provision that demands a high degree of customer orientation towards line management.

Carroll (1991) also envisages a shift in HRM roles, as a consequence of the more pronounced links to business needs and thus the greater need to contribute to organizational effectiveness. In addition to the traditional roles of policy formulator and provider of personnel services, Carroll expects certain roles to take on greater importance:

- *Delegator*   This role enables line managers to serve as primary implementers of HRM systems.
- *Technical expert*   This function encompasses a number of highly specific HRM-related skills in areas such as remuneration and management development.
- *Innovator*   As innovators, HR managers recommend new approaches to solving HRM-related problems such as productivity, or a sudden increase in absenteeism due to illness.

Storey, who was intensively involved in the HRM characteristics debate in the UK in both the 1980s and 1990s, develops the following typology based on two dimensions: action oriented (interventionary) versus non-action oriented (non-interventionary), and strategic versus tactical (Storey 1992: 168; see Figure 9.1):

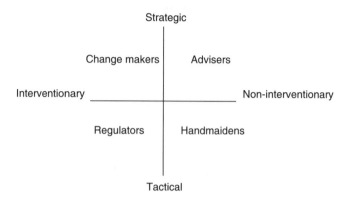

Fig 9.1. Types of personnel management

Source: Storey (1992). Reprinted with permission of Blackwell Publishing.

- *Advisers*   These act as internal consultants; they are in tune with recent developments, but leave the actual running of HRM matters to line and general management colleagues.
- *Handmaidens*   Handmaidens are primarily customer-led in the services they offer, based on a rather subservient, attendant relationship towards line management.
- *Regulators*   These are more interventionary; they formulate, promulgate, and monitor observance of employment rules, which range from personnel procedure manuals to joint agreements with trade unions.
- *Change makers*   Change makers seek to put relationships with employees on a new footing—one that is in line with the 'needs of the business'.

Finally, there is the typology developed by Ulrich (1997), who also uses two dimensions (people versus process, and strategic versus operational) in order to highlight the following roles by which the HR managers can contribute to added value (see Figure 9.2).

- *Administrative expert*   In this role the HR professional designs and delivers efficient HRM processes for staffing, training, appraising, rewarding, promoting, and otherwise managing the flow of employees through the organization. The deliverable from this role is administrative efficiency.
- *Employee champion*   The employee contribution role for HR professionals encompasses their involvement in the day-to-day problems, concerns, and needs of employees. The intended deliverables are increased employee commitment and competence.

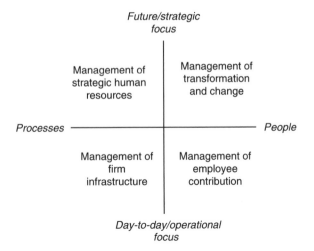

Fig 9.2. HR roles building a competitive organization

Source: Ulrich (1997). Reprinted with permission of Harvard Business School Press.

- *Change agent*   This role focuses on managing transformation and change. The deliverable is aimed at developing a capacity for change. HR managers help employees to let go of the old and adapt to a new culture.
- *Strategic partner*   The strategic HR role focuses on aligning HRM strategies and practices with business strategy. The deliverable is strategy execution. HRM practices help accomplish business objectives.

9.3 A critical reflection on the shift in HR roles

Reflecting on all those typologies and numerous writings in the more popular professional journals on both sides of the Atlantic, the shift in changing HRM roles can simply be summarized by the fact that the HRM function has had to become more business oriented, more strategic, and more oriented towards organizational change. This is also reflected in the outcomes of the surveys carried out by Brockbank *et al.* (Ulrich, 1997), in which, in addition to HRM functional expertise, knowledge of the business and the management of change are among the most prominent competences required by clients of an HRM professional for the purpose of adding value to a business. A 2002 version of the same survey indicated even more strongly the need for a business perspective.

HRM and Performance

Knowledge alone is not enough anymore: it is simply considered a necessary condition. What really matter are strategic contributions in the areas of

- Culture management
- Fast change
- Strategic decision-making
- Market driven connectivity

The latter competence encompasses facilitating the integration of different business functions, managing the arrangement of physical facilities and workplace environment, facilitating the dissemination of customer information, and removing low value added or bureaucratic work (Brockbank and Ulrich, 2002).

These role prescriptions in fact imply that the personnel manager needs to acquire a power base by conforming to the dominant culture and principles of the line management. Legge (1978) refers to the 'conformist innovator', who accepts the dominant utilitarian values and bureaucratic relationships within the organization and tries to demonstrate the value added (contribution to the bottom line) of his activities within this framework. This is an attitude and approach that carries a number of evident risks, such as the eventual inability to differentiate a human resource manager from the regular line manager in terms of contribution or expertise, so that the option of personnel management without an HR manager looms on the horizon (Flood *et al.*, 1996).

An alternative way of acquiring power, or rather influence, is via the 'deviant innovator' approach, whereby the personnel specialist identifies with a set of norms that are distinct from, but not necessarily in conflict with, the norms of organizational success (Legge, 1978: 79–85). In this connection Shipton and McAuley, inspired by Kets de Vries (1990), refer to the need for an

[o]rganizational fool, who without danger to himself can take non-consensual stances ... personnel people are perhaps uniquely fitted for this role because they frequently have the key responsibility for exploring, with members of the organization in which they work, the issues surrounding the management of change and the factors that make it work. (Shipton and McAuley, 1994:9)

This epitomizes the fact that HRM specialists cannot focus only on criteria such as efficiency, effectiveness, and flexibility. Ward Lilley (1991) rightly remarked that personnel specialists must be prepared to risk unpopularity by questioning the short-termism that is rife in much of the British economy—a remark that, over a decade, has lost nothing of its relevance on both sides of the Atlantic. Other appropriate criteria are those of fairness (in the exchange relationship between the individual and the organization) and legitimacy (the relation between society and organization). A staff specialist or manager in the area of human resource management would be the right person to counter or correct an extreme economic rationality, so that the long-term interests of the various organizational members are kept in mind and the outcomes of organizational effectiveness benefit the various stakeholders of the firm.

In this respect, Kamoche (1994) underlines the inherent paradoxes of strategic HRM as a concept encompassing the issues of both 'strategy' and 'human'. On the one hand, strategic HRM is characterized by the dominant organizational imperative for performance and productivity, which according to Kamoche derives from an industry-based view of the firm and is informed by a rationalistic view of human action. On the other hand, HRM is concerned with meeting the complex and often ambiguous needs and expectations of employees, the humanizing of work, and 'equitable' or 'fair' practices, labelled by Hendry and Pettigrew (1990) as 'developmental-humanism'. In this respect Gowler and Legge (1986) refer to the contrast between human *resources* and resourceful *humans*. In the same critical vein, Lefebvre (2001) rightly observes: 'Humans may be called "resources". But they should be treated as "sources" of their own creativity and be allowed to be self-led, not only being led.'

Competing with other functional areas like marketing and finance, the performers of the HRM function are apparently in search of mechanisms to legitimate their proposals (see Figure 9.3). This was a quest in which, until recently, the organizational imperative reflected the dominant criteria. For example, as Ulrich states in an interview, 'a successful HR manager thinks like a marketeer. HR managers should listen to their customers and think in figures. Direct yourself to what line managers want and need. Measure the success of HRM according to their norms' (interview in *PW*, May 2002). But such criteria do not do full justice to the intrinsic complexities of the concept of strategic HRM, which does not consist simply in integrating the human resource dimension into the business strategic planning process (Kamoche, 1994: 40). A better way of reconciling both strategic and humane aspects is to take the resource-based view (see Paauwe, 1994; Kamoche, 1994: 40–1; Wright *et al.*, 1994) as a starting point, because it takes into account the competences and capabilities of human resources instead of focusing exclusively on dominant

Fig 9.3. Legitimation through acceptance

Source: Kamoche (1994). Reproduced with permission from *Human Resource Management Journal*.

businesslike criteria such as those dictated by a specific product–market combination. Kamoche makes a strong plea for this view, because he feels that in this way it will be possible to take into account the specific nature and complexities of human resources:

This paradigm emphasises that the skills of employees are conceived of as a vital resource, which the firm is able to build upon rather than simply to exploit rationally and ideologically. Therefore the full potential of HRM can be realized and can be a key determinant in a firm's performance, without the *a priori* imposition of the organizational imperative. (Kamoche, 1994: 41).

For HRM professionals, this paradigm implies a focus on using multidimensional/multifaceted approaches in their development and rendering of specialist personnel services. A simple one-sided approach, based exclusively on the strategic demands of the marketplace, is out of the question.

The more recent typology of HRM roles based on Ulrich (1997) can be related to the different dimensions of performance (as defined in Chapters 4 and 5) as in Table 9.1.

It is important to emphasize that this is not meant as a strict one-to-one relationship. Both change agent and strategic partner roles also require a certain level of professionalism. And workers and trade unions can benefit from an HRM role that is able to fulfil the requirements of change agent and strategic partner role, etc. The overview is given here only to show how the different logics for effectiveness and multidimensional measures for performance are represented in the different roles. In the following sections I will further argue, develop, and demonstrate this multidimensional approach towards HR effectiveness.

9.4 Measuring HR effectiveness

In 1997 a special issue of the US-based journal *Human Resource Management* (edited by A. K. Yeung) was completely devoted to 'Measuring Human Resource Effectiveness and Impact'. Preceding this issue, numerous articles had

TABLE 9.1 Linking HR roles to the different logics

HR role	Logic
Change agent and strategic partner	Strategic logic
Administrative expert	Professional and delivery logic
Employee champion	Societal logic

addressed the relationship between HRM and its proclaimed contribution to the performance of the firm (see Figure 4.4). As a forerunner to the theme of measuring HR effectiveness, we can consider the approach to HR accounting (HRA) as promoted in the 1970s and 1980s by people such as Bulte (1975) and Flamholtz (1985). Later Fitz-Enz (1990) developed this approach into the so-called concept of 'human value management'. Human resource accounting (HRA) itself was, at least as an academic sub-discipline, quite popular in the 1970s and 1980s. However, in 1989, after reviewing more than 140 articles and several books, Scarpello and Theeke concluded:

At the theoretical level, HRA is an interesting concept. If human resource value could be measured, the knowledge of that value could be used for internal management and external investor decision-making. However, until HRA advocates demonstrate a valid and generalizable means for measuring human resource value in monetary terms, we are compelled to recommend that researchers abandon further consideration of possible benefits from HRA. (Scarpello and Theeke, 1989: 275; cited in Cascio, 1991: 6)

HRA hardly appeared as an academic discipline of inquiry in the 1990s, but the interest in measuring HR effectiveness has since grown enormously, encompassing such approaches as cost–benefit analysis, based on utility analysis, an approach, that attempts to estimate the financial impact of employee behaviours. In its ultimate form, this provides an ability to calculate a return on investment (ROI) for every HRM programme or practice, as Phillips *et al.* (2001) strongly recommend, from labour turnover costs and gains from selection programmes to financial costs and gains of training programmes (see e.g. Cascio, 1991; Noe *et al.*, 2000).

Phillips *et al.* (2001) present an overview of approaches to HR measurement and accountability (see Figure 9.4). They distinguish first a set of so-called 'early approaches', among which is the well-known 'management by objectives', which dates back to the 1960s. Their second set is the 'solid value added approaches' that became popular in the 1980s and 1990s, such as key indicators, monitoring, and benchmarking. Their third category includes more composite approaches, such as the HR profit centre and the whole ROI process as outlined in their book, which focuses on comparing benefits and costs. These authors also foresee a resurgence of HR accounting under the new heading of 'human capital valuation', proponents of which include Watson Wyatt's human capital index (1999), Sveiby's intangible assets monitor (1997) and Mayo's human capital monitor (2001). Based on a distinction between financial and intellectual capital, Peppard and Rylander (2001) present an overview in Figure 9.5.

Although the definitions of intellectual capital differ per author, the distinction made by Peppard and Rylander (2001) gives a good overview of the constituting resources:

HRM and Performance

- *Human capital* comprises the competence, skills, and intellectual agility of the individual employees.
- *Relationship capital* represents all the valuable relationships (networks) with customers, suppliers, and other relevant stakeholders.
- *Organizational capital* includes processes, systems and structures, brands, intellectual property and other intangibles that support value creation.

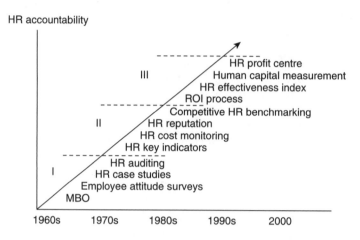

Fig 9.4. Approaches to HR accountability

Source: Phillips *et al.* (2001: 3). Reprinted with permission from Elsevier.
Note: I: early approaches; II: solid, value-added approaches; III: leading-edge approaches

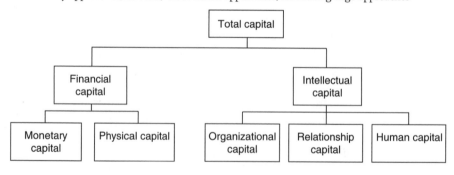

Fig 9.5. Total value scheme: the resource base of the organization

Source: Peppard and Rylander (2001: 515). Reprinted with permission from Elsevier.

Since, from the perspective of financial analysts, the intangibles are crucial in assessing the value of a company (see the Ernst & Young report on *Measures that Matter* 2001), one can easily understand the increased interest in measuring, monitoring, and evaluating the value or potential value creation of human capital.

9.5 Motives, benefits, and critics associated with HR measurement

The overview of approaches and numerous articles and books dealing with adapted versions of the balanced scorecard (Kaplan and Norton, 1992) demonstrate the enormous importance that academics, consultants, and practitioners alike attach to the whole issue of measuring HR effectiveness. Summarizing all the motives for measuring HR, the following reasons can be offered to explain its popularity and drive:

- Growing evidence to support the link between business performance and quality of HRM practices
- Increased competitive pressure as a consequence of rapidly changing technology and increasingly global markets
- Drive for cost-effectiveness; pressure on all specialist staff functions to justify their use of resources
- Pressure to increase earnings per share constantly in order to satisfy shareholders/capital markets
- General trend towards increased benchmarking
- Belief in organizational myths such as 'You cannot manage, what you cannot measure' (Ulrich, 1997) and 'What you measure is what you get' (Yeung and Berman, 1997)
- US-based obsession with measuring effectiveness, which has an impact (through publications in popular business journals) in other countries, albeit with a certain time lag (Pfeffer, 1997)
- Low status of the HRM function, however much it wants to be at the table as a business partner together with accounting, finance, and marketing. For this reason HRM concepts need to be replaced by evidence, preferably quantifiable data; (see Pfeffer (1997) criticizing Ulrich (1997)).

The following potential benefits are associated with paying more attention to HR measurement (based on Daniels, 2002; Noe *et al.*, 2000 and the almost classic and still very valuable paper by Tsui and Gomez-Mejia, 1988):

- *Strengthening the profile of the HRM function* (marketing, PR) This enhances image and visibility.
- *Providing accountability* Measurement and evaluation serve as an important accountability tool to determine whether the HRM function is effectively utilizing its resources and meeting immediate and long-term goals.

189

- *Promoting change* The power of data, perceived as objective, is excellent for gaining attention, concern (by HRM function and other stakeholders), and ultimately action.
- *Assessing financial impact* HR measurement encourages the HRM function to act 'like entrepreneurs whose business happens to be people' (Cascio, 1991).

Critics and pitfalls

A heavy emphasis on measuring can involve risks and unforeseen consequences. For example, Pfeffer (1997: 360) rightly points to the fact that measuring is easiest if you relate it to the expenditure of resources, such as the number of people working in the HRM department and their salary costs, the costs associated with training, etc. However, staffing ratios and measures of resources expended do not reveal effectiveness; nor do they inform us of the value added as a consequence of HRM activities. In this way, expending fewer resources and having fewer people becomes an end in itself and can easily be mistaken for efficiency (Pfeffer, 1997: 360).

Another problem is the time span of HRM activities before their intended consequences become apparent. For example, a range of training sessions across different management layers, aimed at strengthening organizational culture in the direction of a new entity after a merger, might take three or four years before its effects become manifest. Another warning put forward by Pfeffer (1997) relates to the abundance of HRM indicators, which risks our losing sight of the 'forest for the trees'. For example, the book by Phillips *et al.* (2001) gives an enormous overview of possible indicators, all of which should culminate in one figure: the return on investment. However, as Kaplan and Norton emphasize, it is more important to use just a few meaningful indicators per perspective, i.e those that are most successful in attaining their related objectives. Measuring HR effectiveness presupposes that the HRM function is able to influence the outcomes. Pfeffer rightly warns that HRM as a staff specialist function might prove to have little influence. For example, management might design an HRM tool in the area of appraisal, but line management itself might then apply that tool rightly or wrongly in a work setting that is being created by, among others, the style of leadership, the organizational climate, and the team composition. Also, Yeung and Berman (1997) highlight the important influence on and responsibility of line management for people management. So numerous factors play a role in bringing about effects—including side-effects, unintended effects, and disruptive effects.

Both the reasons for measuring HR effectiveness and the potential benefits associated with it are highly effective in stimulating academics and practitioners to pursue approaches, that are academically sound and at the same time useful for practitioners. The next section begins by presenting an overview of some of these approaches, all based on, or at least inspired by, the balanced scorecard. In the final sections I will then outline my own approach—the 4logic HRM scorecard—which conforms with my earlier plea for a multidimensional approach to HR effectiveness and performance.

9.6 The rise of the scorecard for HRM purposes

In 1992 Kaplan and Norton presented their balanced scorecard, aimed at developing a more balanced perspective on monitoring the performance of an organization. It quickly became widely popular. In their original article they distinguished four essential perspectives:

1. *Customer perspective*: How do customers see us?
2. *Internal/business process perspective*: What must we excel at?
3. *Innovation and learning perspective*: Can we continue to create and improve value?
4. *Financial perspective*: How do we look to shareholders?

In essence, the balanced scorecard is a way of looking at the optimal performance of an organization by taking into account all four perspectives. So Kaplan and Norton include not only the well-known financial measures, which report the results of actions already taken, but also operational measures, which are the *drivers* of future financial performance. Whereas traditional finance-based measurement systems have a control bias, the balanced scorecard puts strategy and vision at the forefront.[1]

Given its enormous popularity, it should not come as a surprise that a range of articles and books have been published recently presenting adapted versions of the balanced scorecard, adapted for usage in the area of HRM and in this way filling the gap that has been left by Kaplan and Norton. As Maltz et al. (2003: 190) note, 'the lack of focus on a company's human resource dimension is perhaps the most notable weakness . . .' On the basis of survey research aimed at establishing the relative importance of different measures for performance, Maltz *et al.* add the dimension of people development to reflect the critical importance of human resources. Also, in the above mentioned special edition of *Human Resource Management*, several authors introduced the idea of an adapted balanced scorecard in order to better account for the importance of human resources (Yeung and Berman, 1997; Ulrich, 1997; Pfeffer, 1997; Beatty and Schneier, 1997). Yeung and Berman (1997) state:

For businesses to succeed in the long run, the expectations of three stakeholders—shareholders, customers, and employees—need to be satisfied. Second, all three

191

stakeholders are interrelated. Employee attitudes and behaviours impact the level of customer satisfaction and retention. In turn, customer attitudes and behaviours influence shareholder satisfaction and retention. Finally, shareholder satisfaction affects employee satisfaction through bonuses, stock options or further investment in employee growth. (Yeung and Berman, 1997)

Becker *et al.* (2001) followed with the publication of their book *The HR Scorecard*, which entails a stepwise approach to HR measurement. In this way they claimed to be able to fill the gap that Kaplan and Norton (1996) had noticed:

When it comes to specific measures concerning HR and people related issues, companies have devoted virtually no effort for measuring either outcomes or the drivers of these capabilities. This gap is disappointing, since one of the most important goals for adopting the scorecard measurement and management framework is to promote the growth of individual and organizational capabilities. This reflects the limited progress that most organizations have made linking employees . . . and organizational alignment with their strategic objectives. (Kaplan and Norton, 1996: 144–5; quoted by Becker *et al.* 2001: 23)

Following Kaplan and Norton, Becker *et al.* distinguish *lagging indicators*, such as financial metrics (e.g. ROI), which reflect only what has happened in the past, and *leading indicators* (e.g. R&D cycle time, customer satisfaction, employee strategic focus), which assess the status of the key success factors that drive implementation of the firm's strategy. These emphasize the future instead of the past (Becker *et al.* 2001: 30).

Most important in their approach is the linkage between business strategy and the way in which HRM can help to add value. Becker *et al.* label these *strategic HR deliverables*, i.e. those outcomes of the HRM architecture or HRM system that serve to execute the firm's strategy (2001:30). These strategic HR deliverables come in two different shapes. One category is the so-called *performance drivers*, for example employee productivity, innovativeness; This is the same as what others call HRM outcomes (see Guest, 1987; Paauwe and Richardson, 1997). The other category is the so-called *enablers*, which reinforce the performance drivers, for example training programmes, performance appraisal system. These are the HRM activities or HRM practices.

Yeung and Berman's approach is a bit different. They establish the link between a firm's strategy and its supporting HRM architecture by people-related *organizational capabilities*, which are critical for the successful realization of the firm's strategy. These organizational capabilities (e.g. innovativeness, speed, willingness to change, flexibility) can be built by selecting and designing the right HRM practices (as enablers). I use this distinction in my own approach in the final section.

The building of the HR scorecard is a highly company-specific matter, for which no universal blueprints can be developed, as Becker *et al.* (2001) acknowledge. They outline seven steps to be carried out in order to develop and build an HR scorecard that fits the needs of a specific organization (pp. 36–52):

1. Clearly define business strategy.
2. Build a business case for HR as a strategic asset.
3. Create a strategy map.
4. Identify HR deliverables within the strategy map.
5. Align the HR architecture with HR deliverables.
6. Design the strategic HR measurement system.
7. Implement management by measurement.

Those expecting to encounter an easy-to-handle scorecard may therefore be disappointed, as this is a rather lengthy and difficult process. For a good illustration readers are referred to Walker and MacDonald (2001), who describe the development of a HR scorecard, based on the Becker *et al.* (2001) approach, for the Verizon Company.

Phillips *et al.* (2001) offer a rival perspective, again under the title *The Human Resources Scorecard*. They build on almost twenty years of experience in the development and refinement of a proven ROI process in the HRM area in order to demonstrate the contribution of HRM in generating value. Their approach and measurement tool is targeted at three different user groups: HRM practitioners, senior managers, and evaluation researchers/consultants. Compared with Becker *et al.* (2001), their approach is more narrowly focused on a proper evaluation, monitoring and measuring the effectiveness of HRM programmes themselves, and is not so much related to linkages with a firm's strategy. Figure 9.6 depicts their approach.

For a more extensive overview of all the different approaches currently available in the area of measuring HR effectiveness, see Mayo (2001), who

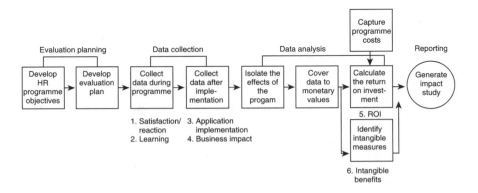

Fig 9.6. ROI process model. Reprinted with permission from Elsevier.

not only presents his own 'Human Capital Monitor', but also summarizes the following approaches:

- Watson Wyatt's Human Capital Index (HCI)
- William Mercer's Human Capital Wheel
- Arthur Anderson's Human Capital Appraisal
- Fitz-Enz's (2000) study on the ROI of human capital
- The Skandia Navigator
- Sveiby's Intangible Assets Monitor

9.7 A real balanced scorecard: the 4logic HRM scorecard

All the previous scorecards originated from the original idea of the balanced scorecard by Kaplan and Norton (1992). They focus mainly on the implementation of a chosen strategy and at improving the effectiveness and efficiency of HRM policies and practices in order to add value. This is in itself a valuable contribution and probably well worth the effort. However, it is very important also to recognize the very essence of human resource management, which is more than just contributing to the generation of added value. Chapter 5 outlined the Contextually Based Human Resource Theory (CBHRT) and its multidimensional view of performance—multidimensional to reflect the different stakeholders that have a say in HRM. Such stakeholders include employees, customers, line and top management, shareholders, trade unions, consumers' organizations, environmental/green associations, and society at large. These different stakeholders and dimensions can be represented by three perspectives or 'logics'.

The *strategic logic* focuses on the expectations of boards of directors, CEOs, shareholders, and financial institutions. These are particularly interested in the inputs (e.g. planning and policies) and outcomes of the strategic dimension and the way in which it will contribute to the whole process of generating added value. So this dimension reflects the notion of economic rationality and can be expressed in criteria such as efficiency, effectiveness, flexibility, agility, quality, and innovativeness.

The *professional logic* focuses on the expectations of line managers, employees, works councils, and colleagues of HR departments. This dimension relates to the degree of customer orientation of the HR function and the quality of its services, for which we can make use of Zeithaml *et al.*'s (1990) criteria:

- *Tangibles* These are the evident products of the personnel function, such as procedures for appraisal, remuneration, evaluation systems, ratios, training, and development facilities.

- *Reliability* This relates to the capacity to implement the required services in an adequate way.
- *Responsiveness* This is the willingness to provide rapid and certainly timely assistance, where help is needed.
- *Assurance* Assurance is the ability to convince the customer that the department can handle its interests because expertise and hence credibility is available and perceived as such.
- *Empathy* This is the ability to perceive and understand different groups of customers and their backgrounds, situations, and perceptions.

(based on Zeithaml *et al.*, 1990, and Paauwe, 1996; 1998)

In this context the meaning of 'professional' is limited to the delivery of services that meet the quality expectations of a firm's customers. I do not intend to use the concept of 'professional' to mean meeting the standards set by a professional association of peers, for example the Dutch Association for Personnel Management, or in the UK the Institute for Personnel Development.

Unlike the strategic locus, with its emphasis on added value, *societal logic* emphasizes moral values and focuses on the expectations of works councils, trade unions, government, and other interest groups, both inside and outside the company. This dimension reflects the notion of relational rationality as outlined in Chapters 4 and 5 and can be monitored on the basis of the following criteria:

- *Fairness* This refers to a 'fair' or just arrangement in the agreed exchange between the individual as an employee and the organization as employer. Elements in this exchange are not only time, money, and labour, but also information, know-how, and voice/consultation/participation.
- *Legitimacy* This refers to the same exchange elements (such as 'fairness'), but at a more collective level, whereby the parties involved are interest groups (employees, unions, government through legislation).
- *Sustainability* This refers to a sustainable development in a way that aims to conserve an ecological balance by avoiding depletion of natural resources.
- *Participation* This refers to the availability of 'voice' options for all relevant parties involved.
- *Solidarity* This refers to a willingness to support those individuals/groups that are in an unfavourable position.

(based on Paauwe, 1998, and Paauwe and Boselie, 2002)

As stated before, I have added one more logic, i.e. the *delivery logic*. This is based on cost effectiveness and works through the following delivery channels:

- HR departments
- Line management

HRM and Performance

- Outsourcing
- Teams and employees themselves
- Self service through e-HRM (implies web-based delivery)

Human resource management itself is central in this scorecard approach, which is subject to a multidimensional concept of performance. It is based not on a set of predefined best practices, but on achieving various fits, e.g. strategic fit, horizontal fit, organizational fit, and environmental fit as outlined in the CBHRT model (see Chapter 5). Every performance perspective, and every logic (strategic, societal, professional, and delivery), has its own distinct set of criteria, which helps management to make choices and to monitor and evaluate the actions chosen. Setting priorities per perspective is an absolute necessity. Nowadays managers are overwhelmed by data and measures. If we want to control and monitor progress in HRM policies and practices and to determine how they contribute to the various logics, it is important to focus on a limited set of targets/objectives. Better to do a few things well than to list too many goals and activities, which cannot be carried out properly and on time.

The HRM function (as an organizational function) is central in this approach, but that does not imply that it can be carried out only by an HR manager. Line managers, teams, external consultants, and web-based

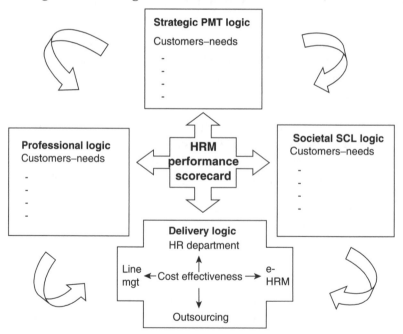

Fig 9.7. The 4logic HRM scorecard

delivery mechanisms can also fulfil parts of the HR function. This implies that different delivery channels can be used, which results in the fourth logic, delivery logic, for which, as stated above, cost effectiveness is the main criterion. Appendix 9.1 gives a helpful overview of the criteria involved when deciding on make (in-house) or buy (outsource) issues (based on Paauwe, in Flood *et al.* 1996: 226). Figure 9.7 presents the basic lay-out of the 4logic HRM scoreboard.

9.8 The 4logic HRM scorecard: a stepwise approach

This section outlines the procedure for working with the 4logic HRM scorecard. For every step, some illustrative examples are included. These are based on two sources. One stems from the range of case studies conducted in order to explore the feasibility of the CBHRT (especially the part on force field analysis; see Appendix 5.2 for an example). The second source is from participants of an international Masters programme in HR leadership at Erasmus University/Rotterdam School of Management. These HR executives, representing a range of internationally operating companies, applied the 4logic HRM scorecard to their own companies and HR departments.

Step 1: Select and define the main customers for every logic

Customers can be both external and internal. Each organization has its own unique context that will influence which customers are relevant for the HR function in the organization. In many cases employees will serve as 'indirect' customers of the HR function, owing to the fact that line management is responsible for putting HRM into action at the workplace. Reflecting on the three logics (strategic, professional, and societal) helps us to think about the different categories of relevant 'customers'.

In one of the post-doctoral seminars for HR executives at Erasmus University, participants ($n = 20$) were asked to create a HRM scorecard, based on the expectations of the main customers of the HR function in their organization. The first task we put to the participants was to list the three most important clients of the HR function in their organization. They mentioned (1) employees (90 per cent of the respondents), (2) the board of directors (85 per cent), and (3) line management (70 per cent); other clients mentioned included works councils, (external) customers, and financial controllers. Employees, line management, and the board of directors appear to be important customers for the HR function in many organizations.

Next, the participants were asked to list the expectations for these three groups of customers. These are set out in Table 9.2.

Step 2: Align every customer or customer category with its main expectations

This step implies a close and interactive link with the overall business goals of the company or subsidiary. Awareness of the overall business goals, and the kind of organizational capabilities required in order to achieve these goals, can be very helpful in defining the firm's customers and their expectations. To stimulate this kind of thinking, the following overview of possible organizational capabilities is presented.

TABLE 9.2 Overview of the three main clients of the HR-function

Customers	Expectations
Employee	Administrative expertise, employee development, fair reward systems, inspirational leadership, flexibility in the contract, a challenging work environment, openness (information sharing and communication), social security (continuity), an acceptable work–life balance, and employee influence
Line manager	HR knowledge transfer, administrative support, facilitating certain HRM practices (and processes) like selecting and training, and having clear goals and targets (information sharing and communication)
Board of directors	HR effectiveness and efficiency in terms of maximizing productivity and creating human capital, creating employee commitment and motivation, establishing fit between overall business strategy and HR strategy and activities, and contributing to sustainability (continuity)

1. Talent
2. Speed
3. Customer alertness
4. Stick to your promises; accountability
5. Starting and managing alliances
6. Strong culture; shared values and norms
7. Innovation
8. Knowledge management

9. Use of state-of-the-art technology
10. Alertness with respect to new developments
11. Safety
12. Leadership
13. Quality/continuous improvement
14. Co-operation
15. Participation; voice
16. Creativity
17. Willingness to change
18. Flexibility
19. Cost-effectiveness
20. . . . .
21. . . . .
22. . . . .

According to Yeung and Berman (1997: 328), it is important to target only a few organizational capabilities, i.e. those that have not yet been totally met, and to which HRM practices and policies might be able to contribute. Given the significance of the link between strategy and HRM, it is important to notice that, especially for the strategic logic, customers and goals are strongly related to the overall business goals and necessary organizational capabilities. Of course it is helpful for the filling in of the 4logic HRM scorecard if top management has a clear view on the strategic objectives and organizational capabilities required. These can act as a useful point of reference and a starting point for filling in the scorecard. Very often the staff of the HR department will be more aware of the customers and expectations for the other two logics, i.e. the professional and societal. However, we should not be too bothered about making a clear distinction between the various logics. It is more important to be triggered by the various logics. And the logics often overlap; for example, avoiding negative publicity for a big accounting firm is both a strategic goal (negative publicity will result in loss of clients) and a societal goal (society at large expects accountancy firms to maintain high standards of conduct in terms of integrity and reliability). The expectations of the customers will vary per logic and per organization. Table 9.3 presents some examples.

As can be seen from the above-mentioned examples, it is helpful to take into account the various perspectives/logics per customer category, including the criteria outlined above for every perspective. So with respect to the societal logic it is advisable to think of criteria like legitimacy, fairness, and sustainability; the strategic logic is represented by criteria like efficiency, flexibility, innovativeness; and the professional logic is represented by service quality criteria like reliability, responsiveness, and assurance.

TABLE 9.3 Examples of customers and their expectations per logic

Customers	Expectations	Logic
Internationally operating accounting firm		
Equity partners	Maximize sustainable earnings per partner while avoiding negative publicity	Strategic logic
General public	Provide assurance and trust about financial reporting of organizations	Societal logic
Works council	Safeguard participation and solidarity among workforce as well as fairness in worker–management relationships	Societal logic
Government	Compliance with regulations	Societal logic
Employees	Maximize both tangible and intangible rewards	Professional logic
Line managers	Provide information on the right mix of human resources	Professional logic
Internationally operating steel mill		
Managing director	Qualified employees; health and safety; overall cost effectiveness (implementing manpower reduction); cultural change	Strategic logic
Works council	Contact person; delivery of reliable information on HR and IR issues	Societal logic
Trade unions	Point of contact and information; fair partner for negotiations	Societal logic
Line management	Staffing and administrative support	Professional logic
Employees	Information and individual help	Professional logic

Step 3: Summarize/merge customers' expectations into overall HR goals

Based on the overview of different customer groupings and their expectations, the third step in our approach involves the setting of priorities and the merging of different expectations into a ranking order of overall goals for the HR function. Some of these expectations are similar for different customers and therefore can easily be prioritized into overall goals. For example, continuity is an important goal for the board of directors in terms of viability, and for employees in terms of job security. Another example is related to information sharing. Employees expect the HR function to be open about issues affecting the employment relationship; line managers expect the HR function to be clear about their HRM goals and targets. In both cases the customers expect a high quality of information sharing and communication from the HR function (professional logic). However, other expectations arising out of the different customer categories and related logics might contradict each other. For example, a top management team may initiate a process of downsizing in order to give a signal to investors and shareholders that the company is seriously trying to make its operations more efficient; however, this endeavour could cause unrest and resistance from trade unions and works councils, which would give priority to maintaining employment levels.

This raises the important question concerning what determines the setting of priorities and the establishment of a ranking order of overall HR goals. With reference to the CBHRT model, this issue belongs to the domain of the so-called 'dominant coalition'. The composition of this coalition will differ per company. Very often actors such as the board of directors, the HR manager, and the works council/shop steward will be included. They will have regulatory mechanisms (authority, consultative, and decision-making meetings) to arrive at a final decision or to settle a dispute. Feedback and evaluation should be important elements in the overall process of decision-making and setting priorities. Circumstances can change overnight, which necessitate a different ranking order of priorities. Table 9.4 gives a few examples of this step, based on our case studies in this area.

It can be seen that filling in the different steps of our 4logic HRM scorecard approach is not a mechanistic endeavour. It requires a lot of intelligent and creative thinking on the part of the actors that are part of the dominant coalition (board of directors, line management, HR staff, works council, trade unions)—and also much consultation. Of course that takes time, but once an agreement has been settled, the implementation can be faster and the acceptance better, thanks to the preceding involvement and voice opportunities for the parties involved (see also Boxall and Purcell, 2003: 231–2). The example of the US-and Dutch-based chemical firms implementing teamwork and flexibility, described in Chapter 8, is both illustrative and convincing in this respect.

TABLE 9.4 Examples of overall goals for the HR function

Internationally operating steel mill

- Providing operational HR support in the areas of staffing, administration, training, and development, in order to have the right manpower (both qualitative and quantitative)

- Punctual and reliable delivery of information related to HR issues

- Implementing and supporting cost savings activities

- Initiating cultural change

Engineering firm involved in a process of privatization

- Management development

- Succession planning

- Employability/multi-skilling

- Establishing a more commercial attitude

- Developing a performance management cycle

- Smooth administrative HR support systems

Step 4: Link prioritized goals to HRM policies and practices

What kind of HRM policies and practices should be present or developed in order to realize the goals? An HRM policy explicitly states what you can or would like to achieve using a certain HRM practice/tool/activity. For example, the HRM policy of achieving adequate staffing in order to realize the right mix of human resources (both quantitatively and qualitatively) implies practices in the areas of labour market communication, advanced recruitment and selection methods, and the right methods for socialization and introduction training (see Table 9.5).

Step 5: Opt for indicators in order to monitor the selected enabling HRM practices

HR management needs to select and/or develop a limited range of indicators that can be used to monitor and measure the effects of the selected HRM

TABLE 9.5 Examples of linking HRM goals to HRM practices

HRM goals/policies	HRM practices
Internationally operating fast-moving consumer goods company in the food sector	
Attract and retain the best people, leveraging the internal knowledge and networks	Culture programmes; management development
Develop capability to build and empower brands	Expatriate management
Encourage breakthrough thinking and entrepreneurial drive, leading to innovation	Climate and atmosphere
Build and use the European muscle to leverage our size	Team development
Have the right leadership to bring both inspiration and aspiration	Leadership development
Develop a culture of trust/high involvement	Global technology centre
	HRM support
	Personal development plans
	Training and development
	Centralized HR support
	Human resource planning
	Open job posting
	Recruitment
Internationally operating travel agency	
Operational HR support	Maintain expertise with respect to remuneration and personnel administration
	Planning resulting in cost-effective allocation of staff
Align HRM with corporate strategy	Active role of HR manager in management team

(Continued)

TABLE 9.5 (*Contd*)

HRM goals/policies	HRM practices
	Stimulate example-setting behaviour by top management
Line managers as HR managers	Train line managers in recruitment, selection, appraisal and motivation of their own staff
Development of competences	Succession planning for key managerial roles and related training and MD programmes
Implementation of cost-saving activities	Stimulate cost-effective behaviour among employees
	Link additional pay to maintaining the budget

practices. Indicators such as employee satisfaction, motivation, retention, presence, absence due to illness, turnover, social climate, involvement, trust, loyalty, and commitment are all examples of typical HRM outcomes. The model of Becker *et al.* (1997) and the scheme of Paauwe and Richardson (1997) suggest that HRM systems or practices are closely linked to those kinds of HRM outcomes and less closely linked to performance indicators such as productivity, product/service quality, customer satisfaction, and research and development. In other words, the distance between HRM systems (or practices) and HRM outcomes is smaller than the distance between HRM systems (or practices) and performance indicators such as productivity. Financial performance indicators such as return on investment (ROI) and return on assets (ROA) are even further away from HRM practices than indicators such as productivity and product/service quality (see Table 9.6).

Appendices 9.2 and 9.3 present a more extensive overview of a range of possible HRM practices and possible indicators.

In connection with the previous example of the fast moving consumer goods company, Table 9.7 gives an example of how the different HRM practices can be linked to indicators.

TABLE 9.6 HRM outcomes and other performance indicators

HRM outcomes	Performance outcomes	Financial outcomes
Employee satisfaction, motivation, retention, social climate, involvement, trust, loyalty, security, intention to leave, commitment	Productivity, product/service quality, customer satisfaction, research and development	ROI, ROA, ROE, ROS, GRATE and Tobin's q (Sales, market share, growth, profits, and market value)

TABLE 9.7 Linking HRM practices to indicators

Fast moving consumer goods company operating at a European level	
HRM practices	Indicators
Cultural programmes, management development	% high potentials attracted from operating companies
Expatriate management	% high potentials leaving voluntary
Climate and atmosphere	% increase in skills and profile regarding the building and maintenance of power brands
Team development	Number of innovative ideas per brand
Leadership development	Number of pan-European innovations delivered
HRM support	Progress made in factory rationalization
Personal development plans Training and development Centralized HRM support Human resource planning Open job posting Recruitment	Global employee survey scores

Step 6: Make people accountable; specify reporting intervals and indicators

This step involves three important issues. First of all, there is the issue related to who is accountable (responsible) for a specific HRM practice. Possible candidates are (1) the HRM department, (2) line management (employees' direct supervisors), (3) teams (e.g. self-managing teams and quality circles), (4) self-service through e-HRM, and (5) external partners (outsourcing). So for each HRM practice we have to determine who is responsible.

Second is the issue of (a) when to start, (b) when to finish, and (c) what kind of reporting intervals to create. The necessary evaluation can be successful only if there is general agreement between stakeholders on these temporal issues in advance.

Third is the issue of what kind of indicators to apply. There is a fundamental difference between the 'indicator' itself (e.g. absence due to illness), the way we measure it (e.g. the average duration of absence due to illness), the objective or 'target' we want to achieve (e.g. less than 5 days on average per year absence due to illness), and the 'actual outcomes' (e.g. the organization on average had an absence rate of 6.1 days in the year 2001). In Table 9.8 we present some examples in order to clearly illustrate the differences.

TABLE 9.8 The difference between concept, measurement, objective, and reality

Indicator	Measurement	Target/objective	Reality
Absence due to illness	The average duration of absence due to illness per year	< 5.0 days per person per year	6.1 days absence per person, per year
Employee turnover	The number of employees that (whether voluntarily or not) have left the organization in relation to the total number of employees in a specific year (%)	10% < employee turnover > 20% (Target is an employee turnover rate above 10% and below 20% per year)	8.3% employee turnover
Employee satisfaction	The degree of employee satisfaction on a 5-point scale (1 = low and 5 = high)	Average satisfaction > 3.5	3.87

Step 7: Determine the proper delivery channel (or combination of it) for every HRM practice

In the past, HRM delivery mechanisms were limited to discussions about HR staff specialist versus line management and centralized versus decentralized delivery. Nowadays we see an increase in types of delivery mechanism, including various degrees of internalizing and externalizing. By 'internalizing' we mean the shift from HRM department to line managers and / or employees themselves. By 'externalizing' we mean the shift from in-house activities to outsourcing or, in the words of Adams (1991: 44), 'the application of market forces to the delivery of personnel activities'. Figure 9.8, based on Paauwe (Chapter 6, in Flood *et al.* 1996:200), presents an overview distinguishing between minor changes (which can be implemented without radically altering the existing organizational structure, systems, and culture) and major changes (which have an impact upon the whole organization and cannot be implemented in an isolated way).

More recently has come the need to include the possibilities of self-service by employees (and potential employees!) through e-HRM or web-enabled HRM delivery by making use of intranet and internet. It is to be expected (see Wright and Dyer, 2000) that a range of so-called transactional activities, such as compensation and benefits administration and record keeping, but also parts of training and development, will increasingly be delivered through the use of information technology. Many companies nowadays have an HRM website for information, vacancies, the updating of personnel files, benefits administration, internal labour market, training and development, assessment, etc., a development that is paralleled by a centralization and reallocation of the more transactional HRM activities into so-called 'shared services centres'. Combined with

	Focus of change	
Extent of change	Internalizing (shift from staff to regular line/workers)	Externalizing (outsourcing)
Minor change	• Integral management • Self managing teams • Core and peripheral personnel activities	• Outsourcing partially • Contract management • Specialized in-house units • Internal consultancy/profit center
Major change	• Personnel management without personnel management	• Agencies • Leased employees • Teleworking

Fig 9.8. Alternative HRM delivery mechanisms found in practice

Source: Paauwe, in Flood *et al.* (1996)

information technology, this development enables a more cost-effective execution of a range of standardized HRM activities and the rapid answering of frequently asked questions by employees. So today the options for HRM delivery include HRM department, line management, teams, outsourcing, and e-HRM. It is advisable to develop action overview sheets for every delivery channel. Appendix 9.4 gives an example based on one of the participating companies that took part in our executive programme on HR leadership.

9.9 Summary and conclusions

The topic of HRM effectiveness and measurement has become very important since the mid-1990s. This development has been stimulated on the one hand by the interest among academics and practitioners in the relationship between HRM and performance, and on the other by the growing conviction within the business community that all kinds of specialist staff function have to prove their contribution to the process of generating added value. Approaches like value-based management are popular among the big internationally operating companies. Scorecards and monitoring through key indicators can be of help in this respect. However, choosing a certain approach does not remove the necessity to think about the far more important topic of what to measure, and whether we can really measure the things that are important. So the underlying philosophy of the approach is crucial.

In the above approach I have deliberately paid a lot of attention to the basic fundamentals underlying the 4logic HRM scorecard. The different perspectives or logics are fully in line with my approach of combining both economic and normative rationality, and both added value (the economic point of view) and moral values such as fairness and legitimacy. In this way I hope to have contributed to a balanced perspective on performance in the area of human resource management.

Moreover, the 4logic HRM scorecard provides a way of reconciling the inherent tensions in the field of HRM—between the short and long run, between productivity/profitability and legitimacy/fairness, etc.—based not on a mechanistic approach, but on intelligent and imaginative scanning of the different forces (PMT dimension, SCL dimension, organizational configuration) involved. These forces create scope and leeway for the dominant coalition to shape best HRM practices in a way that fits the very context of the organization and can contribute to long-term viability.

Note

1. Since its conception, the balanced scorecard has diffused rapidly and become widely used. This has led on the one hand to a range of papers describing its adapted use in

areas other than those originally intended, and on the other hand to papers criticizing its approach. For a critical overview readers are referred to Meyer (2002), who, under the heading of 'Rethinking Performance Measurement: Beyond the Balanced Scorecard', critically analyses its approach and offers an alternative activity based probability analysis. A paper by Maltz *et al.* (2003) offers under the same heading ('Beyond the Balanced Scorecard') more refined measures for organizational success.

Appendix 9.1 Decision Tree for Weighing Staff-line and Make/Buy Alternatives

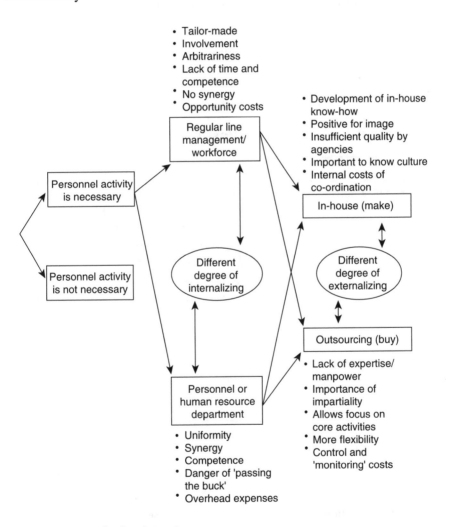

- Tailor-made
- Involvement
- Arbitrariness
- Lack of time and competence
- No synergy
- Opportunity costs

- Development of in-house know-how
- Positive for image
- Insufficient quality by agencies
- Important to know culture
- Internal costs of co-ordination

Regular line management/ workforce

Personnel activity is necessary

In-house (make)

Personnel activity is not necessary

Different degree of internalizing

Different degree of externalizing

Outsourcing (buy)

Personnel or human resource department

- Lack of expertise/ manpower
- Importance of impartiality
- Allows focus on core activities
- More flexibility
- Control and 'monitoring' costs

- Uniformity
- Synergy
- Competence
- Danger of 'passing the buck'
- Overhead expenses

Source: Paauwe, in Flood *et al.* (1996).

Appendix 9.2 Overview of Possible Human Resource Practices

HR planning	Decentralization
Selection	Autonomy
Socialization	Teamwork
Training	Status and security
Appraisal	Internal promotion opportunity
Rewards/compensation	Coaching
Job design	Formal procedures
Participation	

Source: based on Paauwe and Richardson (1997) and Boselie (2002).

Appendix 9.3 Overview of Possible Indicators

Indicators	Examples
Perceived HRM outcomes	Employee satisfaction, employee motivation, employee trust, employee commitment, employee loyalty, employee involvement, organizational citizenship, social atmosphere (management/employees), intention to leave the organization (attitude)
Objective HRM outcomes	Employee turnover, employee retention, (internal) conflicts, absence due to illness, time needed to fill a vacancy, percentage of internally filled vacancies, average number of applicants per vacancy advertised, percentage of employees eligible for training, percentage of employees with a career planning, selection of young people, women, minorities, and incapacitated workers
Manufacturing performance	Product/service quality, customer complaints, customer satisfaction, productivity, scrap rate, number of accidents, innovation (R&D outcomes)
Firm performance	Negative publicity, sales, market share, growth, profits, market value

Source: based on Paauwe and Richardson (1997); Boselie (1999); Boselie *et al.* (2001*a*); Boselie and van der Wiele (2002).

Appendix 9.4 Action Overview

HRM practices	HRM practice in detail	Delivery channel	Start/ready	Indicator	Measurement	Target
Training and skill development	For every function a training schedule has to be made	Line manager/HR manager	08/2003–12/2003	No. of completed curriculum	% of total functions	100%
	Every employee must have a personal development plan	Line manager/HR manager	08/2003–12/2003	No. of completed personal development plans	% of total population	100%
	Selection of training agencies	HR manager	09/2003–10/2003	Selection of agency	Y/N	Selection agency
Recruitment and selection process	Clear competences have to be defined for every function	Line manager/HR manager	06/2003–09/2003	No. of completed with defined competencies	% of functions	100 %
	Interview process to be described	HR manager	06/2003–07/2003	Description of the procedure	Y/N	Procedure ready
	Selection of professional recruitment agencies	HR manager	10/2003–12/2003	Selection of agency	Y/N	Selection agency ready

(Continued)

Appendix 9.4 (*Contd*)

HRM practices	HRM practice in detail	Delivery channel	Start/ready	Indicator	Measurement	Target
	Selection of psychological test agency	HR manager	10/2003–12/2003	Selection of agency	Y/N	Selection agency
Performance review process	Every employee must get clear and measurable targets	Local MT/Line manager	10/2003–01/2004	Number of employees with clear targets	% of population	95%
	Target setting has to start with local management team	Local MT	10/2003–01/2004	Number of MT members that sets targets	% of MT	100%
	Train supervisors to set targets and to give feedback	HR manager	09/2003–10/2003	Select training agency and plan training	Y/N	90%
Compensation policy	Base salaries must be in Q3 compared with benchmark	HR manager	02/2004–05/2004	Execution of salary survey	Y/N	Survey completed
	Low performers must be below market average	HR manager	immediately	Low performers do not get increases	Y/N	Immediately
	Study on incentive pay to be carried out	HR manager	02/2004–06/2004	Execution of study	Y/N	Study completed

10 Epilogue

Our journey of developing a contextually based human resource theory has come to an end. We started with the discovery of the building blocks in strategy, industrial relations, human resource management, and related performance. The theoretical model itself then had to prove its value at the level of the individual organization, the sector, and the international comparative level. Finally there were some practical insights into HR roles and the development of the 4logic HRM scorecard—a relevant chapter for those practitioners who sincerely want to achieve a fair balance between competitiveness and social justice in order to achieve uniqueness in the area of human resource management.

This is a tentative end, because endeavours will continue to generate more insights into the factors that are important in shaping HRM policies and practices. Some people proclaim that the research topic of HRM and performance is dead, either because they think that everything has already been investigated, or because of the many flaws and methodological pitfalls encountered thus far (Gerhart, Wright and McMahan, 2000; Wright and Gardner, 2001; Sels, 2002). I am convinced that the research track into the factors that are decisive in shaping HRM is a fruitful one, irrespective of whether or not such practices contribute to performance.

The topic of HRM and performance is an important one, but it does not tell the whole story. The number of variables having an effect on the bottom line, on the performance of a firm, might easily add up to more than 300, of which HRM will be just one. But the field of HRM has a lot to say in the areas of bringing about fairness and legitimacy, contributing to sustainability, willingness to change, improving agility, etc. In the end, these topics will prove to be far more important than 'proving' that an improvement in HRM sophistication implies an increase in added value per employee.

So the quest to unravel the factors that are decisive in shaping HRM policies and practices is a rewarding and promising one, and—as the empirical chapters indicate—is also important for practitioners who want to develop a unique approach in HRM, one that fits their organization in its context and serves viability in the long run.

Bibliography

Adams, K. (1991). 'Externalisation vs. specialisation: what is happening to personnel?' *Human Resource Management Journal*, 4/1: 40–54.

Ackerman, K. F. (1983) 'A contingency model of HRM strategy'. *Management Forum*, 6: 65–83.

Albeda, W. B. and Dercksen, W. J. (1994). *Arbeidsverhoudingen in Nederland*. Alphen aan den Rijn: Samson Bedrijfsinformatie.

Albert, M. (1990). *Capitalism against Capitalism*. London: Whurr.

Aldrich, H. (1999). *Organizations Evolving*. London: Sage.

Appelbaum, E. and Batt, R. (1994). *The New American Workplace: Transforming Work Systems in the United States*. Ithaca, NY: Cornell University Press.

—— Bailey, T., Berg, P., and Kalleberg, A. (2000). *Manufacturing Advantage: Why High-Performance Work Systems Pay Off*. Ithaca, NY: Cornell University Press.

d'Arcimoles, C. H. (1997). 'Human resource policies and company performance: a quantitative approach using longitudinal data'. *Organization Studies*, 18: 857–74.

Argyris, C. and Schön, D. A. (1978). *Organizational Learning: A Theory of Action Perspective*. Reading, Mass.: Addison-Wesley.

Arthur, J. B. (1992). 'The link between business strategy and industrial relations systems in American steel minimills'. *Industrial and Labor Relations Review*, 45: 488–506.

—— (1994). 'Effects of human resource systems on manufacturing performance and turnover'. *Academy of Management Journal*, 37: 670–87.

Atkinson, J. (1984). 'Manpower strategies for flexible organizations'. *Personnel Management*, 66: 28–31.

—— (1987). 'Flexibility or fragment? The United Kingdom labour market in the eighties'. *Cahiers economiques de Bruxelle*, 113: 87–104.

Atleson, J. B. (1983). *Values and Assumptions in American Labor Law*. Amherst: University of Massachusetts Press.

Backes-Gellner, U., Frick, B., and Sadowski, D. (1997). 'Codetermination and personnel policies of German firms: the influence of works councils on turnover and further training'. *International Journal of Human Resource Management*, 8: 328–74.

Baden-Fuller, C. and Stopford, J. M. (1994). 'Creating corporate entrepreneurship'. *Strategic Management Journal*, 15: 521–36.

Bae, J. and Lawler, J. J. (2000). 'Organizational performance and HRM in Korea: impact on firm performance in an emerging economy'. *Academy of Management Journal*, 43: 502–17.

HRM and Performance

Bae, J. and Lawler, J. J. Chen, T. W., Wan, J. J., Lawler, J. J., and Roh, H. (2001). 'Human resource strategy and firm performance in pacific countries: a comparative study of Korea, Taiwan, Singapore and Thailand'. Paper presented at the Global HRM Conference, Barcelona.

Bain, G. S. and Clegg, H. A. (1974). 'A strategy for industrial relations research in Great Britain'. *British Journal of Industrial Relations*, 12/1: 91–113.

Bamberger, P. and Phillips, R. (1991). 'Organizational environment and business strategy: parallel versus conflicting influences on human resource strategy in the pharmaceutical industry'. *Human Resource Management*, 30: 153–82.

Banker, R. D., Field, J. M., Schroeder, R. G., and Sinha, K. K. (1996). 'Impact of work teams on manufacturing performance: a longitudinal field study'. *Academy of Management Journal*, 39: 920–49.

Barney, J. B. (1991). 'Firm resources and sustainable competitive advantage'. *Journal of Management*, 17/1: 99–120.

—— (1995). 'Looking inside for competitive advantage'. *Academy of Management Executive*, 9/1: 49–67.

—— (1997). *Gaining and Sustaining Competitive Advantage*. Reading, Mass.: Addison-Wesley.

—— and Wright, P. M. (1998). 'On becoming a strategic partner: the roles of human resources in gaining competitive advantage'. *Human Resource Management*, 37/1: 31–46.

Baron, J. N. and Kreps, D. M. (1999). *Strategic Human Resources: Frameworks for General Managers*. New York: John Wiley.

Bartlett, C. A. and Ghosal, S. (1989). *Managing across Borders: The Transnational Solution*. Boston: Harvard Business School Press.

Baum, J. A. C. and Singh, J. V. (1994). *Evolutionary Dynamics of Organizations*. New York: Oxford University Press.

Bean, R. (1985). *Comparative Industrial Relations*. London: Croom Helm.

Beatty, R. W. and Schneier, C. E. (1997). 'New HR roles to impact organizational performance: from "partners" to "players"'. *Human Resource Management*, 36/1: 29–37.

Becker, B. E., Huselid, M. A., Pickus, P. S., and Spratt, M. F. (1997). 'HR as a source of shareholder value: research and recommendations'. *Human Resource Management*, 36/1: 39–47.

—— Huselid, M. A., and Ulrich, D. (2001). *The HR Scorecard: Linking People, Strategy and Performance*. Boston: Harvard Business School Press.

Beer, M., Spector, B., Lawrence, P. R., Mills, D. Q., and Walton, R. E. (1984). *Managing Human Assets*. New York: Free Press.

—— Spector, B., Lawrence, P., Quinn Mills, D., and Walton, R. (1985). *Human Resource Management: A General Manager's Perspective*. New York: Free Press.

Begin, J. P. (1997). *Dynamic Human Resource Systems*. Berlin: Willem de Gruyter.

Biemans, P. J. (1999). *Professionalisering van de Personeelsfunctie: een Empirisch Onderzoek bij Twintig Organisaties*. Dissertation, Uitgeverij Eburon, Delft.

Blain, A. N. J. and Gennard, J. (1970). 'Industrial relations theory: a critical review'. *British Journal of Industrial Relations*, 8: 389–407.

Bolweg, J. F. (1989). 'Internalisering van de arbeidsverhoudingen en politisering van het personeelsmanagement', in J. F. Bolweg and F. Kluytmans (eds.), *De Noodzaak van Nieuwe Verhoudingen: Beschouwingen over Arbeidsverhoudingen en Personeelsmanagement*. Deventer: Kluwer Bedrijfswetenschappen.

—— and Kluytmans, F. (eds.) (1989). *De Noodzaak van Nieuwe Verhoudingen: Beschouwingen over Arbeidsverhoudingen en Personeelsmanagement*. Deventer: Kluwer Bedrijfswetenschappen.

Boselie, J. P. (1999). 'Effectief personeelsmanagement in de Nederlandse context'. *Checklisten Personeelsmanagement*, 29: 1–29.

—— (2002). *Human Resource Management, Work Systems and Performance: A Theoretical–Empirical Approach*. Tinbergen Institute Research Series, no. 274. Amsterdam: Thela Thesis.

—— and Dietz, G. (2003). 'Commonalities and contradictions in research on human resource management and performance'. Paper presented at the Academy of Management conference, Seattle.

—— and Paauwe, J. (2002). 'Het geheim ontrafeld?: De bijdrage van strategisch human resource management aan prestatic verbelering'. *M&O*, 56/4: 5–24.

—— and van der Wiele, A. (2002). 'Employee perceptions of HRM and TQM and the effects on satisfaction and intention to leave'. *Managing Service Quality*, 12: 165–72.

—— Koene, B. A. S., and Paauwe, J. (1998). *Human Resource Management and Performance: A Trade Union Perspective*. Paper presented at the HRM Study Group IIRA, 11th World Conference, Bologna, September.

—— Paauwe, J., and Jansen, P. J. (2001a). 'Human resource management and performance: lessons from the Netherlands'. *International Journal of Human Resource Management*, 12: 1107–25.

—— Hesselink, M., Paauwe, J., and T. Wiele, van der (2001b). 'Human Resource Management and Performance: Commitment Oriented Work Systems through the Eyes of Employees'. Paper presented at the Academy of Management Meeting, Washington.

Bouwman, T., Camp, A. van de, and Tom, T. (1994). Net Werk: Over Werken in de Automatisering. Amsterdam: STZ.

Boxall, P. (1996). 'The strategic human resource debate and the resource-based view of the firm'. *Human Resource Management Journal*, 6/3: 59–75.

—— and Purcell, J. (2003). *Strategy and Human Resource Management*. Basingstoke, Hants: Palgrave Macmillan.

—— and Steeneveld, M. (1999). 'Human resource strategy and competitive advantage: a longitudinal study of engineering consultancies'. *Journal of Management Studies*, 36: 443–63.

Boyer, R. (1996). 'The convergence hypothesis revisited: globalization, but still the century of nations', in S. Berger and R. Dore (eds.), *National Diversity and Global Capitalism*. Ithaca, NY: Cornell University Press.

HRM and Performance

Bracker, J. (1980). 'The historical development of the strategic management concept'. *Academy of Management Review*, 5: 219–24.

Brewster, C. (1993). 'Developing a "European" model of human resource management'. *International Journal of Human Resource Management*, 4: 763–84.

—— (1995). 'Toward a "European" model of human resource management'. *Journal of International Business Studies*, 26/1: 1–21.

—— Hegewisch, A., and Mayne, L. (1994). 'Trends in European HRM: signs of convergence', in P. Kirkbride (ed.), *Human Resource Management in Europe: Perspectives for the 1990s*. London: Routledge.

Brockbank, W. and Ulrich, D. (2002). *The New HR Agenda: 2002 HRCS Executive Summary*. East Lansing, Mich.: University of Michigan Business School.

Buitendam, A. (2001). *Een Open Architectuur voor Arbeid en Organisatie*. Assen: Van Gorcum.

Bulte, J. (1975). *Human Resource Accounting*. Leiden: Stenfert Kroese.

Caroll, S. J. (1991). 'The new HRM roles, responsibilities, and structures', in R. S. Schuler (ed.), *Managing Human Resources in the Information Age*. Washington: Bureau of National Affairs.

Cascio, W. F. (1991). *Costing Human Resources*. Boston: PWS-Kent.

CBS (Centraal Bureau voor de Statistiek) (1996). *Flexibilisering: het Nederlandse Antwoord op Internationalisering?* Voorburg: CBS.

Chandler, A. D. (1962). *Strategy and Structure: Chapters in History of the Industrial Enterprise*. Cambridge, Mass.: MIT Press.

Child, J. (1972). 'Organisational structure, environment and performance: the role of strategic choice'. *Sociology*, 6/1: 1–22.

—— (2000). 'Theorizing about organizations cross-nationally', in J. L. Cheng and R. B. Peterson (eds.), *Advances in International Comparative Management*. Stamford, Conn.: JAI Press.

Coff, R. (1997). 'Human assets and management dilemmas: coping with hazards on the road to resource-based theory'. *Academy of Management Review*, 22: 374–402.

—— (1999). 'When competitive advantage doesn't lead to performance: the resource-based view and stakeholder bargaining power'. *Organization Science*, 10: 119–32.

Colomy, P. (1998). 'Neofunctionalism and neoinstitutionalism: human agency and interest in institutional change'. *Sociological Forum*, 13: 265–300.

Dacin, M. T. (1997). 'Isomorphism in context: the power and prescription of institutional norms'. *Academy of Management Journal*, 40/1: 46–81.

—— Goodstein, J., and Scott, W. R. (2002). 'Institutional theory and institutional change: introduction to special research forum'. *Academy of Management Journal*, 45/1: 45–57.

Daniels, C. (2002). *Creating Lasting Value through People*. Masters thesis, Rotterdam School of Management.

Delaney, J. T. and Huselid M. A. (1996). 'The impact of human resource management practices on perceptions of organizational performance'. *Academy of Management Journal*, 39: 949–69.

Delbridge, R. and Whitfield, K. (1999). 'Employee Perceptions of Job Influence under Varying Forms of Organizational Participation'. Paper presented at the Dutch HRM Network Conference, Erasmus University, Rotterdam.

Delery, J. E. and Doty, D. H. (1996). 'Modes of theorizing in strategic human resource management: tests of universalistics, contingency, and configurational performance predictions'. *Academy of Management Journal*, 39: 802–35.

——and Shaw, J. D. (2001). 'The strategic management of people in work organizations: review, synthesis, and extension'. Paper presented at the Academy of Management Meeting, Washington.

Deming, W. E. (1986). *Out of the Crisis*. Cambridge, Mass.: MIT Press.

Den Hartog, D. and Verburg, R. (2001). 'High performance work practices, organizational culture and perceived organizational performance'. Paper presented at the Dutch HRM Network Conference, Nijmegen.

DiMaggio, P. J. and Powell, W. W. (1983). 'The iron cage revisited: institutional isomorphism and collective rationality in organizational fields'. *American Sociological Review*, 48: 147–60.

—— —— (eds.) (1991). *The New Institutionalism in Organizational Analysis*. Chicago: University of Chicago Press.

Doorewaard, H. and Meihuizen, H. E. (2000). 'Strategic performance options in professional service organizations'. *Human Resource Management Journal*, 10/2: 39–57.

Dore, R. (1973). *British Factory, Japanese Factory: The Origins of Diversity in Industrial Relations*. Berkeley: University of California Press.

——(1986). *Flexible Rigidities: Industrial Policy and Structural Adjustment in the Japanese Economy*. Stanford, Calif.: Stanford University Press.

Dowling, B. and Richardson, R. (1997). 'Evaluating performance-related pay for managers in the national health service'. *International Journal of Human Resource Management*, 8: 348–66.

Dowling, P. J., Welch, D. E., and Schuler, R. (1999). *International Human Resource Management: Managing People in a Multinational Context*. Cincinnati: Southwestern College.

Dunlop, J. T. (1958). *Industrial Relations Systems*. Boston: Harvard Business School.

Dyer, L. (1983). 'Bringing human resources into the strategic formulation process'. *Human Resource Management*, 22: 257–71.

——(1984). 'Studying human resource strategy: an approach and an agenda'. *Industrial Relations*, 23: 156–69.

——and Shafer, R. A. (1999). 'From human resource strategy to organizational effectiveness: lessons from research on organizational agility'. *Research in Personnel in Human Resource Management*, 4: 145–74.

Economist (1996). 'Le defi Americain, again?' *The Economist*, 13 July: 21–4.

Edwards, P. K. (1994). 'A comparison of national regimes of labor regulation and the problems of the workplace, in J. Belanger, P. K. Edwards, and L. Haiven (eds.), *Workplace Industrial Relations and the Global Challenge*. Ithaca, NY: Cornell University Press.

HRM and Performance

Eelens, L. (1995). 'The fallacy of fit'. Working Paper for the seminar group on HRM, Erasmus University, Rotterdam.

Ernst and Young (2001). *Measures that Matter: An Outside-In Perspective on Shareholder Value Recognition*. London: Ernst & Young.

Fernie, S., Metcalf, D., and Woodland, S. (1994). 'What has human resource management achieved in the workplace?' *Employment Policy Institute Economic Report*, 8/3.

Fey, C. F. and Bjorkman, I. (2001). 'The effect of human resource management practices on MNC subsidiary performance in Russia'. *Journal of International Business Studies*, 32/1: 59–75.

—— Bjorkman, I., and Pavlovskaya, A. (2000). 'The effect of human resource management practices on performance in Russia'. *International Journal of Human Resource Management*, 11/1: 1–18.

Financieele Dagblad (2002). 'Randstad ontmoet nieuwe concurrent'. *Financieele Dagblad*, 21 August.

Fitz-Enz, J. (1990). *Human Value Management*. San Francisco: Jossey-Bass.

—— (2000). *The ROI of Human Capital*. New York: Amacom.

Flamholtz, E. G. (1985). *Human Resource Accounting*. San Francisco: Jossey Bass.

Flood, P. C., Gannon, M. J., and Paauwe, J. (1996). *Managing without Traditional Methods: International Innovations in Human Resource Management*. Wokingham, Berks: Addison-Wesley.

—— Turner, T. and Pearson, J. (1999). 'Knowledge workers and the psychological contract'. Paper presented at the Dutch HRM Network conference, Rotterdam.

Fombrun, C., Tichy, N. M., and Devanna, M. A. (eds.) (1984). *Strategic Human Resource Management*. New York: John Wiley.

Friedman, M. (1982). *Capitalism and Freedom*. Chicago: University of Chicago Press.

Futuyama, D. J. and Slatkin, M. (eds) (1983). *Coevolution*. Sunderland: Sinauer.

Gallie, D. (1978). *In Search of the New Working Class: Automation and Social Integration within the Capitalist Enterprise*. Cambridge: Cambridge University Press.

Gasperz, J. and Ott, M. (1996). *Management van Employability: Nieuwe Kansen in Arbeidsrelaties*. Assen: Van Gorcum.

Geppart, M., Matten, D., and Williams, K. (eds.) (2003). *Challenges for European Management in a Global Context*. New York: Palgrave Macmillan.

Gerhart, B. (1999). 'Human resource management and firm performance: measurement issues and effect on causal and policy inferences'. *Research in Personnel and Human Resource Management*, 4: 31–51.

—— Trevor, C. O., and Graham, M. E. (1996). 'New directions in compensation research: synergies, risk, and survival'. *Research in Personnel and Human Resources Management*, 14: 143–203.

—— Wright, P. M., and McMahan, G. (2000). 'Measurement in error in research on the human resource and firm performance relationship: further evidence and analysis'. *Personnel Psychology*, 53: 855–72.

Godard, J. (1998). 'Workplace reforms, managerial objectives and managerial outcomes and perceptions of Canadian IR/HRM managers'. *International Journal of Human Resource Management*, 9/1: 18–40.

Golden, K. A. and Ramanujam, V. (1985). 'Between a dream and a nightmare: on the integration of the human resource management and strategic planning processes'. *Human Resource Management*, 24: 429–52.

Gollan, P. and Davis, E. (1999). 'The Australian experience of high involvement management and organisational change'. Paper presented at the Dutch HRM Network Conference, Rotterdam.

Gomez-Meija, L. R. and Balkin, D. B. (1992). *Compensation, Organizational Strategy and Firm Performance*. Cincinatti: Southwestern College Press.

Goslinga, S. and Klandermans, B. (1996). 'Flexibilisering en individualisering van arbeidsvoorwaarden'. *Tijdschrift voor Arbeidsvraagstukken*, 12: 155–63.

Gowler, D. and Legge, K. (1986). 'Personnel and paradigms: four perspectives on the future'. *Industrial Relations Journal*, 17: 225–35.

Grant, R. M. (1991). 'The resource-based theory of competitive advantage: implications for strategy formulation'. *California Management Review*, 33/3: 114–35.

Gratton, L. (2000). *Living Strategy: Putting people at the Heart of Corporate Purpose*. Hernel Hempstead, Herts: Prentice-Hall.

—— Hope Hailey, V., Stiles, P., and Truss, K. (1999). 'Linking individual performance to business strategy: the people process model'. *Human Resource Management*, 38/1: 17–32.

Greenwood, R. and Hinings, C. R. (1996). 'Understanding radical organizational change: bringing together the old and the new institutionalism'. *Academy of Management Review*, 21: 1022–55.

Groenewegen, J. (1997). 'Institutions of capitalism: American, European and Japanese systems compared'. *Journal of Economic Issues*, 31: 333–48.

Guest, D. E. (1987). 'Human resource management and industrial relations'. *Journal of Management Studies*, 24: 503–21.

—— (1990). 'Human resource management and the American Dream'. *Journal of Management Studies*, 27: 377–97.

—— (1997). 'Human resource management and performance: a review and research agenda'. *International Journal of Human Resource Management*, 8: 263–76.

—— (1999a). 'Human resource management: the workers' verdict'. *Human Resource Management Journal*, 9/3: 5–25.

—— (1999b). 'Human resource management: when reality confronts theory'. Paper presented at the Dutch HRM Network Conference, Rotterdam.

—— (2001). 'Human resource management: when reality confronts theory'. *International Journal of Human Resource Management*, 12: 1092–1106.

—— and Peccei, R. (1994). 'The nature and causes of effective human resource management'. *British Journal of Industrial Relations*, 32: 219–41.

HRM and Performance

Guest, D. E. Michie, J., Conway, N. and Sheehan, M. (2003). 'Human resource management and corporate performance in the UK'. *British Journal of Industrial Relations*, 41: 291–314.

Guthrie, J. P. (2001). 'High-involvement work practices, turnover and productivity: evidence from New Zealand'. *Academy of Management Journal*, 44/1: 180–90.

Haan, E., Vos, P. de, and Jong, P. de (1994). *Flexibiliteit van de Arbeid: Op Zoek naar Zekerheid*. Amsterdam: Welboom bladen.

Hannan, M. T. and Freeman, J. (1977). 'The population ecology of organizations'. *American Journal of Sociology*, 82: 929–64.

Harzing, A. W. and Sorge, A. M. (2003). 'The relative impact of country-of-origin and universal contingencies on internationalization strategies and corporate control in multinational enterprises: worldwide and European perspectives'. *Organization Studies*, 24: 187–214.

Have, K. ten (1993). *Markt, Organisatie en Personeel in de Industrie: een Empirisch Onderzoek naar Produktieregimes als Configuraties van Arbeidsdeling en Arbeidsrelaties*. Tilburg: Tilburg University Press.

Hendry, C. and Pettigrew, A. (1986). 'The practice of strategic human resource management'. *Personnel Review*, 15/5: 3–8.

—— —— (1990). 'Human resource management: an agenda for the 1990s'. *International Journal of Human Resource Management*, 1/1: 17–43.

—— —— and Sparrow, P. (1989). 'Linking strategic change, competitive performance and human resource management: results of a UK empirical study', in R. Mansfield (ed.), *Frontiers of Management*. London: Routledge.

Hiltrop, J. M. (1999). 'The quest for the best: human resource practices to attract and retain talent'. *European Management Journal*, 17: 422–30.

Hollander, E. P. (1964). *Leaders, Groups and Influence*. New York: Oxford University Press.

Hollingsworth, J. R. (1997). 'Continuities and changes in social systems of production: the cases of Japan, Germany and the United States', in J. R. Hollingsworth and R. Boyer (eds.), *Contemporary Capitalism: The Embeddedness of Institutions*. Cambridge: Cambridge University Press.

—— and Boyer, R. (eds.) (1997). *Contemporary Capitalism: The Embeddedness of Institutions*. Cambridge: Cambridge University Press.

—— and Streeck, W. (1994). 'Countries and sectors: concluding remarks on performance, convergence and competitiveness', in J. R. Hollingsworth, P. C. Schmitter and W. Streeck (eds.), *Governing Capitalist Economies: Performance and Control of Economic Sectors*. New York: Oxford University Press.

Horbeek, H. J. (2003). *De Buigzame Werkvloer: De Implementatie van Interne Flexibiliseringsmaatregelen Nader Beschouwd*. Tinbergen Instituut Research series, no. 319. Amsterdam: Thela Thesis.

Huang, T. (2001). 'Effects of HRM practices on different dimensions of firm performance'. Paper presented at the Global HRM Conference, Barcelona.

Huiskamp, M. J. (1995). 'Regulating the employment relationship: an analytical framework', in J. van Ruysseveldt, M. J. Huiskamp and J. van Hoof (eds.), *Comparative Industrial and Employment Relations*. London: Sage.

——(2003). *Arbeidsrelaties en Onderneming: Vernieuwing in Theorie, Empirie en Praktijk*. Utrecht: Lemma BV.

Huselid, M. A. (1995). 'The impact of human resource management practices on turnover, productivity, and corporate financial performance'. *Academy of Management Journal*, 38: 635–72.

Ichniowski, C. and Shaw, K. (1999). 'The effects of human resource management systems on economic performance: an international comparison of US and Japanese plants'. *Management Science*, 45: 704–21.

————and Prennushi, G. (1997). 'The effects of human resource management practices on productivity: a study of steel finishing lines'. *American Economic Review*, 87: 291–313.

Institute for Management Development (2002). *IMD World Competitiveness Yearbook 2002*. Lausanne: IMD.

d'Iribarne, P. (1989). *La Logique de l'honneur: gestion des enterprises et traditions nationals*. Paris: Seuil.

Jacoby, S. M. (1991). 'American exceptionalism revisited: the importance of management', in S. M. Jacoby (ed.), *Masters to Managers: Historical and Comparative Perspectives on American Employers*. New York: Columbia University Press.

Jaffee, D. (2001). *Organization Theory: Tension and Change*. New York: McGraw-Hill.

Jaggi, B. (1992). 'A comparative analysis of worker participation in the United States and Europe', in G. Dlugos and W. Dorrow (eds.), *Management under Differing Labour Market and Employment Systems*. Berlin: Walter de Gruyter.

Kalleberg, A. L. and Moody, J. W. (1994). 'Human resource management and organizational performance'. *American Behavioral Scientist*, 7: 948–62.

Kamoche, K. (1994). 'A critique and proposed reformulations of strategic human resource management'. *Human Resource Management Journal*, 4/4: 29–43.

——(1996). 'Strategic human resource management within a resource-capability view of the firm'. *Journal of Management Studies*, 33: 213–33.

Kanfer, R. (1994). 'Work motivation: new directions in theory and research'. In C. L. Cooper and I. T. Robertson (eds.), *Key Reviews in Managerial Psychology*. New York: John Wiley.

Kaplan, R. S. and Norton, D. P. (1992). 'The balanced scorecard: measures that drive performance'. *Harvard Business Review*, January/February: 71–9.

————(1996). 'Using the balanced scorecard as a strategic management system'. *Harvard Business Review*, January/February: 75–87.

Kato, T. and Morishima, M. (2002). 'The productivity effects of participatory employment practices: evidence from new Japanese panel data'. *Industrial Relations*, 41: 487–520.

HRM and Performance

Katz, H. C., Kochan, T. A., and Weber, M. R. (1985). 'Assessing the effects of industrial relations systems and efforts to improve the quality of working life on organisational effectiveness'. *Academy of Management Journal*, 3: 509–26.

Keenoy, T. and Anthony, P. (1992). 'HRM: metaphor, meaning and morality'. In P. Blyton, and P. Turnbull, (eds.), *Reassessing Human Resource Management*. London: Sage.

Kerr, C. (1983). *The Future of Industrial Societies: Convergence or Continuing Divergence*. Cambridge, Mass.: Harvard University Press.

——Dunlop, J. T., Harbinson, F. H., and Myers, C. A. (1960). *Industrialism and Industrial Man: The Problems of Labor and Management in Economic Growth*. Cambridge, Mass.: Harvard University Press.

Kets de Vries, M. F. R. (1990). 'The organisational fool: balancing a leader hubris'. *Human Relations*, 4: 751–70.

Kluytmans, F. (1999). *Arbeidsrelaties: tussen Schijn en Werkelijkheid*. Deventer: Kluwer Bedrijfswetenschappen.

——and Paauwe, J. (1991). 'HRM-denkbeelden: de balans opgemaakt'. *M&O*, 45: 279–303.

——and Sluijs, E. van (1995). 'De relatie tussen ondernemingsstrategie en personeels-management'. *Tijdschrift voor Arbeidsvraagstukken*, 1/1: 34–44.

Koch, M. J. and McGrath, R. G. (1996). 'Improving labor productivity: human resource policies do matter'. *Strategic Management Journal*, 17: 335–54.

Kochan, T. A. and Katz, H. C. (1988). *Collective Bargaining and Industrial Relations*. Homewood, Ill.: Irwin.

——McKersie, R. B. and Capelli, P. (1984). 'Strategic choice and industrial relations theory'. *Industrial Relations*, 23/1: 16–39.

——Katz, H. C., and McKersie, R. B. (1986). *The Transformation of American Industrial Relations*. New York: Basic Books.

Koene, B. A. S. and Paauwe, J. (2002). 'The institutionalisation of temporary work agencies in the Netherlands'. Paper presented at the Academy of Management Conference, Denver.

Konter, D. J., Boer, M. E. de, and Hoeksema, L. H. (2002). 'What about tailoring the HR function?' Paper presented at the PREBEM conference, Nijmegen.

Kraatz, M. S. and Moore, J. H. (2002). 'Executive migration and institutional change'. *Academy of Management Journal*, 45/1: 120–43.

Kydd, C. T. and Oppenheim, L. (1990). 'Using human resource management to enhance competitiveness: lessons from four excellent companies'. *Human Resource Management*, 29: 145–66.

Lado, A. and Wilson, M. (1994). 'Human resource system and sustained competitive advantage: competency-based perspective'. *Academy of Management Review*, 19: 699–727.

Lahteenmaki, S., Storey, J., and Vanhala, S. (1998). 'HRM and company performance: the use of measurement and the influence of economic cycles'. *Human Resource Management Journal*, 8/2: 51–66.

Lammers, C. J. (1990). 'Sociology of organizations around the globe: similarities and differences between American, British, French, German and Dutch brands'. *Organization Studies*, 11: 179–205.

——Mijs, A. A., and Noort, W. J., van (2000). *Organisaties Vergelijkender Wijs: Ontwikkeling en Relevantie van het Sociologisch Denken over Organisaties*. Utrecht: Het Spectrum.

Laroche, P. (2001). 'The impact of human resource management practices and industrial relations on the firm performance: an empirical study in the French context'. Paper presented at the Global HRM Conference, Barcelona.

Lawler, E. E. (1986). *High Involvement Management: Participative Strategies for Improving Organizational Management*. San Francisco: Jossey-Bass.

——Mohrman, S. A., and Ledford, G. (1992). *Employee Involvement and TQM: Practice and Results in Fortune 5000 Companies*. San Fransisco: Jossey-Bass.

Lawrence, P. (1996). *Management in the United States*. London: Sage.

Lazear, E. P. (1996). *Performance Pay and Productivity*. NBER working paper 5672, Cambridge, Mass.

Lefebvre, E. R. L. (2001) 'Lecture notes for the HR Leadership program'. Module on HR Effectiveness. Rotterdam: Rotterdam School of Management.

Leget, J. (1997). *Personeelsbeleid en Succes van Organisaties: Resultaatgericht Human Resources Management in Nederland*. Deventer: Kluwer Bedrijfsinformatie.

Legge, K. (1978). *Power, Innovation and Problem-Solving in Personnel Management*. Maidenhead, Berks: McGraw-Hill.

——(1995). *Human Resource Management: Rhetorics and Realities*. Basingstoke, Hants: Macmillan.

Leijten, A. Th. (1992). *Stimulerend personeelsmanagement: een effectiviteitsdiagnose*. Amsterdam: Thela Thesis.

Lengnick-Hall, C. A. and Lengnick-Hall, M. L. (1988). 'Strategic human resources management: a review of the literature and a proposed typology'. *Academy of Management Review*, 13: 454–70.

Levinthal, D. A. and March, J. G. (1993). 'The myopia of learning'. *Strategic Management Journal*, 14 (special issue): 95–112.

Lewin, A. Y. and Volberda, H. W. (1999). 'Prolegomena on coevolution: a framework for research on strategy and new organisational forms'. *Organization Science*, 10: 519–34.

——Long, C. P., and Caroll, T. N. (1999). 'The coevolution of new organizational forms'. *Organization Science*, 10: 535–50.

Lindblom, C. E. (1959). 'The science of muddling through'. *Public Administration Review*, 19/2: 79–88.

Looise, J. C. (1996). *Sociale innovatie Moet, maar Hoe?* Enschede: Universiteit Twente.

——and Paauwe, J. (1998). 'Human resource management: evolving paradigms and research issues from an integrated stakeholder perspective', in G. Evers, B. van Hees, and J. Schippers (eds.), *Work, Organisation and Labour in Dutch Society: A State of the Art of Research*. Dordrecht: Kluwer Academic.

Lowe, J., Delbridge, R., and Oliver, N. (1997). 'High-performance manufacturing: evidence from the automotive components industry'. *Organization Studies*, 18: 783–98.

MacDuffie, J. P. (1995). 'Human resource bundles and manufacturing performance: organizational logic and flexible production systems in the world auto industry'. *Industrial and Labor Relations Review*, 48: 197–221.

MacMillan, H. and Tampoe, M. (2000). *Strategic Management: Process, Content and Implementation*. Oxford: Oxford University Press.

McFarlin, D. B., Sweeney, P. D., and Cotton, J. L. (1992). 'Attitudes toward employee participation in decision-making'. *Human Resource Management*, 31: 363–83.

McNabb, R. and Whitfield, K. (1997). 'Unions, flexibility, team working and financial performance'. *Organization Studies*, 18: 821–38.

Mahoney, J. T. and Pandian, J. R. (1991). 'The resource-based view within the conversation of strategic management'. *Strategic Management Journal*, 13: 363–80.

Maltz, A. C., Shenhar, A. J., and Reilly, R. R. (2003). 'Beyond the balanced scorecard: refining the search for organizational success measures'. *Long Range Planning*, 36: 187–204.

March, J. G. (1991). 'Exploration and exploitation in organizational learning'. *Organisation Science*, 2/1: 71–87.

—— and Simon, H. A. (1958). *Organizations*. New York: John Wiley.

Martell, K. and Caroll, S. (1995). 'Which executive human resource management practices for the top management team are associated with higher firm performance?' *Human Resource Management*, 34: 497–512.

Maurice, M. and Sorge, A. (eds.) (2000). *Embedded Organizations: Societal Analysis of Actors, Organizations and Socio-economic Context*. Amsterdam/Philadelphia: Benjamins.

—— Sorge, A., and Warner, M. (1980). 'Societal differences in organizing manufacturing units: a comparison of France, West Germany and Great Britain'. *Organization Studies*, 1: 59–86.

—— Sellier, F., and Silvestre, J. J. (1986). *The Social Foundations of Industrial Power: A Comparison of France and Germany*. Cambridge, Mass.: MIT Press.

Mayo, A. (2001). *The Human Value of the Enterprise: Valuing PEOPLE as Assets: Monitoring, Measuring, Managing*. London: Nicholas Brealey.

Meer, M. van der, Visser, J., Wilthagen, T., and Heijden, P. F., van der (2003). '*Weg van het Overleg?* Amsterdam: Amsterdam University Press.

Meerveld, N. A. (2001). *Strategievorming in de Nieuwe Economie naar een Conceptueel Raamwerk*. M.Sc. thesis, Erasmus University Rotterdam.

Meihuizen, H. (1999). 'Productivity effects of employee stock ownership and employee stock option plans in firms listed on the Amsterdam stock exchanges: an empirical analysis'. Paper presented at the Dutch HRM Network Conference, Rotterdam.

Merchant, K. A. (1985). *Control in Business Organizations*. New York: Ballinger.

Meyer, M. W. (2002). *Rethinking Performance Measurement: Beyond the Balanced Scorecard*. Cambridge: Cambridge University Press.

Meyer, J. W. and Rowan, B. (1977). 'Institutionalized organizations: formal structures as myth and ceremony', reprinted in W. W. Powell and P. J. DiMaggio (eds.), *The New Institutionalism in Organizational Analysis*. Chicago: University of Chicago Press, 1991.

—— Scott, W. R., and Strang, D. (1987). 'Centralisation, fragmentation and school district complexity'. *Administrative Science Quarterly*, 32: 186–201.

Miles, R. and Snow, C. (1981). 'Designing strategic human resource systems'. *Organizational Dynamics*, 13: 36–52.

Ministerie van Sociale Zaken en Werkgelegenheid (1995). *Flexibiliteit en Zekerheid*. The Hague: SDU Uitgevers.

Mintzberg, H. (1979). *The Structuring of Organizations*. Hemel Hempstead, Herts: Prentice-Hall.

—— (1987). 'The strategy concept 1: five PS for strategy'. *California Management Review*, 30/1: 11–24.

—— (1990). 'The design school: reconsidering the basic premises of strategic management'. *Strategic Management Journal*, 11: 171–95.

—— (1994). *The Rise and Fall of Strategic Planning*. Englewood Cliffs, NJ: Prentice-Hall.

—— (1998). 'Covert leadership: notes on managing professionals'. *Harvard Business Review*, November/December: 140–7.

—— Ahlstrand, B., and Lampel, J. (1998). *Strategy Safari: A Guided Tour through the Wilds of Strategic Management*. New York: Free Press.

Mirvis, P. H. (1997). 'Human resource management: leaders, laggards, and followers'. *Academy of Management Executive*, 11/2: 43–56.

Mitchell, C. (1983). 'Case and situation analysis'. *Sociological Review*, 31: 187–211.

Mitsuhashi, H., Park, H. J., Wright, P. M., and Chua, R. S. (2000). 'Line and HR executives' perceptions of HR effectiveness in firms in people's republic China'. *International Journal of Human Resource Management*, 11: 197–216.

Monks, K. and Schuster, F. (2001). 'Understanding the HRM performance linkage: insights and explanations'. Paper presented at the Global HRM Conference 2001, Barcelona.

Morgan, G., Kristensen, P. H., and Whitley, R. (eds.) (2001). *The Multinational Firm*. Oxford: Oxford University Press.

Nijs, W. F. de (1996). 'Arbeidsverhoudingen en personeelsmanagement', in A. G. Nagelkerke and W. F de Nijs (eds.), *Regels rond Arbeid*. Leiden: Stenfert Kroese.

Noe, R. A., Hollenbeck, J. R., Gerhart, B., and Wright, P. M. (2000). *Human Resource Management: Gaining a Competitive Advantage*. New York: McGraw-Hill.

Ohmae, K. (1990). *The Borderless World: Power and Strategy in the Interlinked Economy*. London: HarperCollins.

Oliver, C. (1991). 'Strategic responses to institutional processes'. *Academy of Management Review*, 16/1: 145–79.

—— (1992). 'The antecedents of deinstitutionalization'. *Organization Studies*, 13: 563–88.

HRM and Performance

Oliver, C. (1997). 'Sustainable competitive advantage: combining institutional and resource-based views'. *Strategic Management Journal*, 18: 697–713.

Osterman, P. (1994). 'How common is workplace transformation and how can we explain who does it?' *Industrial and Labor Relations Review*, 47: 173–88.

Paauwe, J. (1989). *Sociaal Ondernemingsbeleid: tussen Dwang en Ambities*. Alphen aan den Rijn: Samson Bedrijfsinformatie.

—— (1991). 'Limitations to freedom: is there a choice for human resource management?' *British Journal of Management*, 2: 1–17.

—— (1994). *Organiseren: een Grensoverschrijdende Passie*. Alphen aan den Rijn: Samson Bedrijfsinformatie.

—— (1995). 'Kernvraagstukken op het gebied van strategisch HRM in Nederland'. *M&O*, 49: 369–89.

—— (1996). 'Key issues in strategic human resource management: lessons from the Netherlands'. *Human Resource Management Journal*, 6/3: 76–93.

—— (1998). 'HRM and performance: the linkage between resources and institutional context'. RIBES Working Paper, Erasmus University Rotterdam.

—— and Boselie, J. P. (2000). 'HRM en het presteren van de organisatie: een vergelijkend overzicht'. *Maandblad voor Accountancy en Bedrijfseconomie*, April: 111–28.

—— —— (2003a). 'Challenging "strategic HRM" and the relevance of the institutional settings'. *Human Resource Management Journal*, 13/3: 56–70.

—— and Boselie, P. (2003b). 'Challenging (strategic) human resource management theory: integration of resource-based approaches and new institutionalism'. *ERIM Report*. Rotterdam: Erasmus Universiteit Rotterdam.

—— and Richardson, R. (1997). 'Introduction to Special Issue on HRM and performance'. *International Journal of Human Resource Management*, 8: 257–62.

Paine, L. S. (2003). *Value Shift: Why Companies Must Merge Social and Financial Imperatives to Achieve Superior Performance*. New York: McGraw-Hill.

Panayotopoulou, L. (2001). 'Strategic human resource management and its link to firm performance: an implementation of the competing values framework'. Paper presented at the Global HRM Conference, Barcelona.

Peppard, J. and Rylander, A. (2001). 'Using an intellectual capital perspective to design and implement a growth strategy: the case of APiON'. *European Management Journal*, 19: 510–25.

Peters, T. J. and Waterman, R. H. (1982). *In Search of Excellence: Lessons from America's Best-Run Companies*. New York: Warner Books.

Pfeffer, J. (1994). *Competitive Advantage through People*. Boston: Harvard Business School Press.

—— (1995). 'Producing sustainable competitive advantage through the effective management of people'. *Academy of Management Executive*, 9/1: 55–69.

—— (1997). 'Pitfalls on the road to measurement: the dangerous liaison of human resources with ideas of accounting and finance'. *Human Resource Management*, 36: 357–65.

Bibliography

—— (1998). *The Human Equation: Building Profits by Putting People First*. Boston: Harvard Business School Press.

—— and Salancik, G. (1978). *The External Control of Organizations: A Resource Dependence Perspective*. New York: Harper & Row.

Phillips, J. J., Stone, R. D., and Phillips, P. P. (2001). *The Human Resources Scorecard: Measuring the Return on Investment*. Woburn, Mass.: Butterworth–Heinemann.

Pil, F. K. and MacDuffie, J. P. (1996). 'The adoption of high-involvement work practices'. *Industrial Relations*, 35: 423–55.

Poole, M. (1986). *Industrial Relations: Origins and Patterns of National Diversity.* London: Routledge.

—— (1990). Editorial: 'HRM in an international perspective'. *International Journal of Human Resource Management*, 1/1: 1–15.

Porter, M. E. (1980). *Competitive Strategy: Techniques for Analyzing Industries and Competitors*. New York: Free Press.

—— (1985). *Competitive Advantage: Creating and Sustaining Superior Performance*. New York: Free Press.

Pot, F. (1998). *Continuity and Change of Human Resource Management: A Comparative Analysis of the Impact of Global Change and Cultural Continuity on the Management of Labour in the Netherlands and the United States*. Tinbergen Institute Research Series, no. 188. Amsterdam: Thela Thesis.

—— (2000). *Employment Relations and National Culture*. Cheltenham, Glos.: Edward Elgar.

Powell, W. W. (1990). 'Neither market nor hierachy: network forms of organization'. *Research in Organizational Behavior*, 12: 295–336.

—— (1998). 'Institutional theory', in C. L. Cooper and C. Argyris (eds.), *Encyclopaedia of Management*. Oxford: Blackwell.

Prahalad, C. K. and Hamel, G. (1990). 'The core competence of the corporation'. *Harvard Business Review*, May–June: 79–91.

Pugh, D. S. (1981). 'The Aston Program perspective: retrospect and prospect', in A. H. Ven and W. F. Joyce (eds.), *Perspectives on Organization and Behavior*. New York: John Wiley.

—— and Hickson, D. J. (1976). *Organizational Structure in its Context: the Aston Programme I*. Farnborough, Hants.: Saxon House.

—— and Hinings, C. R. (1976). *Organizational Structure in its Context: the Aston Programme II*. Farnborough, Hants.: Saxon House.

—— and Payne, R. L. (1977). *Organizational Structure in its Context: the Aston Programme III*. Farnborough, Hants.: Saxon House.

Purcell, J. (1999). 'Best practice and best fit: chimera or cul-de-sac?' *Human Resource Management Journal*, 9/3: 26–41.

—— and Ahlstrand, B. (1994). *Human Resource Management in the Multi-Divisional Company.* Oxford: Oxford University Press.

Quinn, J. B. (1980). *Strategies for Change: Logical Incrementalism*. Homewood, See.: Irwin.

Remery, C., Doorne-Huiskes, A. van, and Schippers, J. (2002). 'Labour market flexibility in the Netherlands: looking for winners and losers'. *Work, Employment and Society*, 16: 477–95.

Roughgarden, J. (1983). 'The theory of coevolution', in D. J. Futuyama and M. Slatkin (eds.), *Coevolution*. Sunderland: Sinauer.

Saa Perez, P. de and Garcia Falcon, J. M. (2001). 'Human resource management and organisational performance from a resource-based view'. Paper presented at the Global HRM Conference, Barcelona.

Sangers, V. M. and Paauwe, J. (supervisor) (1996). *De effectiviteit van HRM in kaart gebracht*. M.Sc. thesis, Erasmus University Rotterdam.

Scarpello, V. and Theeke, H. E. (1989). 'Human resource accounting: a measured critique'. *Journal of Accounting Literature*, 8: 265–80.

Scheurer, L., Krancher, E., and Manders, F. (1993). 'Human resource management is geen vanzelfsprekendheid'. *Gids voor Personeelsmanagement*, 1: 31–69.

Schilstra, K. (1998). *Industrial Relations and Human Resource Management*. Tinbergen Institute Research Series, no. 185. Amsterdam: Thela Thesis.

—— and Jongbloed, A. (2003). 'Geslaagd decentralisatie', in A. G. Nagelkerke and W. F. Nijs (eds.), *Sturen in het Laagland: Over Contuiniteit en Verandering van de Nederlandse Arbeidsverhoudingen*. Delft: Eburon.

—— Smit, E. and Paauwe, J. (1996) (eds.). *Markt, Overlegeconomie of Bedrijfsgemeenschap*. Alphen aan de Rijn: Samson Bedrijfsinformatie.

Schipper, F. (1993). *Zin in Organisatie: Een Filosofische Beschouwing over Organisatiecultuur en Rationaliteit*. Amsterdam: Boom.

Scholarios, D., Ramsay, H., and Harley, B. (1999). 'High noon on the high road: testing high commitment management theory'. Paper presented at the Dutch HRM Network Conference, Rotterdam.

Schuler, R. S. (1990). 'Repositioning the human resource function: transformation or demise?' *Academy of Management Executive*, 4/3: 49–59.

—— and Jackson, S. E. (1987). 'Linking competitive strategies with human resource management practices'. *Academy of Management Executive*, 1: 209–13.

—— —— (2001). 'HR roles, competences, partnerships and structure', in M. Warner and M. Poole (eds.), *International Encyclopedia of Business and Management*. London: ITP.

Schumpeter, J. A. (1934). *The Theory of Economic Development: An Inquiry into Profits, Capital, Credit, Interest and the Business Cycle*. Oxford: Oxford University Press.

Scott, W. R. (1992). *Organisations: Rational, Natural and Open Systems*. Englewood Cliffs, NJ: Prentice-Hall.

—— (1994) (ed.). *Institutional Environments and Organizations: Structural Complexity and Individualism*. Thousands Oaks, Calif.: Sage.

Sels, L. (2002). *Strategisch Management van Human Resources: Maakt het een Verschil?* Antwerp: Universiteit Antwerpen Faculteit Toegepaste Economische Wetenschappen.

Selznick, P. (1957). *Leadership in Administration: A Sociological Perspective*. New York: Harper & Row.

Senge, P. M. (1990). *The Fifth Discipline: The Art and Practice of the Learning Organization*. New York: Doubleday.

SER (Sociaal Economische Raad) (1991). *Flexibele Arbeidsrelaties: Advies inzake Flexibele arbeidsrelaties*. The Hague: SER.

Sherer, P. D. and Lee, K. (2002). 'Institutional change in large law firms: a resource dependency and institutional perspective'. *Academy of Management Journal*, 45/1: 102–19.

Shipton, J. and McAuley, J. (1994). 'Issues of power and marginality in personnel'. *Human Resource Management Journal*, 4/1: 1–13.

Simon, H. A. (1947). *Administrative Behavior: A Study of Decision-Making in Administrative Organizations*. New York: Macmillan. Second edn. 1957.

Smit, E., Schilstra, K., and Paauwe, J. (1995). *Belangenbehartiging van Werknemers: Een Toekomstverkenning*. The Hague: Vuga.

Smith, C. and Meiksins, P. (1995). 'System, society and dominance effects in cross-national organisational analysis'. *Work, Employment and Society*, 9: 241–67.

Snell, S. A. (1992). 'Control theory in strategic HRM'. *Academy of Management Journal*, 35: 292–327.

Sorge, A. (1983). 'Cultured organization'. *International Studies of Management and Organization*, 12/4: 106–38.

—— and Warner, M. (1986). *Comparative Factory Organisation*. Aldershot, Hants.: Gower.

Sparrow, P., Schuler, R. S., and Jackson, S. E. (1994). 'Convergence or divergence: human resource practices and policies for competitive advantage worldwide'. *International Journal of Human Resource Management*, 5: 267–99.

Starkey, K. and McKinlay, A. (1993). *Strategy and the Human Resource: Ford and the Search for Competitive Advantage*. Oxford: Blackwell.

Stichting van de Arbeid (1996). *Nota 'Flexibiliteit en Zekerheid'*. The Hague: Stichting van de Arbeid.

Storey, J. (ed.) (1989). *New Perspectives on Human Resource Management*. London: Routledge.

—— (1992). *Developments in the Management of Human Resources*. Oxford: Blackwell.

—— (1995). *Human Resource Management: A Critical Text*. London: Routledge.

—— and Sisson, K. (1993). *Managing Human Resources and Industrial Relations*. Milton Keynes: Open University Press.

Strange, S. (1997). 'The future of global capitalism; or, will divergence persist forever?' in C. Crouch and W. Streeck (eds.), *Political Economy of Modern Capitalism: Mapping Convergence and Divergence*. London: Sage.

Streeck, W. (1992). *Social Institutions and Economic Performance: Studies of Industrial Relations in Advanced Capitalist Economies*. London: Sage.

Sveiby, K. E. (1997). *The New Organizational Wealth*. San Francisco: Berrett-Koehler.

Teece, D. J., Pisano, G., and Shuen, A. (1997). 'Dynamic capabilities and strategic management'. *Strategic Management Journal*, 18: 509–33.

Townley, B. (2002). 'The role of competing rationalities in institutional change'. *Academy of Management Journal*, 45/1: 163–79.

Trist, E. (1977). 'A concept of organizational ecology'. *Australian Journal of Management*, 2: 162–75.

Truss, K. and Gratton, L. (2003). 'The three-dimensional people strategy: putting human resources policies into action'. *Academy of Management Executive*, 17/3: 74–86.

Tsui, A. S. and Gomez, Mejia, L. R. (1988). 'Evaluating human resource effectiveness', in L. Dyer and G. Holder (eds.), *Human Resource Management Evolving Roles and Responsibilities*. Washington: Bureau of National Affairs.

Tyson, S. (1987). 'The management of the personnel function'. *Journal of Management Studies*, 24: 523–32.

—— (1996). 'HR strategy: a process for managing the contribution of HRM to organisational preformance'. Paper presented at the ESRC Seminar on HR Contribution to Business Performance, Milton Keynes.

—— (1999). 'How HR knowledge contributes to organisational performance'. *Human Resource Management Journal*, 9/3: 42–52.

—— and Fell, A. (1986). *Evaluating the Personnel Function*. London: Hutchinson.

Ulrich, D. (1997). *Human Resource Champions: The Next Agenda for Adding Value and Delivering Results*. Boston: Harvard Business School Press.

—— Brockbank, W., Yeung, A. K., and Dale, G. L. (1995). 'Human resource competences: an empirical assessment'. *Human Resource Management*, 34: 473–95.

Venkatraman, N. (1989). 'The concept of fit in strategy research: toward verbal and statistical correspondence'. *Academy of Management Review*, 14: 423–44.

Verburg, R. M. (1998). *Human Resource Management: optimale HRM-praktijken en Configuraties*. Amsterdam: Vrije Universiteit.

Visser, J. (1998). 'Two cheers for corporatism, one for the market: job growth, welfare reform and corporatism in the Netherlands'. *British Journal of Industrial Relations*, 36: 269–92.

—— and Hemerijck, A. (1997). *A Dutch Miracle: Job Growth, Welfare Reform and Corporatism in the Netherlands*. Amsterdam: Amsterdam University Press.

Vloeberghs, D. (1997). *Handboek Human Resource Management: Managementcompetenties voor de 21ste eeuw*. Leuven/Amersfoort: Acco.

Volberda, H. W. (1998). *Building the Flexible Firm: How to Remain Competitive*. New York: Oxford University Press.

—— and Elfring, T. (2001). *Rethinking Strategy*. London: Sage.

Walker, G. and MacDonald, J. R. (2001). 'Designing and implementing an HR scorecard'. *Human Resource Management*, 40: 365–77.

Walker, K. F. (1969). 'Strategic factors in industrial relations systems: a programme of international comparative industry studies'. *International Institute for Labour Studies Bulletin*, 6 (June): 187–209.

Wallace, J. E. (1995). 'Corporatist control and organizational commitment among professionals: the case of lawyers working in law firms', *Social Forces*, 3: 811–40.

Walton, R. E. (1985). 'From control to commitment in the workplace'. *Harvard Business Review*, March/April: 25–32.

Ward Lilley, B. (1991). 'Be ready to be unpopular'. *Personnel Management Plus*, April: 2.

Waters, M. (1995). *Globalization*. London: Routledge.

Watson Wyatt (1999). See www.watsonwyatt.com for the Human Capital Index.

Weber, M. (1946). *From Max Weber: Essays in Sociology*. Oxford: Oxford University Press.

Weick, K. E. (1979). *The Social Psychology of Organizing*. Reading, Mass.: Addison-Wesley.

Wernerfelt, B. (1984). 'A resource-based view of the firm'. *Strategic Management Journal*, 5: 171–80.

Whitley, R. (1999). *Divergent Capitalisms: The Social Structuring and Change of Business Systems*. Oxford: Oxford University Press.

Whittington, R. (1993). *What is Strategy, and Does It Matter?* London: Routledge.

Wilson, D. (1992). *A Strategy of Change: Concepts and Controversies in the Management of Change*. London: Routledge.

Wit, B. de and Meyer, R. (1998). *Strategy: Process, Content, Context: An International Perspective*. London: Thompson.

Wood, S. (1999). 'Human resource management and performance'. *International Journal of Management Review*, 4/1: 367–413.

Woodward, J. (1965). *Industrial Organization: Theory and Practice*. Oxford: Oxford University Press.

Wright, P. and Dyer, L. (2000). *People in E-business: New Challenges, New Solutions*. New York: Human Resource Planning Society.

—— and Gardner, T. M. (2001). 'Theoretical and empirical challenges in studying the HR practices: firm performance relationship'. Paper presented at the ERIM Seminars, Erasmus University Rotterdam.

—— and McMahan, G. C. (1992). 'Theoretical perspectives for strategic human resource management'. *Journal of Management*, 18: 295–320.

—— and Snell, S. (1998). 'Towards a unifying framework for exploring fit and flexibility in strategic human resource management'. *Academy of Management Review*, 23: 756–72.

—— McMahan, G. C., and McWilliams, A. (1994). 'Human resources and sustained competitive advantage: a resource-based perspective'. *International Journal of Human Resource Management*, 5: 301–26.

Yeung, A. K. and Berman, B. (1997). 'Adding value through human resources: reorienting human resource measurement to drive business performance'. *Human Resource Management*, 36: 321–35.

Yin, R. K. (1994). *Case Study Research: Design and Methods*. Thousand Oaks, Calif.: Sage.

Zedeck, S. and Cascio, W. F. (1984). 'Psychological issues in personnel decisions'. *Annual Review of Psychology*, 35: 461–518.

HRM and Performance

Zeithaml, V. A., Parasuraman, A., and Berry, U. (1990). *Delivering Quality Services: Building Customer Perspectives and Expectations*. New York: Free Press.

Zilber, T. (2002). 'Institutionalization as an interplay between actions, meanings and actors: the case of a rape crisis center in Israel'. *Academy of Management Journal*, 45: 234–54.

Zucker, L. (1977). 'The role of institutionalisation in cultural persistence'. *American Sociological Review*, 42: 726–43.

Index

Index

Index

Index

Index

Index

Index

Index

Index

Index